A Distant View of the Pamunkey Reservation

THE CONQUEST OF VIRGINIA
THE FOREST PRIMEVAL

An Account, Based on Original Documents, of the
Indians in That Portion of the Continent
in Which was Established the First
English Colony in America

with
Illustrations

Conway Whittle Sams, B.L.
Author of "Sams on Attachment," "Shall Women Vote?" etc.
Member of the Virginia Bar

HERITAGE BOOKS
2012

HERITAGE BOOKS
AN IMPRINT OF HERITAGE BOOKS, INC.

Books, CDs, and more—Worldwide

For our listing of thousands of titles see our website
at
www.HeritageBooks.com

A Facsimile Reprint
Published 2012 by
HERITAGE BOOKS, INC.
Publishing Division
100 Railroad Ave. #104
Westminster, Maryland 21157

Copyright © 1916 Conway Whittle Sams
The Knickerbocker Press, New York

— Publisher's Notice —
In reprints such as this, it is often not possible to remove blemishes from the original. We feel the contents of this book warrant its reissue despite these blemishes and hope you will agree and read it with pleasure.

International Standard Book Numbers
Paperbound: 978-0-7884-0899-1
Clothbound: 978-0-7884-9229-7

To

THE MEMORY OF

SIR WALTER RALEIGH

AND

HENRY WRIOTHESLEY, EARL OF SOUTHAMPTON,

THE GREAT LEADERS IN THE

MOVEMENT WHICH RESULTED IN

THE FOUNDING OF

VIRGINIA

THIS WORK IS DEDICATED

THE VIRGINIANS' INTENTIONS WITH
REGARD TO THE INDIANS

"To teach them moral and physical good, which is the end of our planting amongst them; to let them know what virtue and goodness is, and the reward of both; to teach them religion, and the crown of the righteous; to acquaint them with grace, that they may participate with glory; which God grant in mercy unto them."

WILLIAM STRACHEY

PREFACE

THE present volume is the first of a series on which the author has been engaged for several years. As the work grew, it became apparent that it would be better to issue its parts, written originally merely as chapters, in the form of separate volumes.

Before beginning the narrative of the events which occurred on this continent when the English proceeded to take possession of it, it has seemed proper to view the country itself, the stage upon which so important a drama was to be presented, and the race which then occupied it.

We are enabled to do this with the aid of the writings of those who lived at that period, and who participated in these scenes.

The earliest of these writers, and a very important one, is Thomas Hariot. This man was well known to Sir Walter Raleigh, who allowed him a pension for instructing him in mathematics. He was sent over by Sir Walter with the expedition to Virginia in 1585. He was employed in connection with the Roanoke Island settlement, under the command of Sir Ralph Lane, from June, 1585, to June, 1586. He was a man distinguished for his great talents, excelling as he did in many departments of learning. He was a noted astronomer, and withal a gentleman of an affable disposition. His work is of enduring value and interest.

Captain George Percy, also cited, was a son of the Earl of Northumberland. He sailed for Virginia in the first expedition, 1606. He was twice Governor of Virginia, first from September, 1609, until the arrival of Gates in May, 1610; and again, when appointed by Lord De la Warr at the time of the latter's departure, in March, 1611, pending the arrival of Dale in May, 1612. Percy was a man of great importance. His writings are preserved in part in the valuable compilation made by the Rev. Samuel Purchas.

Captain John Smith's first work, the *True Relation*, was followed some years later by his *General History of Virginia, New-England, and the Summer Isles*, which, unless otherwise indicated, is the work herein referred to under his name. He was a voluminous writer.

High in authority among these early writers stands William Strachey, of Saffron Walden, in England, who sailed from Falmouth on June 18, 1609, on one of the ships of the fleet of nine vessels then sent out by the Company.

In this fleet were persons of the first importance: Sir Thomas Gates, Sir George Somers, Captain Christopher Newport, Ralph Hamor, and others equally well known. The vessel he was in was wrecked on the Bermudas, and there he stayed from July, 1609, until May, 1610, when he set sail in one of the two vessels built on the Bermudas by the shipwrecked mariners. He reached Virginia on the 23d of that month. Here for three years he was employed as Secretary of State and one of the Council with Lord De la Warr, the Lord Governor and Captain General of the Colony. A good scholar and of an observant mind, Strachey gathered during this time the material for his *Historie of Travaile into Virginia*. This was composed, as he expresses it, of what had been "gathered and observed as well by those who went first thither, as collected" by himself.

Two manuscript copies of this work, with but little variation between them, are in existence. One is in the British Museum, Sloane Collection. In 1618, it was presented to Lord Bacon. This copy was published by the Hakluyt Society in 1849. From it our extracts are taken. The other, in the Bodleian Library at Oxford, has not been published.

Strachey returned to England in 1611, and Alexander Brown fixes the time when this treatise was written between the date of his return and July 23, 1612, when Captain Argall sailed for Virginia.[1]

Strachey must have returned to Virginia, as he states that he was "three years thither employed." He was still living in 1618, then presumably in England.

He wrote other works, among them an account

[1] *Genesis of the United States*, vol. ii., p. 562.

of the wreck on the Bermudas. Alexander Brown says of him: "We know but little of Strachey; his command of language seems to me very striking, and his initials, W. S., are the most interesting of the period." This tribute was well deserved, for Strachey is one of the clearest, most direct, and satisfactory writers of that period. It is a pity that his fine work should have lain unpublished so long.

Henry Spelman, who is quoted so often, writes from a close personal knowledge of the Indians, having lived among them for some time. He was the third son of Sir Henry Spelman, of Congham, Norfolk, and came over to Virginia in the same fleet in which Strachey shipped in 1609. Spelman's ship was the *Unity*. It was not wrecked, but reached Virginia safely. Shortly after his arrival he was carried by Captain Smith on an expedition to the Falls of the James. Here, unknown to Spelman, he was sold to Taux-Powhatan, or, the Little Powhatan, a son of the great Powhatan. This son was king of the Indian town of Powhatan. Smith sold Spelman in exchange for the town, and left him with the Indians. Smith wanted Captain William West, a nephew of Lord De la Warr, to build a town here. But Captain West had selected another site and a serious dispute arose in consequence.

After seven or eight days, however, Spelman managed to return to the ship and sailed to Jamestown. Hither came, soon after, Thomas

Savage, who was then living with Powhatan, bringing venison from Powhatan to Captain Percy, then President. Savage desired one of his fellow-countrymen to go back with him, and Spelman was selected. Spelman went willingly, food being scarce at Jamestown. Powhatan received him kindly, he and Savage sitting regularly at his table. He was sent back to Jamestown by Powhatan, to tell the English that if they would bring to him a ship containing some copper, he would give corn in exchange. When in response they came, Powhatan killed twenty-six or seven of their number.

While these proceedings were taking place, Powhatan sent Spelman, and a Dutchman named Samuel, to a town about sixteen miles off, called Yaw-ta-noo-ne, where they were to wait for him. Here Spelman seems to have stayed for some six months. At the expiration of that period, the King of Potomac came to visit Powhatan, and showed such kindness to Spelman, Savage, and the Dutchman that upon his departure they decided to go away with him. They had not traveled far when Savage deserted them, and going back to Powhatan informed him of the departure of his companions. Powhatan sent after them, demanding their return. They refused to comply and proceeded with the King of Potomac. One of Powhatan's messengers with his tomahawk killed the Dutchman. Spelman ran off, his pursuers after him, and the King of Potomac and his men following in turn.

The last mentioned overtook and subdued Powhatan's men. Spelman, escaping, made his way to the Potomac country.

Here he lived a year or more, making his domicile at a town called Pas-ptan-zie. At the expiration of that period, Captain Argall, sailing up the Potomac River, heard that there was an English boy in the region, and sought for him. The King of Potomac, hearing of Argall's endeavor, sent Spelman to him. Spelman returned from the interview, and conducted the king to the ship. Then a bargain was struck, Captain Argall purchasing Spelman from the king for a stipulated amount of copper.

"Thus," says Spelman, "was I set at liberty and brought into England."

He returned to England in 1611 with Lord De la Warr. Later he went back to Virginia, and was employed by the Colony as an interpreter. In 1618, he was again in England, but returned presently to Virginia. In 1619, he was in trouble with the authorities for speaking disrespectfully of Governor Yeardley to O-pe-chan-ca-nough, and was removed from his office as interpreter.

At the time of the massacre in 1622, he was trading with the Potomac Indians, and on March 23, 1623, he was killed by the Anacostan Indians, on the Potomac, at some point near the present site of Washington. His head was cut off, and thrown down the bank of the river to his companions.

His work, a short treatise, was not published

until 1872, and then only in an edition of one hundred copies. It is, therefore, very rare. There is a good deal of difficulty in the style of its composition, but it has strength and is a valuable addition to the records of the time in which he lived.

Ralph Hamor, whose *Relation* is frequently mentioned, came to Virginia, like Strachey and Spelman, in 1609. He remained in Virginia until June 18, 1614, when he returned to England. During this period he published his book, which appeared in London in 1615.

During this stay, the Company presented him with eight shares, which carried title to eight hundred acres. This was no doubt in recognition of his valuable service to the Colony. He was also a subscriber to the stock of the Company, and on that account, and by reason of the transportation of other persons to Virginia at his expense, he must have become entitled to a large amount of land.

His brother Thomas decided to return to Virginia with him, and in the spring of 1617 they jointly set sail.

Ralph Hamor became a person of considerable importance in the Colony. He was a member of the Council both under the Company and under the King—that is, from 1621 to 1628, and probably later.

His brother Thomas is believed to have died early in 1624. We do not know the time of the death of the author.

Thomas Glover, described as "an ingenious chirurgion," who had lived some years in Virginia, communicated his account, a tract of only thirty-one pages, to the Royal Society in 1676. A very limited edition of it was reprinted from the philosophical transactions of that society, in 1904.

The Beverley referred to so often is Robert Beverley, whose entertaining work, *The History and Present State of Virginia*, belongs to a much later period than the above-mentioned works, and, unlike the other narratives, is written "by a Native and Inhabitant of the Place." It was published in London in 1705.

This gentleman belonged to a well-known family of Middlesex County. He married Ursula, daughter of the first William Byrd. His father, Major Robert Beverley, was Clerk of the House of Burgesses, "noted in the early history of Virginia as a martyr in the cause of liberty," says Bishop Meade. During Bacon's Rebellion the elder Beverley sided with the King, and helped to re-establish the authority of Governor Berkeley. But later he fell under the dire displeasure of the Governor and others in authority by refusing to deliver to them copies of the journal of the House of Burgesses without that body's consent. All of which arose out of popular disapproval of the enforcement of the law in regard to establishing towns in each county, and other disorders.

The historian himself lived in King and Queen County, and there he died.

Though belonging to a much later period than the writers we have mentioned above, there were still Indians in Virginia when Beverley wrote,—few indeed in the eastern part of the Colony, but the Indian power in the west and south was as yet unbroken.

In his writing he seems to have followed in many respects the earlier narrators. His work is of considerable value. It is well known, and much of it is evidently original information.

These are the principal writers we rely upon in the following account. We prefer to reproduce their own words, changed, for the convenience and pleasure of the reader, only to the extent of bringing much of what they wrote into conformity with the present spelling. No modern writer can equal in authority, nor surpass in interest, the statements found in the original records made by the very men who saw these Virginia Indians, and whose feet trod the forest primeval in which they dwelt.

C. W. S.

NORFOLK, VIRGINIA,
June 28, 1915.

BIBLIOGRAPHY
PRINCIPAL AUTHORITIES REFERRED TO IN THIS WORK, AND THEIR PARTICULAR EDITIONS

BEVERLEY'S *History and Present State of Virginia*, London, 1705.
BURK'S *History of Virginia*.
CAMPBELL, CHARLES, *History of Virginia*, Philadelphia, Pa., 1860.
GLOVER, *An Account of Virginia*, 1676, Oxford Reprint, 1904.
HAKLUYT, *Early English Voyages to America*, Edinburgh, 1891.
HAMOR'S *Relation*, Reproduction of the London Edition of 1615.
HARIOT'S *Narrative*, London Reprint, 1893.
HENING'S *Statutes at Large*.
HOWE'S *Virginia, its History and Antiquities*, Charleston, 1845.
JONES'S *Present State of Virginia*, Sabin's Reprints, No. 5, New York, 1865.
KEITH'S *History of Virginia*.
KERCHEVAL'S *History of the Valley*, Edition of 1850.
MEADE'S *Old Churches and Families of Virginia*, Original Edition, Philadelphia, 1857.
NEWPORT'S "Discoveries in Virginia," Printed in the *Archæologia Americana, Transactions and Collections of the American Antiquarian Society*, vol. iv., Boston, 1860.
PURCHAS, *His Pilgrims*, London Edition of 1625.
Records of the Virginia Company, Publication by the Library of Congress, 1906.

Bibliography

SMITH'S *True Relation*, Annotated by Charles Deane, Boston, 1866.

SMITH'S *History of Virginia* (General History), Richmond Reprint, 1819.

SPELMAN, HENRY, *Relation of Virginia*, Printed by James F. Hunnerwell, London, 1872.

STITH'S *History of Virginia*, Sabin's Reprint, New York, 1865.

STRACHEY, *Historie of Travaile into Virginia*, Printed for the Hakluyt Society, London, 1849.

WINGFIELD'S *Discourse of Virginia*, Privately Printed by Charles Deane, Boston, 1860.

CONTENTS

CHAPTER	PAGE
I.—INTRODUCTORY	1
II.—THE INDIAN CHARACTER	25
III.—THE FASHION AND DOMESTIC CONSTRUCTION OF INDIAN SOCIETY	53
IV.—MARRIAGE	77
V.—SEASONS AND FESTIVALS	84
VI.—FISHING, HUNTING, AND AGRICULTURE	91
VII.—CANOE-, ARROW-, AND POTTERY-MAKING	109
VIII.—HOUSES AND TOWNS	128
IX.—THE TOWNS LOCATED	141
X.—THE FALLS OF THE JAMES	161
XI.—POLITICAL LAWS AND THE ART OF WAR	165
XII.—THE PRIESTLY MEDICINE MAN	183
XIII.—HUS-KA-NAW-ING	191
XIV.—THE EMBALMED KINGS AND FUNERAL RITES	198
XV.—BURIAL MOUNDS	204
XVI.—PRIESTS AND CONJURERS	223

CHAPTER	PAGE
XVII.—Religion	238
XVIII.—Powhatan and Wingina	267
XIX.—Some Indian Words	285
XX.—The Tribes and Nations	324
XXI.—Conclusion	406
Index	409

ILLUSTRATIONS

	PAGE
A DISTANT VIEW OF THE PAMUNKEY RESERVATION . . . . . *Frontispiece*	
A WER-Ó-ANCE OR GREAT LORD OF VIRGINIA .	38
A CHIEF LORD OF ROANOKE	54
AGED MEN OF POM-E-I-OCK	56
AN AGED MAN IN HIS WINTER GARMENT .	58
THE WOMEN CARRYING THEIR CHILDREN . .	60
ONE OF THE CHIEF LADIES OF SE-CO-TA . .	62
A CHIEF LADY OF POM-E-I-OCK . . .	64
A COUPLE OF YOUNG WOMEN	66
COOKING FISH	68
SEETHING OF MEAT IN EARTHEN POTS . .	70
A MAN AND HIS WIFE AT DINNER . . .	74
DANCING AT THE GREAT FEAST . . .	86
MANNER OF PRAYING	88
FISHING IN THE CANOE	94
CANOE MAKING AND FELLING TREES . .	110

Illustrations

	PAGE
PLATE 1.—PALEOLITHIC IMPLEMENTS FROM THE DISTRICT OF COLUMBIA	112
From the *American Anthropologist*.	
PLATE 2.—PALEOLITHIC IMPLEMENTS FROM THE DISTRICT OF COLUMBIA	114
From the *American Anthropologist*.	
PLATE 3.—RUDE CHIPPED IMPLEMENTS FROM THE DISTRICT OF COLUMBIA	116
From the *American Anthropologist*.	
PLATE 4.—RUDE CHIPPED IMPLEMENTS FROM THE DISTRICT OF COLUMBIA	118
From the *American Anthropologist*.	
PLATE 5.—EXAMPLES OF FABRICS IMPRESSED UPON POTTERY OF THE POTOMAC VALLEY	120
From the *American Anthropologist*.	
AN INDIAN TOWN WITH CORNFIELD	132
THE TOWN OF POM-E-I-OCK	135
THE UNENCLOSED TOWN OF SE-CO-TA	137
MAP SHOWING PRINCIPAL PORTION OF THE TERRITORY RULED BY POWHATAN	142
MAP SHOWING INDIAN LOCALITIES NEAR ROANOKE ISLAND	160
THE BURIAL OF THE KINGS	201
THE MARIETTA MOUND	210
THE GREAT MOUND, SHOWING THE OBSERVATORY BUILT ON IT IN 1837	212

Illustrations

	PAGE
CARVED STONE FOUND IN THE MOUND	216
THE GREAT MOUND IN 1909	220
A PRIEST AND A CONJURER IN THEIR PROPER HABITS	232
THEIR IDOL IN HIS TABERNACLE	240
THE IDOL CALLED OKÈE, QUI-ÓC-COS, OR KI-WA-SÀ	248
THE HOME OF A PAMUNKEY INDIAN	334

The Conquest of Virginia

CHAPTER I

INTRODUCTORY

MANY excellent histories of Virginia have been written, but the whole story has never been told, and probably never will be. It has been the method of the other writers on this subject to regard the acquisition of the territory we occupy as a "Settlement" by the English, a peaceful kind of settlement, one might infer, and the Indians, and the troubles with the Indians, have been made to occupy a comparatively inconspicuous place in the narrative. Our relations with England is the theme these writers have preferred to dwell upon, and but little is said of our relations with the Indians.

On the other hand, in the series of historical studies of which this is the initial volume, the purpose has been to bring out the long and difficult struggle which our forefathers had in acquiring this goodly heritage. We have, therefore, called the work as a whole *The Conquest of*

Virginia, for conquest it was as truly as that of Granada by Ferdinand and Isabella, Mexico by Cortes, or Peru by Pizarro. The conquest on the part of England was complicated by European rivalry. Spain, the great World-Power of that day, claimed this territory as her own, and France was equally ambitious to acquire it. These three great Powers, therefore, were rival claimants, and England had to deal with them as well as with the Indians who were in actual possession. Spain had led the way in the conquest of the New World, and claimed it under the discovery of Columbus, and a grant from the Pope. She had established herself in the southern part of North America, and called it Florida. France came behind Spain, but claimed title to the country on account of the voyage of Verazzano and by virtue of the traditions of earlier expeditions. She entered upon and attempted permanently to appropriate a portion of this southern land, but she was forcibly driven out by Spain, and, selecting a new location for her Colony, went where European opposition was less effective. She founded her new settlement in the colder regions of the north, on the great River St. Lawrence, and called the country Canada. From this beginning she expanded west and south, and came later into a long and dreadful conflict with England and the English Colonies.

With the Spaniards then to the south, and the French to the north, England, also claiming the whole continent on account of the discovery of Cabot, decided to proceed to take actual possession of the central part of the continent, and called it Virginia.

At the time when our history begins, 1584, Elizabeth was Queen of England, having ascended the throne twenty-five years before. She was a staunch Protestant. Henry III., the son of Catharine de' Medici,—she who had instigated the leaders in the Massacre of St. Bartholomew,—was King of France, having reigned already ten years. Philip II., the most bigoted and persecuting of monarchs, who had dedicated himself and the resources of his kingdom to the extermination of Protestantism, sat absolute monarch upon the throne of Spain. He had then reigned for twenty-eight years.

The condition of Europe at this period, and far into the seventeenth century, was that of one vast battle-field. From every quarter ascended to heaven the smoke of burning homes or villages or cities. On all sides was heard the heavy tramp of marching troops. The news of each day was a battle, a conspiracy, or an assassination. The world was divided against itself on an issue which seemed to threaten one side or the other with extermination, as no ground of compromise or adjustment seemed possible. This war involved many countries and took various names, but one and the same principle was at issue—freedom of religion. In Germany it was the Thirty Years' War. In France it was the religious wars between the Catholics and the Huguenots. In Holland it was the war for independence from Spain, which lasted eighty years. In England it involved endless intrigue and a revolution, and had as its most dramatic incident and culminating point the defeat and destruction of the Spanish Armada, which was sent by Philip II. to overthrow and subjugate that heretical kingdom, which was, next to Holland, the great champion of Protestantism.

These long and bloody wars were most disastrous, and are responsible in part for the prejudice entertained by some to religion itself. But they were fought by the Protestants for self-preservation. To have surrendered the principle of freedom of religion would have changed the whole course of the world's history. It was not to be thought of. Self-preservation in the cause of freedom of religion was, therefore, the principle for which the Protestant hosts were contending. The destruction of this freedom, and the extirpation of all dissent from the doctrines of the Church of Rome, was the principle for which the Catholic Powers were contending.

Many of the incidents characteristic of this long and terrible struggle are familiar to us all, but some of them at least should be here briefly reviewed, in order to understand the political conditions under which Virginia was founded, and so properly to appreciate and comprehend its deep significance and importance. The founding of Virginia was a movement undertaken by England for the extension of Protestantism at the time when the following occurrences were taking place. Beginning our list of events some thirty years before the first move in that direction was made, we therefore mention:—

The burning alive of Bishops Ridley and Latimer and other Protestants by Mary, the Catholic Queen of England, in 1555.

The persecution of the Protestants, which had gone on under Queen Isabella and Charles V., actively undertaken upon a formidable scale by Philip II., 1561, with a view to their complete extermination.

The petition of the Four Hundred nobles against the Inquisition in the Netherlands, 1565.

The revolt of the Protestants in Scotland, 1565.

The revolt of the Netherlands from Philip II., 1566.

The war which followed this revolt lasted, as we have said, eighty years, and covered, therefore, the entire period here reviewed. This war, in which England took part, is one of the most remarkable struggles recorded in history. It resulted in the establishment of freedom of religion and the independence of Holland, but only after the most appalling losses and heroic sacrifices. At the head of the Hollanders stood the majestic figure of the great William the Silent of Nassau, Prince of Orange, who earned his sobriquet of "The Silent" by reason of his course on one occasion when, walking with Henry II. of France, this monarch, who had only recently ascended the throne, unfolded to him his plans and purposes respecting the Protestants, whom he had determined utterly to destroy. Philip II. was to aid him in this plot. William listened in silence to what Henry had to say, letting the French King disclose all that was in his heart, while he dedicated himself to defeat those plans.

The dispatch of the Duke of Alva of Spain, for the purpose of subduing the Netherlands, 1567.

The beheading of the Counts Egmont and Horn, by the Duke of Alva, 1568.

The defeat of Mary, Queen of Scots, in her attempt to conquer Protestant Scotland, 1568.

The defeat of the Huguenots in St. Denis by the French Catholics, 1568.

The establishment of the Duke of Alva's "bloody tribunal" at Brussels, 1568.

The rout of the Huguenots at Jarnac; Condé killed, 1569.

The elevation to the leadership of the Huguenots in 1571 of Henry of Béarn, afterwards Henry IV. of France.

The Massacre of St. Bartholomew, 1572, in the course of which 70,000 Protestants were murdered.

The recognition, in 1572, on the part of the Northern States of the Netherlands, of William the Silent as Stadtholder.

The siege of Leyden, 1574, by the armies of Spain.

The peace of Chastenoy, 1576, granting the

Protestants free exercise of their religion in all parts of France, except Paris.

The formation in France, 1576, of the Catholic League, supported by Philip II., whose object it was utterly to destroy the French Protestants.

The superseding of Don Juan by Alexander Farnese as leader of the Spanish forces in the Netherlands, in 1578.

The formation of the Union of Utrecht in 1579 by the Seven Provinces under William the Silent against Philip II.

The declaration on the part of the United Provinces of Holland of their independence from Spain, 1581.

Sir Walter Raleigh's first expedition for Virginia, to establish a Protestant Colony in the New World, April 27, 1584.

This event took place at the very height of the long and dreadful struggle. Sir Walter Raleigh, one of the most interesting figures that has moved across the stage of history, hated Spain and what Spain stood for, as Hannibal hated Rome, and Raleigh's work was in large part directed toward establishing in the New World a Protestant Power, as a rival to Catholic Spain and Catholic France. In the attempt he perished. Spain regarded him with the deepest hatred as an intruder on the domains which she claimed as her own, and because he was an avowed and audacious opponent of her religion, her policies, and her power. At the hands of James I., whose influence Sir Walter had sought to extend across the ocean, but who now wished to make a family alliance with the Spanish King, who was James's natural enemy, and at the Spanish King's instigation, and in deference to the desire of pleasing that monarch, Raleigh, generally regarded as one of the finest types England has produced, met his death, and the Colony on which he had lavished his care and wealth came to naught. But the work which he had been bold enough to attempt was taken up by others and carried, with labor and difficulty, and again with overwhelming loss to those engaged in the enterprise, to a finally successful issue.

Many of the most stirring incidents of the titanic struggle between Catholicism and Protestantism were still hidden in the future when Sir Walter undertook to plant his Colony.

Virginia was England's bold and determined effort, participated in and encouraged by Elizabeth and, at first, likewise by James I., and by cities, peers, nobles, members of Parliament, men of affairs, and representatives of all classes of English citizens, to claim and hold for England and for Protestantism a part of the New World which was in danger of falling entirely into Catholic hands. Had Catholicism acquired this domain, such a preponderating influence in the affairs of the world at large would have been hers that the aim and dream of Philip II., which were utterly to exterminate Protestantism from the face of the earth, might conceivably have been realized. This was the object dearest to the

Introductory

heart of Philip, and it was the intention of Raleigh, as it had been that of the great William the Silent, that this object should be defeated.

Catholicism tolerated no dissent from its beliefs. The Moors were conquered and driven out of Spain, on the ground that they were heretics. The Jews came in for equal condemnation, and the Protestant Christians were most hated of all. Holding the doctrine that no faith was to be kept with heretics, the wars which were waged against them were of the bloodiest and most cruel character. Around the struggle which began with Holland, when Spain, under Charles V. and his son Philip II., undertook to suppress all religious dissent from the doctrines of the Church of Rome, by means of the cruelties and terrors of the Spanish Inquisition, all the policies and armed forces of the nations of Europe gradually revolved, as one after the other was drawn into the vortex of that mortal struggle.

After Raleigh's ships had sailed for Virginia, then, in the year 1584, these events were still to happen:—

The assassination, July 10, 1584, of William the Silent, Prince of Orange and Stadtholder of Holland, by a tool of Philip II.

This event, one of Earth's great tragedies, occurred only seventy-four days after the ships of Raleigh left England on their voyage for Virginia.

Babington's conspiracy in the cause of Mary

Queen of Scots to assassinate Elizabeth and seize her throne, 1586.

The death of Sir Philip Sidney at the battle of Zütphen, 1586.

The beheading by direction of Elizabeth at Fotheringay Castle, 1587, of Mary Queen of Scots, the Catholic pretender to the throne of England, for complicity in Babington's conspiracy.

The appearance in the English Channel on July 19, 1588, of the Spanish fleet, called the *Invincible Armada*, built by Philip II., and dispatched, under the command of the Duke of Medina Sidonia, to conquer Protestant England and subjugate it to Catholicism. Its defeat and destruction by Lord Charles Howard, Sir Francis Drake, and other English commanders. Sir Walter Raleigh himself took an active part in this defence.

The breaking out in 1588 of a rebellion in Paris, at the instigation of Henry, Duke of Guise, the head of the Catholic party of France.

The assassination of Henry III. of France, and the ascension to the throne in 1589 of Henry IV. of France and Navarre, a Protestant, the first of the House of Bourbon.

The besieging, 1590, by Henry IV., of Paris, which refuses him admittance because he is a Protestant.

Henry IV.'s conversion to Catholicism, 1593.

The destruction by Howard, Essex, and Raleigh of a Spanish fleet at Cadiz, 1596.

Introductory

The overthrow of the Roman Catholic League by Henry IV. of France, 1596.

The demise of Philip II., September 13, 1598, and his succession by his son Philip III., who was the persistent enemy of the Virginia Colony at Jamestown, as his father had been of the one attempted by Sir Walter Raleigh at Roanoke Island.

The establishment through Henry IV. of liberty of conscience and religion for the Protestants by the issuance of the celebrated Edict of Nantes, 1599.

The expulsion of the Jesuits from England by proclamation of James I., 1604.

The concocting by Catholics of the Gunpowder Plot designed to throw the English Government into confusion. It was to have been accomplished by springing a mine under the House of Parliament and destroying at the same time the three estates of the realm,—the King, the House of Lords, and the Commons. Guy Fawkes was detected on November 5, 1605, in the vaults under the House of Lords, preparing the train for exploding the mine the next day.

The foundation of Quebec by the French Catholics, 1605.

The requirement in England of oaths of allegiance recognizing only the Protestant succession to the Crown, 1606.

The departure from London, December 19, 1606, for the purpose of founding a Colony in Virginia, of the *Sarah Constant,* the *Goodspeed,* and the *Discovery*, owned by the Virginia Company, which had succeeded to the claims of Sir Walter Raleigh. These ships landed at Cape Henry on the 26th of April, 1607, and on May 13th, founded Jamestown, or James City, as it was at first called, the first permanent English settlement in the New World.

The assassination, May 14, 1610, of Henry IV. of France, the great supporter of the Protestants.

The succession to the throne of Sweden in 1611 of Gustavus Adolphus, destined to become the great champion of Protestantism.

War in Germany between the two parties, the Evangelic Union under Frederick, Elector Palatine, and the Catholic League, under the Duke of Bavaria, 1618.

The execution, on October 29, 1618, of Sir Walter Raleigh, then in the sixty-fifth year of his age, by James I. of England, to please Philip III. of Spain.

The beginning in 1618 of the Thirty Years' War between the Protestants and Catholics, involving the States of Central Europe.

The battle of Prague, 1620, resulting in the total defeat and ruin of the cause of the Protestants in Bohemia, and the loss of his crown by Frederick V., the son-in-law of King James I. of England.

The driving from Bohemia into exile in 1620 of the Protestants at the instigation of Ferdinand II.

Introductory

The settlement of New England, at Plymouth, December 21, 1620.

The death in March, 1621, of Philip III. of Spain, and his succession by his son Philip IV., who continued the religious war with Holland.

The overthrow by King James I., June 26, 1624, of the Virginia Company which had established the Colony.

The death on March 27, 1625, of King James I., and his succession by his son Charles I., who married Henrietta Maria, daughter of the great Henry IV. of France.

The defeat by Tilly, who had been commander of the Catholic League, of Christian IV., King of Denmark and Norway, and leader of the Protestants, at the battle of Lutter, August 27, 1626.

The choosing in 1629 of Christian IV. as head of the Protestant League.

The inauguration of the career of Gustavus Adolphus, the great champion of Protestantism, by the conquest of Pomerania, 1630.

The capture and sack of Magdeburg by Tilly, May 16, 1631.

The defeat of Tilly by Gustavus Adolphus at the battle of Leipsic, September 17, 1631.

The mortal wounding of Tilly, in contest with Gustavus Adolphus, near the Lech, April 15, 1632.

The defeat by Gustavus Adolphus, in alliance with Charles I. of England, of Wallenstein at the battle of Lützen, and the death of Gustavus

Adolphus in the moment of victory, November 16, 1632.

The founding of Maryland by Lord Baltimore, a Catholic, 1632.

The assassination of Wallenstein by his officers, February 25, 1634.

The Peace of Prague between the Protestant German Princes and the Catholic Emperor, 1634.

The formation, 1635, under the leadership of Richelieu, of an alliance between France and Sweden against the two great Catholic states, Spain and Austria.

The death on February 15, 1637, of the Emperor Ferdinand II. of Germany, the great persecutor of the Protestants, and his succession by his son, Ferdinand III.

The hatching of a conspiracy by the Irish Catholics to expel the English and massacre the Protestant settlers in Ulster to the number of forty thousand, commenced on St. Ignatius' day, October 23, 1641.

The defeat by the Swedes of the Austrians at Leipsic, 1642.

The death of Louis XIII., May 14, 1643, and his succession by his son Louis XIV., then an infant, Cardinal Mazarin controlling the affairs of France.

The soliciting by the Protestant Princes of Germany, oppressed by the House of Austria, of the aid of Sweden, 1648, resulting in the Treaty of Westphalia, signed on October 24, 1648.

This famous treaty, which included all the

Introductory

great and nearly all the minor Powers of Europe, established the general condition of Europe for one hundred and fifty years, and concludes this list of the leading events which marked the period just before and during the time of the settlement of the Colony of Virginia by England.

By this treaty the Protestants in Germany were protected in their freedom of religion nearly to the same extent to which they had enjoyed religious toleration under Maximilian II. The Pope protested against this toleration, but his protest was disregarded.

In France the Protestants were still protected by the Edict of Nantes, established by Henry IV., but which was to be revoked by Louis XIV. in 1685, as a result of which fifty thousand families were driven from his kingdom, many of whom came to Virginia.

Religious persecution and strife was, therefore, by no means ended even with the establishment of the Treaty of Westphalia.

The condensed summary of events above reproduced shows the state of Europe when Raleigh, and after him, the Virginia Company, undertook to plant an English Protestant Colony on the western shore of the Atlantic.

This Colony was, therefore, the outpost of Protestantism, braving not only the ocean and the savage inhabitants of a vast and unknown continent, but braving the two great rival Catholic Powers of Europe, Spain and France.

A wide and deep distinction exists in this respect between the Virginia Settlement and the Massachusetts Settlement. The Jamestown Settlement was in harmony with, and an extension of, the national aims and aspirations and with the Orthodox Church of England, having no grievance against the mother country, but loving her, and seeking to extend her ideas and her power to another continent, which was to be held by and for Old England.

The Plymouth Settlement represented only a fraction of the English nation. Puritanism was obnoxious to the English Government. King James I. hated the Puritans as much as Philip II. and Ferdinand II. abhorred the Protestants, and determined to suppress them. The founders of the Plymouth Colony, having with difficulty left England, on account of persecution, had gone to Amsterdam in Holland a year before the twelve years' truce of the war between Holland and Spain was signed. Here they hoped to find refuge and a toleration not granted them in England, with whose Established Church they were at variance on account of its adherence to certain features of the worship which they thought partook of the Roman ceremonial. After one year's stay at Amsterdam, they removed to Leyden. Here they lived ten years in peace and security.

For various reasons they decided to go elsewhere. They first thought of lands beneath the equator. New Amsterdam (New York) next loomed as a possible home. Then they applied

Introductory

to the Virginia Company for a patent, which they could have obtained. On applying to King James I. for a guarantee of religious liberty in Virginia, to be given under his seal, the King refused. They understood, however, that the King would not molest them if they conducted themselves peaceably. On the strength of this understanding, they decided to go.

From Delftshaven in Holland, these people, known in later years as the Pilgrim Fathers of New England, sailed in the *Speedwell* for England. They joined others at Southampton, and in the *Mayflower* sailed to Plymouth, Massachusetts.

These Pilgrim Fathers did not found the United States of America. South of them, at Jamestown, Virginia, another Colony, more truly representative of the ideas of England, their common mother country, had been established for thirteen years before the *Mayflower* began her journey. In this older Colony representative government had already been established and Protestantism planted in the New World.

But for the existence in that part of the world of this older Colony, America might not have been selected by these people for their settlement. They did not have to leave Holland. They were protected there. That they could not accommodate themselves to the form of Protestantism approved by England made them desire to separate themselves from England. This was no more heroic than the action of the other men of their kindred, who, having no grievance at home, carried the banner of their beloved country and its religion and laws voluntarily into the wilderness, to extend its power and influence in the world at large, and, by resisting Catholicism successfully in another continent, prevent the total destruction of all the forms of Protestantism, Puritanism among them.

The Virginia Settlement was, therefore, a larger, more significant, and nobler movement than that of the Plymouth Settlement. It was the great national struggle of the whole of England, while the Plymouth Settlement was that of a part which was out of harmony with the whole.

Real religious freedom was nowhere. The Catholics did not tolerate the Protestants, which fact was the beginning and cause of all the subsequent trouble. Virginia did not tolerate the Catholics, and was founded with the intention of prohibiting any of them from coming to this country. New England had no idea of toleration, and persecuted those who dissented from her.

Maryland, encroaching upon Virginia, and led by members of the weaker party in England did declare for toleration, but this toleration was obligatory under the terms of the charter granted to Lord Baltimore, a Catholic. This was no doubt prompted by the desire to prevent that Colony from oppressing the Protestants—the leaders and founders of the Colony being Catholics.

Introductory

The founding of Virginia was not the work of a single man, nor of a group of men, nor was it indeed in any sense a private undertaking. Virginia was founded by England, and the man at the head of the movement was no less a personage than the King of England. James, by the grace of God, King of England, Scotland, and Ireland, Defender of the faith, etc., was the director and the guiding hand of the movement, though not its immediate originator. The actual work was undertaken by others, but they were acting under his immediate instructions both on sea and land. The form of the charter under which they were acting was that of a permission to locate and establish a colony in Virginia, the transaction thus having a private character to the extent of enabling the King to disclaim it at any time if he so saw fit, in order to avoid international complications if they should arise, especially with Spain, the national enemy, but with whom England was then at peace.

The fleet which was to carry over the settlers was placed under the sole command of Captain Christopher Newport. The King made elaborate provisions for conducting the affairs of the Colony. He put his instructions in writing, delivered them, duly signed and sealed, and fastened up in a box, to Captain Newport, Bartholomew Gosnold, and John Ratcliff. This box, kept tightly closed during the voyage, was not to be opened until within twenty-four hours after they had reached Virginia. These instructions contained a large amount of practical advice, the combined experience of other colonization enterprises, and worked out a general scheme of colonial government. It is believed that the King did not allow the box to be opened until the destined land was reached, in order to prevent any conflict of authority arising between the commander at sea and the commander who would be chosen for the land. Thus the settlers did not know who their rulers in the New World were to be until the night following the day of their arrival. Then they opened this mysterious box and learned for the first time that by the King's appointment they were to be ruled by "His Majesties Council for the first Colony in Virginia," and that this Council was to be composed of Captain Edward-Maria Wingfield, Captain Bartholomew Gosnold, Captain John Smith, Captain Christopher Newport, Captain John Ratcliff, Captain John Martin, and Captain George Kendall. Captain John Smith was at the time under arrest, on account of a mutiny which had occurred during the voyage, and was not allowed at first to serve. He was kept in confinement in all for thirteen weeks, and was not released until June, after the settlement at Jamestown had been begun. The other men designated selected Captain Wingfield as president.

The movements of the colonists after their landing were largely regulated by instructions given to them by the Council in England, which,

Introductory

having been also appointed by the King, of course, represented his authority.

The beginning of this movement under the first Charter, that granted on April 10, 1606, was, therefore, under the royal authority, and this period of the settlement has now come to be understood as the period of the King's Government. It was not eminently successful, and a revolution took place when, in 1609, a new Charter was granted, the Company reorganized, and power vested more fully in the hands of the London Company, as we call it, with a vast accession of territory covered by its new grant. For fifteen years this Company carried on patriotically the movement under that and still a third Charter, further enlarging its scope. At the close of this decade and a half, the Company was finally overthrown by the same King James I., who, by a Quo Warranto proceeding, revoked these charters on June 26, 1624, and resumed the government of the Colony, which then continued under the jurisdiction of the Crown until the Revolution.

The undertaking was too great for any individual, or set of individuals. The King's first Government or Company did not succeed. The London Company depleted its treasury in the attempt, and met with even greater losses than Raleigh himself had suffered. This work was governmental in its conception, continental in scope, and hazardous in execution. It required the resources of an established government to bear such burdens, and to carry to a successful issue so gigantic an undertaking, and it was the established government of England which began, and which finally accomplished, the colonization of Virginia. The founders of the Colony have suffered a slight injury due to the change in the meaning of a word. Two classes of persons who aided in this great enterprise were called "adventurers." This word has in the course of three hundred years acquired a meaning different from what it bore at the time of the founding of Virginia. A more or less bad signification now attaches to the word adventurer, and a still worse to the feminine form—adventuress. No such meaning applied in 1607. The two kinds of adventurers then spoken of were: those who adventured their money in the enterprise, whom we would now call investors; and those who went further, and adventured their persons, these we would now call colonists or immigrants. The idea underlying its use in both cases was that in the first instance one risked his means in furtherance of the enterprise, and the latter that he risked his life. The men of that day would have been amazed if they had been told that by the use of the well-known and deeply significant word adventurer, any deduction would in the future be drawn that they were of such a class as we now think of when we call persons "adventurers." The patriotic gentlemen, men of affairs, members of Parliament, nobles, peers, and great municipal corporations who subscribed to the stock of this company would surely have laughed at being called "adventurers" in the modern meaning of the word.

The religious principles which characterized the movement at its inception were steadily adhered to for many years thereafter. The colonists came over with fixed convictions and a settled policy as to the government of both State and Church.

As civil government extended, *pari passu* ecclesiastical government extended. Over every square mile under the jurisdiction of the county court, the jurisdiction of some parish, equally as vigorous and well defined, also extended. Scattered all over Virginia were parish churches, chapels of ease, and glebes of ministers. Roman Catholics for a long time were not allowed in the Colony. Lord Baltimore himself was driven out on this ground.

This ecclesiastical polity of Virginia, as to its adherence to the Church of England and its parish system, continued in full vigor down to the Revolution.

What made Virginia so much respected by the other colonies, by the mother-country, and by her own sons was the character of her leading people, her orderly governmental construction, and the principles for which she stood. Aristocratic in all social matters, well governed by the members of its aristocracy, who filled all public offices, and sincerely attached to the Church of

England, Virginia, during the Colonial period, presented to an admiring world a well governed, vigorous Colony, loyal to the Crown and loyal to the Church.

CHAPTER II

THE INDIAN CHARACTER

ANTHROPOLOGISTS, in studying the early races of mankind, and characterizing the ages in which they lived by the implements they used, have called one the Stone Age. This they divide into two principal periods; the first, the rudest and least developed, when their stone implements were only chipped and rough, they call the paleolithic or ancient Stone Age. Then came an advance upon this stage, when the men using the stone implements were able to make them smooth. This age they call the neolithic, or new—that is, the more recent Stone Age. To this latter period belonged the Indians living in Virginia at the time of the Conquest.

Viewed from the standpoint of their development, being cultivators of the soil, they are classed as barbarous. West of the Rocky Mountains, stretching north into Canada and covering Alaska, were Indians who lived only by hunting and fishing, and so are classed as savage. To the south, in Mexico and Central America, were other Indians who, possessing some of the arts and sciences, are classed as half-civilized.

Viewed generically, the Virginia Indians were a part of the great Algonquin stock, whose branches covered a large portion of the continent east of the Mississippi, and reached up into the eastern part of Canada. Of this race were the Powhatans, the Shawnees, the Delawares, the Illinois, the Miamis, the Kickapoos, the Pottawatomies, the Ottawas, the Sacs and Foxes, the Chippewas, the Objibwas, the Mohegans, the Pequots, the Narragansetts, the Wampanoags, the Tarratines, the Abenakis, and a host of others.

As a little island in this sea of Algonquinism were the Winnebagos, on the western shore of Lake Michigan, and, as a very large island, the Iroquois, stretching from Lake Huron to the Hudson, and comprehending the Hurons, the Eries, the Six Nations—that is, the Senecas, the Cayugas, the Onondagas, the Oneidas, the Mohawks, and the Susquehannocks.

To the south of the Algonquins, whose line roughly corresponded to that dividing Virginia from North Carolina, lay a branch of the Iroquois comprised of the Cherokees and the Tuscaroras. They occupied, however, only a part of this southern boundary.

South, southeast, and southwest of these, stretching down to the end of Florida, were the Maskoki, or Mobilians, comprising the Catawbas and the Yemassees; in North Carolina and South

Carolina, the Chickasaws and Choctaws; on the Mississippi, with a small territory of the Natchez Indians between them, the Creeks in Georgia, and the Seminoles in Florida.

All of these nations were subject to many subdivisions of tribes.

It was with some of the tribes of the Catawbas that the Roanoke Island settlers had to deal, as it was with the Powhatans that the Jamestown settlers were brought into conflict.

Although grouped under one general name the various nations or tribes included under it were by no means therefore friends or allies. They were often bitter enemies. Examples of this abound in all the records of those times. To such an extent was this true, that if the Indians had not been conquered by the white man, they were still in danger of being exterminated by each other.

Of all the things in the forest in which the Virginia Indians lived, that which seems to have first attracted the attention of the early writers was the grapevines. Captain Barlow, in his account of the first voyage made on behalf of Sir Walter Raleigh, mentions them. They climbed to the tops of high cedars, they abounded on the sand and on the green soil, on the hills, in the plains, on every little shrub. They spread their leafy, Briarean arms into the very sea itself. Glover tells of this same profusion, and says that they twined about the oaks and poplars, and ran to the tops of these stately monarchs of the forest.

Other trees which were important and characteristic were the pine, walnut, cypress, juniper, ash, elm, gum, locust, maple, willow, magnolia, mimosa, honeypod, horse-chestnut, chestnut, beech, holly, hickory, sycamore, and the live oak; with the dogwood, sassafras, and chinkapin of the size of large bushes. The pines rose often to a majestic height, and many of the others were equally imposing with their centuries of growth behind them.

This forest was inhabited not only by Indians, but by wolves, in such numbers that it took many years to exterminate them, deer, bears, wild cats, raccoons, possums, flying-squirrels, rabbits, squirrels, beavers, otters, rattlesnakes, moccasins, long black snakes, and short and thick black snakes, which also abounded there, and in the fields were the corn-snakes.

There were also eagles, hawks, cormorants, fish-hawks, turkey-buzzards, owls, crows, wild turkeys, pheasants, partridges, turtle-doves, pigeons, mocking-birds, redbirds, blackbirds, blue-birds, blue-jays, robins, cedar-birds, cat-birds, and humming-birds.

On the marshes were marsh-hens, snipe, yellow shanks, and cranes.

On the water, in season, were wild ducks, brant, geese, and swan, in flocks which were innumerable.

In the water were sharks, porpoises, turtles,

The Indian Character

stingrays, toad-fishes, sheepsheads, drums, sturgeons, perches, croakers, tailors, trout, spots, eels, crabs, and great shoals of mussels and oysters.

Gnats, flies, and mosquitoes were also there.

Such, in the rudest outline merely, were the flora and fauna of the country inhabited by such of the Virginia Indians as were first seen by the white man. It was a flat country, only a few feet above the level of the sea. It abounded in watercourses. The great Atlantic itself washed its low-lying, sandy shore; in part it was intersected by the great Chesapeake Bay, and further cut to pieces by broad sounds, majestic rivers, and vast arms of the sea. Its prairie-like stretches of marsh often formed a characteristic feature of the landscape.

The race of people which lived here was strongly marked, and possessed a perfectly well defined government. They were of a warlike character, blood-thirsty and cruel. They had been stationary, so far as progress in the arts is concerned, from aboriginal times, apparently, and have left us no works by which we can remember them; not a ruin, except some scattered burial-mounds, not a road, scarcely a visible vestige of them remains in this part of the world to tell the present generation that another, a vanished, rather than a conquered, race once dwelt upon the soil we occupy. They have, however, one set of monuments still left, which will probably defy the erosion of time—a few of their words still live in the names of streams, lakes, places, and counties. These have been accepted, and so perpetuated, by the destroyers of the race which gave them.

Still, we know these people fairly well, and some of their leading characters, existing at the time of the invasion, stand out boldly upon the pages of history. The three principal invaders of America—the Spaniards, the French, and the English,—each pursued, as to the natives, a different and a characteristic policy. The Spaniards proceeded at once to crush, exterminate, annihilate them. The French, with adroitness, and a deeply laid policy, courted them, studied them, entered into alliances with them, plunged into their politics, and fought side by side with them in their battles. The English, without carrying their diplomacy so far as did the French, yet entered into many treaties with them, which extended in importance as the Colony stretched farther and farther into the west, and came into contact with larger nations, and involved also other colonies. While a great deal of the forward movement was by force of arms, an equal amount at least was due to these negotiations and treaties. Like the French, Virginia, in the course of its history, had many treaties of friendship and alliance with Indian tribes and nations.

The Indians were in possession of the country when the white man came, and they had not

The Indian Character 31

invited him to come over and take their country from them. The natural relation of the two races was, therefore, one of enmity, which must have been accentuated, on the part of the savage, by the visible superiority and the irresistible encroachments of the invader, and on the part of the English, by the barbarous habits and savage surroundings of the Indian.

War with these people was therefore inevitable, although we would gladly have avoided it. Indeed the conversion of the Indians to Christianity was one of the reasons for making the settlement, although a subordinate one. That settlement had to be made, peaceably, if possible, but still it had to be made. There were the Indians. With no desire to make war upon them nor to exterminate them, but rather with a sincere intention of improving them, the English came. But they came prepared to defend themselves. They brought cannon with them.

Let us now see what kind of a race of barbarians it was which our English ancestors, men who in many cases were fresh from fighting the well trained Spaniards in the great war then still going on in the highly cultivated Netherlands, were now called upon to confront in the tangled forests of the New World.

Strachey thus describes their color and features:

"They are generally of a color brown or rather tawny, which they cast themselves into with a kind of arsenick stone, like red patise or orpiment,[1] or rather red tempered ointments of earth and the juice of certains crused[2] roots, when they come unto certain years, and this they do (keeping themselves still so smudged and besmeered) either for the custom of the country, or the better to defend them (since they go most what naked) from the stinging of musquitoes, kinds of flies or biting gnats, such as the Greeks called scynipes, as yet in great swarms within the Arches,[3] and which here breed abundantly amongst the marish-whorts[4] and fen-berries,[5] and of the same hue are their women; howbeit, it is supposed neither of them naturally born so discolored; for Captain Smith (living sometimes amongst them) affirmeth how they are from the womb indifferent white, but as the men, so do the women, dye and disguise themselves into this tawny color, esteeming it the best beauty to be nearest such a kind of murrey[6] as a sodden[7] quince is of (to liken it to the nearest color I can) for which they daily anoint both face and bodies all over with such a kind of fucus[8] or unguent as can cast them into that stain; after their anointing (which is daily) they dry in the sun, and thereby make their skins (besides the color) more black and spotted, which the sun kissing oft and hard, adds to their painting the more rough and rugged.

"Their heads and shoulders they paint often-

[1] The trisulphide of arsenic. [2] Crushed.
[3] The sailors' term for the Archipelago. [4] The cranberry.
[5] Another name or kind of cranberry. [6] Mulberry. [7] Boiled.
[8] Latin, a red dye, generally understood for alkanet, or rouge.

est, and those red, with the root pochone,[1] brayed[2] to powder, mixed with oil of the walnut or bear's grease; this they hold in summer doth check the heat, and in winter arms them in some measure against the cold. Many other forms of paintings they use; but he is the most gallant who is the most monstrous and ugly to behold.

"Their hair is black, grosse, long, and thick; the men have no beards; their noses are broad, flat, and full at the end, great big lips, and wide mouths, yet nothing so unsightly as the Moors; they are generally tall of stature, and straight, of comely proportion, and the women have handsome limbs, slender arms, and pretty hands, and when they sing they have a pleasant tange[3] in their voices."[4]

"The men are very strong, of able bodies, and full of agility, accustoming themselves to endure hardness, to lie in the woods, under a tree, by a small fire, in the worst of winter, in frost and snow, or in the weeds and grass, as in ambuscado, to accomplish their purposes in the summer.'[5]

"The people differ very much in stature, especially in language. Some being very great as the Sus-que-han-nocks; others very little, as the Wigh-co-com-o-coes; but generally tall and straight, of a comely proportion, and of a color brown, when they are of an age, but they are born white. Their hair is generally black, but few have any beards. The men wear half their beards shaven, the other half long; for barbers

---

[1] Puccoon; the bloodroot.   [2] Beaten.   [3] Tone.
[4] *Historie of Travaile into Virginia*, p. 63   [5] *Ibid.*, p. 68.

they use their women, who with two shells will grate away the hair, of any fashion they please. The women's are cut in many fashions, agreeable to their years, but ever some part remaineth long."

"They are inconstant in everything, but what fear constraineth them to keep. Crafty, timorous, quick of apprehension and very ingenious. Some are of disposition fearful, some bold, most cautious, all savage. Generally covetous of copper, beads, and such like trash. They are soon moved to anger, and so malicious, that they seldom forget an injury; they seldom steal one from another, lest their conjurers should reveal it, and so they be pursued and punished.

"Their women are careful not to be suspected of dishonesty without the leave of their husbands.[1]

"They are treacherous, suspicious and jealous, difficult to be persuaded or imposed upon, and very sharp, hard in dealing, and ingenious in their way, and in things that they naturally know, or have been taught; though at first they are very obstinate, and unwilling to apprehend or learn novelties, and seem stupid and silly to strangers.

"An instance of their resolute stupidity and obstinacy in receiving a new custom, I have seen in the prodigious trouble of bringing them to sell their skins, and buy gunpowder by weight; for they could not apprehend the power and jus-

[1] Smith's *General History of Virginia*, vol. i, p. 129 *et seq.*

tice of the stilliard[1]; but with the scales at length they apprehended it tolerably well; though at first they insisted upon as much gunpowder as the skin weighed, which was much more than their demand in measure.

"They have tolerably good notions of natural justice, equity, honor and honesty, to the rules whereof the great men strictly adhere; but their common people will lie, cheat and steal.

"An instance of their resolutions for satisfaction, we have in the death of Major Wynne, who was shot by an Indian, because one of our servants had killed one of their great men; and upon the trial of the Indian, they pleaded that we were the aggressors, and that they never rest without revenge and reprisals; and that now they said we and they were equal, having each lost a great man: wherefore, to avoid more bloodshed, there was a necessity to pardon the Indian."[2]

Beverley says: "The Indians are of the middling and largest stature of the English. They are straight and well proportioned, having the cleanest and most exact limbs in the world. They are so perfect in their outward frame, that I never heard of one single Indian, that was either dwarfish, crooked, bandy-legged, or otherwise misshapen. But if they have any such practice among them, as the Romans had, of exposing such children till they died, as were weak and misshapen, at their birth, they are very shy of

[1] Steelyard—an instrument for ascertaining weight.
[2] Jones's *Present State of Virginia*, pp. 11, 13, 17.

confessing it, and I could never yet learn that they had.

"Their color, when they are grown up, is a chestnut brown and tawny; but much clearer in their infancy. Their skin comes afterwards to harden and grow blacker, by greasing and sunning themselves. They have generally coal black hair, and very black eyes, which are most commonly graced with that sort of squint which many of the Jews are observed to have. Their women are generally beautiful, possessing an uncommon delicacy of shape and features, and wanting no charm but that of a fair complexion.

"The men wear their hair cut after several fanciful fashions, sometimes greased and sometimes painted. The great men, or better sort, preserve a long lock behind for distinction. They pull their beards up by the roots with a mussel-shell; and both men and women do the same by the other parts of their body for cleanliness sake. The women wear the hair of the head very long, either hanging at their backs, or brought before in a single lock, bound up with a fillet of peak[1] or beads; sometimes also they wear it neatly tied up in a knot behind. It is commonly greased, and shining black, but never painted.

"The people of condition of both sexes, wear a sort of coronet on their heads, from four to six inches broad, open at the top, and composed of peak or beads, or else of both interwoven to-

[1] Beads made from shells.

The Indian Character 37

gether, and worked into figures, made by a nice mixture of the colors. Sometimes they wear a wreath of dyed furs; as likewise bracelets on their necks and arms. The common people go bare-headed only sticking large shining feathers about their heads, as their fancies lead them.

"Their clothes are a large mantle, carelessly wrapped about their bodies, and sometimes girt close in the middle with a girdle. The upper part of this mantle is drawn close upon the shoulders, and the other hangs below their knees. When that's thrown off they have only for modesty sake a piece of cloth, or a small skin, tied round their waist, which reaches down to the middle of the thigh. The common sort tie only a string round their middle, and pass a piece of cloath or skin round between their thighs, which they turn at each end over the string.

"Their shoes, when they wear any, are made of an entire piece of buck-skin; except when they sew a piece to the bottom, to thicken the sole. They are fastened on with running strings, the skin being drawn together like a purse on the top of the foot, and tied round the ankle. The Indian name of this kind of shoe is moccasin.

"But because a draft of these things will inform the reader more at first view, than a description in many words, I shall present him with the following prints[1]; wherein he is to take notice, that the air of the face, as well as

[1] This refers to all the pictures illustrating Indian life which are distributed through this volume.

the ornaments of the body, are exactly represented, being all drawn by the life."[1]

With reference to the pictures above referred to illustrating the Indian habits, customs, and houses, we will say that they are those drawn in Virginia, in 1585, by John White, one of the party which founded the celebrated settlement of Sir Walter Raleigh, at Roanoke. The drawings of White were carried to Europe the next year, and engraved by the famous artist Theodorus de Bry, of Frankfort. The original leaves of these drawings are now preserved in the British Museum.

These pictures are so well drawn and engraved, that they have been reproduced more than once before. Fourteen of them are found in Beverley. They are also seen in enlarged form in various places, and are the most authentic presentation we have of this vanished people.

In this same settlement, was Thomas Hariot, from whose narrative of the first plantation in Virginia in 1585 we liberally borrow. His work was first printed in London in 1588, and afterwards, with White and De Bry's illustrations, in Frankfort in 1590. A commentator, speaking of these, says: "The illustrations are of distinct anthropological importance and exactness, and convey a clearer notion of the ways and manners of the Red Indians at the time of the English plantation than any narrative could express."

It adds an additional interest to these pictures,

---

[1] Beverley's *History of Virginia*, book 3, pp. 1-3.

"A Wer-ó-ance or Great Lord of Virginia"

The Indian Character 39

to know that Sir Walter Raleigh sent White over to draw for him pictures of the natives, so as to illustrate their habits and customs. They relate particularly to the towns of Roanoke, Pom-e-i-ock, and Se-co-ta, which were near the Roanoke settlement, but they are characteristic of the whole section, and strictly accord with what is written directly relating to the inhabitants of Virginia.

The engraver, De Bry, himself thus speaks of these pictures in his dedication to Raleigh of the work of Hariot, which was illustrated by them. After stating that he thought every one should strive to express to Raleigh his appreciation of his labors at colonization, he says: "I have thought that I could find no better occasion to declare it, than taking the pains to cut in copper, the most diligently and well that were in my possible to do, the figures which do lively represent the form and manner of the inhabitants of the same country with their ceremonies, solemn feasts, and the manner and situation of their towns or villages."

"The princes of Virginia are attired in such manner as is expressed in this figure.[1] They wear the hair of their heads long and bind up the end of the same in a knot under their ears. Yet they cut the top of their heads from the forehead to the nape of the neck in manner of a coxcomb, sticking a fair long feather of some bird at the beginning of the crest upon their foreheads, and

[1] This refers to the first picture.

another short one on both sides about their ears. They hang at their ears either thick pearls, or somewhat else, as the claw of some great bird, as cometh in to their fancy. Moreover they either pounce[1] or paint their forehead, cheeks, chin, body, arms, and legs, yet in another sort than the inhabitants of Florida. They wear a chain about their necks of pearls or beads of copper, which they much esteem, and thereof wear they also bracelets on their arms. Under their breasts about their bellies appear certain spots, where they use to let themselves bleed, when they are sick. They hang before them the skin of some beast very finely dressed in such sort, that the tail hangeth down behind. They carry a quiver made of small rushes holding their bow ready bent in one hand, and an arrow in the other, ready to defend themselves. In this manner they go to war, or to their solemn feasts and banquets. They take much pleasure in hunting of deer whereof there is great store in the country, for it is fruitful, pleasant, and full of goodly woods. It hath also store of rivers full of divers sorts of fish. When they go to battle they paint their bodies in the most terrible manner that they can devise.

"The inhabitants of all the country for the most part have marks rased[2] on their backs, whereby it may be known what prince's subjects they be, or of what place they have their original. For which cause we have set down those marks in

[1] Tattoo.   [2] Scratched.

The Indian Character 41

this figure, and have annexed the names of the places, that they might more easily be discerned. Which industry hath God indued them withal although they be very simple, and rude. And to confess a truth, I cannot remember that ever I saw a better or quieter people than they.[1]

"The marks which I observed among them, are here put down in order following:

"The mark which is expressed by A.[2] belongeth to Win-gi-na, the chief lord of Roanoac.

"That which hath B. is the mark of Win-gi-na his sister's husband.[3]

"Those which be noted with the letters of C. and D. belong unto divers chief lords in Se-co-tam.

"Those which have the letters of E. F. are certain chief men of Pom-e-i-ock, and A-quas-cog-oc.[4]

"The upper part of his hair is cut short, to make a ridge, which stands up like the comb of a cock, the rest is either shorn off, or knotted behind his ear. On his head are stuck three feathers of the wild turkey, pheasant, hawk, or such like. At his ear is hung a fine shell, with pearl drops. At his breast is a tablet or fine shell, smooth as polished marble, which sometimes

---

[1] It is to be remembered, in considering this statement, that Hariot had no desire to frighten off possible settlers. This would prejudice the interests of his patron, Raleigh, to whom this report was made.

[2] See plate, p. 38. Roanoac was the town of Roanoke, on Roanoke Island.

[3] That is, Wingina's brother-in-law.

[4] The places here referred to were in the neighborhood of Roanoke Island, where Sir Walter Raleigh's settlement was attempted. Hariot's *Narrative*, iii. and xxiii.

also has etched on it, a star, half moon, or other figure, according to the maker's fancy. Upon his neck, and wrists, hang strings of beads, peak and roanoke.[1] His apron is made of a deer skin, gashed round the edges, which hang like tassels or fringe; at the upper end of the fringe is an edging of peak, to make it finer. His quiver is of a thin bark; but sometimes they make it of the skin of a fox or young wolf, with the head hanging to it, which has a wild sort of terror in it; and to make it yet more warlike, they tie it on with the tail of a panther, buffalo or such like, letting the end hang down between their legs. The pricked lines on his shoulders, breast and legs, represent the figures painted thereon. In his left hand he holds a bow, and in his right an arrow. The mark upon his shoulder blade, is a distinction used by the Indians in travelling, to show the nation they are of. And perhaps is the same with that which Baron Lahontan calls the arms and heraldry of the Indians. Thus several lettered marks are used by several other nations about Virginia, when they make a journey to their friends and allies.

"The Landscape is a natural representation of an Indian field."[2]

"For fishing, hunting and wars, they use much their bow and arrows. Their arrows are made of some straight young sprigs, which they head

[1] A kind of shell money, made of the cockle shell, of less value than peak.
[2] Beverley, book 3, p. 3-4.

The Indian Character

with bone, some two or three inches long. These they use to shoot at squirrels on trees. Another sort of arrow they use made of reeds. These are pieced with wood, headed with splinters of crystal, or some sharp stone, the spurs of a turkey, or the bill of some bird.

"For his knife he hath the splinter of a reed to cut his feathers in form. With this knife also, he will joint a deer, or any beast, shape his shoes, buskins, mantles, etc.

"To make the notch of his arrow he hath the tooth of a beaver, set in a stick, wherewith he grateth it by degrees.

"His arrow head he quickly maketh with a little bone, which he ever weareth at his bracert,[1] of any splint of a stone, or glass in the form of a heart, and these they glew to the end of their arrows. With the sinews of deer, and the tops of deer's horns boiled to a jelly, they make a glew that will not dissolve in cold water."[2]

"If any great commander arrive at the habitation of a wer-ó-ance,[3] they spread a mat as the Turks do a carpet for him to sit upon. Upon another right opposite they sit themselves. Then do all with a tunable[4] voice of shouting bid him welcome. After this do two or more of their chiefest men make an oration, testifying their love. Which they do with such vehemency, and so great passions, that they sweat till they

---

[1] Bracer, the wrist-guard worn on the left arm as a protection from the stroke of the bow-string.
[2] Smith, vol. i., p. 132.   [3] War captain.   [4] Musical.

drop, and are so out of breath they can scarce speak. So that a man would take them to be exceeding angry, or stark mad. Such victual as they have, they spread freely.

"Their manner of trading is for copper, beads, and such like, for which they give such commodities as they have, as skins, fowl, fish, flesh, and their country corn. But their victuals are their chiefest riches."[1]

"The savages bear their years well, for when we were at Pa-mon-kies[2] we saw a savage who by their report was above eight score years of age. His eyes were sunk into his head, having never a tooth in his mouth, his hair all gray with a reasonable big beard, which was as white as any snow. It is a miracle to see a savage have any hair on their faces, I never saw, read, nor heard, any have the like before. This savage was as lustie and went as fast as any of us, which was strange to behold."[3]

"They walk one after another in a line."[4]

"They are frequently at war with all their neighbors, or most of them, and treat their captive prisoners very barbarously; either by scalping them (which I have seen) by ripping off the crown of the head, which they wear on a thong, by their side as a signal trophey and token of victory and bravery. Sometimes they tie

[1] Smith, vol. i., pp. 136-7.
[2] The territory of the Pa-mun-key Indians, between the Pa-mun-key and Mat-ta-po-ny rivers, in Virginia.
[3] Purchas, vol. iv., p. 1689.
[4] Jones's *Present State of Virginia*, pp. 8, 12.

their prisoners, and lead them bound to their town, where with the most joyful solemnity they kill them, often by thrusting in several parts of their bodies skewers of light-wood which burn like torches. The poor victim all the while (which is sometimes two or three days) not shewing the least symptom of grief, nor sign of pain, but bearing it with a scornful sullenness.

"In their rejoicings and war dances they with the most antic gestures, in the most frightful dress, with a hideous noise, enumerate the enemies, that they have murdered, and such like exploits.

"They attack always by surprise, and will never stand their ground when discovered; but fly to ambush whither the enemy may pursue with peril of his life.

"They bred no sort of cattle, nor had anything that could be called riches. They valued skins and furs for use, and peak and re-o-noke[1] for ornament.

"The Indians never forget nor forgive an injury, till satisfaction be given, be it national or personal: but it becomes the business of their whole lives, and even after that, the revenge is entailed upon their posterity, till full reparation be made."[2]

This statement is corroborated, and partly explained, by Glover, who says: "They are very revengeful; for if any one chance to be slain, some

---

[1] Roanoke, a form of shell money already described.
[2] Beverley, book 3, pp. 56-7.

of the relations of the slain person will kill the murderer or some of his family, though it be two or three generations after, having no justice done amongst them in this respect but what particular persons do themselves; if that may be termed justice."[1]

The use of the conch shell with these people was diversified and important. Besides the wampum peak, and white peak which as money and ornament was made of it, we are told:

"The Indians also make pipes of this, two or three inches long, and thicker than ordinary, which are much more valuable. They also make runtees of the same shell, and grind them as smooth as peak. These are either large like an oval bead, and drilled the length of the oval, or else they are circular and flat, almost an inch over, and one-third of an inch thick, and drilled edgeways. Of this shell they also make round tablets of about four inches diameter, which they polish as smooth as the other, and sometimes they etch or grave thereon, circles, stars, a half-moon, or any other figure suitable to their fancy. These they wear instead of medals before or behind their neck, and use the peak, runtees and pipes for coronets, bracelets, belts or long strings hanging down before the breast, or else they lace their garments with them, and adorn their tomahawks, and every other thing that they value.

"They have also another sort which is as

[1] *Account of Virginia*, p. 26.

current among them, but of far less value; and this is made of the cockle shell, broke into small bits with rough edges, drilled through in the same manner as beads, and this they call ro-e-noke, and use it as the peak.

"These sorts of money have their rates set upon them as unalterable and current as the values of our money are.

"The Indians have likewise some pearl amongst them, and formerly had many more, but where they got them is uncertain, except they found them in the oyster banks, which are frequent in this country."[1]

"Their travels they perform altogether on foot, the fatigue of which they endure to admiration. They make no other provision for their journey, but their gun or bow, to supply them with food for many hundred miles together. If they carry any flesh in their marches, they barbicue[2] it, or rather dry it by degrees, at some distance, over the clear coals of a wood fire; just as the Charibees are said to preserve the bodies of their kings and great men from corruption. Their sauce to this dry meat (if they have any besides a good stomach), is only a little bear's oil, or oil of acorns; which last they force out, by boiling the acorns in a strong lye. Sometimes also in their travels, each man takes with him a pint or quart of rock-a-hom-o-nie, that is, the finest Indian corn parched, and beaten to powder.

[1] Beverley, book 3, pp. 58–9.
[2] Roast whole after their manner.

When they find their stomach empty, (and cannot stay for the tedious cookery of other things,) they put about a spoonful of this into their mouths, and drink a draught of water upon it, which stays their stomachs, and enables them to pursue their journey without delay. But their main dependence is upon the game they kill by the way, and the natural fruits of the earth. They take no care about lodging in these journeys; but content themselves with the shade of a tree, or a little high grass.

"When they fear being discovered, or followed by an enemy in their marches, they, every morning having first agreed where they shall rendezvous at night, disperse themselves into the woods, and each takes a several way, that so, the grass or leaves being but singly prest, may rise again, and not betray them. For the Indians are very artful in following a track, even where the impressions are not visible to other people, especially if they have any advantage from the looseness of the earth, from the stiffness of the grass, or the stirring of the leaves, which in the winter season lie very thick upon the ground; and likewise afterwards, if they do not happen to be burned.

"When in their travels, they meet with any waters, which are not fordable, they make canoes of birch bark, by flipping it whole off the tree, in this manner. First, they gash the bark quite round the tree, at the length they would have the canoe of, then slit down the length from end to end; when that is done, they with their tomahawks easily open the bark, and strip it whole off. Then they force it open with sticks in the middle, slope the underside of the ends, and sew them up, which helps to keep the belly open, or if the birch trees happen to be small, they sew the bark of two together; the seams they dawb with clay or mud, and then pass over in these canoes by two, three, or more at a time, according as they are in bigness. By reason of the lightness of these boats, they can easily carry them over land, if they foresee that they are like to meet with any more waters, that may impede their march; or else they leave them at the water-side, making no further account of them; except it be to repass the same waters in their return.

"They have a peculiar way of receiving strangers, and distinguishing whether they come as friends or enemies; tho' they do not understand each other's language: and that is by a singular method of smoking tobacco; in which these things are always observed.

"1. They take a pipe much larger and bigger than the common tobacco pipe, expressly made for that purpose, with which all towns are plentifully provided; they call them the Pipes of Peace.

"2. This pipe they always fill with tobacco before the face of the strangers, and light it.

"3. The chief man of the Indians, to whom the strangers come, takes two or three whiffs, and then hands it to the chief of the strangers.

"4. If the stranger refuses to smoke in it, 'tis a sign of war.

"5. If it be peace, the chief of the strangers takes a whiff or two in the pipe, and presents it to the next great man of the town, they come to visit: he, after taking two or three whiffs, gives it back to the next of the strangers, and so on alternately, until they have past all the persons of note on each side, and then the ceremony is ended.

"After a little discourse, they march together in a friendly manner into the town, and then proceed to explain the business upon which they came. This method is as general a rule among all the Indians of those parts of America, as the flag of truce is among the Europeans. And tho' the fashion of the pipe differ, as well as the ornaments of it, according to the humor of the several nations, yet 'tis a general rule, to make these pipes remarkably bigger, than those for common use, and to adorn them with beautiful wings, and feathers of birds, as likewise with peak, beads, or other such foppery. Father Lewis Henepin gives a particular description of one, that he took notice of, among the Indians, upon the lakes wherein he travelled. He describes it by the name of Calumet of Peace, and his words are these, Book I, chap. 24:

"'This calumet is the most mysterious thing in the world, among the savages of the continent of Northern America; for it is used in all their important transactions: however, it is nothing else but a large tobacco pipe, made of red, black or white marble: the head is finely polished, and the quill, which is commonly two feet and a-half long, is made of a pretty strong reed, or cane, adorned with feathers of all colors, interlaced with locks of women's hair. They tie to it two wings of the most curious birds they can find, which makes their calumet not much unlike Mercury's wand, or that staff ambassadors did formerly carry, when they went to treat of peace. They sheath that reed into the neck of birds they call huars, which are as big as geese, and spotted with black and white: or else of a sort of ducks, which make their nests upon trees, tho' the water be their ordinary element: and whose feathers be of many different colors. However, every nation adorns their calumet as they think fit, according to their own genius, and the birds they have in their country.

"'Such a pipe is a pass and safe-conduct among all the allies of the nation who has given it. And in all embassies, the ambassador carries that calumet, as the symbol of peace, which is always respected. For the savages are generally persuaded, that a great misfortune would befall them, if they violated the public faith of the calumet.

"'All their enterprises, declarations of war, or conclusions of peace, as well as all the rest of their ceremonies, are sealed (if I may be permitted to say so), with this calumet. They fill that pipe with the best tobacco they have, and then present it to those, with whom they have concluded any great affair; and smoke out of the same after them.'

"In Table 6,[1] is seen the calumet of peace, drawn by Lahontan, and one of the sort which I have seen.

"They have a remarkable way of entertaining all strangers of condition, which is performed after the following manner. First, the king or queen with a guard, and a great retinue march out of the town, a quarter or half a mile, and carry mats for their accommodation: when they meet the strangers, they invite them to sit down upon those mats. Then they pass the ceremony of the pipe, and afterwards, having spent about half an hour in grave discourse, they get up all together and march into the town. Here the first compliment, is to wash the courteous traveller's feet; then he is treated at a sumptuous entertainment served up by a great number of attendants. After which he is diverted with antique Indian dances, performed both by men and women, and accompanied with great variety of wild music."[2]

[1] See picture, page 60.
[2] Beverley, book 3, pp. 18–22.

CHAPTER III

THE FASHION AND DOMESTIC CONSTRUCTION OF INDIAN SOCIETY

SMITH gives us an account of the fashions prevailing among the native inhabitants of Virginia, in the year 1607, which presents somewhat of a contrast to those of the present day. He says: "For their apparel, they are sometimes covered with the skins of wild beasts, which in winter are dressed with the hair, but in summer without. The better sort use large mantles of deer-skins, not much differing in fashion from the Irish mantles. Some embroidered with white beads, some with copper, others painted after their manner. But the common sort have scarce to cover their nakedness, but with grass, the leaves of trees, or such like. We have seen some use mantles made of turkey-feathers, so prettily wrought and woven with threads that nothing could be discerned but the feathers. That was exceedingly warm and very handsome. They adorn themselves most with copper beads and paintings. Their women, some have their legs, hands, breasts, and face cunningly embroidered[1] with divers works, as beasts, serpents, artificially wrought into their flesh with black spots. In each ear commonly they have three great holes, whereat they hang chains, bracelets, or copper. Some of their men wear in those holes, a small green and yellow colored snake, near half a yard in length, which crawling and lapping herself about his neck, oftentimes familiarly would kiss his lips. Others wear a dead rat tied by the tail. Some on their heads wear the wing of a bird, or some large feather with a rattle. Many have the whole skin of a hawk or some strange fowl, stuffed with the wings abroad. Others a broad piece of copper, and some the hand of their enemy dried. Their heads and shoulders are painted red with the root po-cone, brayed[2] to powder mixed with oil, this they hold[3] in summer to preserve them from the heat, and in winter from the cold. Many other forms of paintings they use, but he is the most gallant, that is the most monstrous to behold."[4]

Spelman assigns a reason for the style of wearing their hair:

"The common people have no beards at all for they pull away their hair as fast as it grows. And they also cut the hair on the right side of their head that it might not hinder them by flapping about their bow-string, when they draw it to shoot. But on the other side they let it

[1] Tattooed. [2] Beaten. [3] Believe.
[4] Smith, vol. i., pp. 129–30.

"A Chief Lord of Roanoke"

Construction of Indian Society 55

grow and have a long lock hanging down their shoulder."[1]

These long locks were what we have heard of as the scalp-locks, which were cut around and torn dripping with blood from their heads by their victorious enemies, who kept and prized them as trophies of their valor.

"The chief men of the island and town of Roanoac[2] wear the hair of the crown of their heads cut like a coxcomb, as the others do. The rest they wear long as women and truss them up in a knot in the nape of their necks. They hang pearls strung upon a thread at their ears, and wear bracelets on their arms of pearls, or small beads of copper or of smooth bone called minsal, neither painting nor pouncing[3] themselves; but in token of authority and honor, they wear a chain of great pearls, or copper beads, or smooth bones about their necks and a plate of copper hanging upon a string. From the navel unto the middle of their thighs they cover themselves before and behind as the women do, with a deer skin handsomely dressed and fringed. Moreover they fold their arms together as they walk, or as they talk one with another in sign of wisdom. The Isle of Roanoac is very pleasant, and hath plenty of fish by reason of the water that environeth the same."[4]

"In their opinion, they are finest when dressed

[1] Spelman's *Relation of Virginia*, p. 52.
[2] The island near the seacoast of North Carolina, between Albemarle and Pamlico Sounds.
[3] Tattooing.   [4] Hariot's *Narrative*, vii.

most ridiculously or terribly. Thus some have their skins all over curiously wrought with bluish lines and figures, as if done with gun-powder and needles, and all of them delight in being painted; so that when they are very fine, you may see some of them with their hair cut off on one side, and a long lock on the other. The crown being crested and bedaubed with red lead and oil; their forehead being painted white, and it may be their nose black, and a circle of blue round one eye, with the cheek red, and all the other side of the face yellow, or in some such fantastical manner. These colors they buy of us, being persuaded to despise their own, which are common and finer."[1]

"The people of condition of both sexes, wear a sort of coronet on their heads, from 4 to 6 inches broad, open at the top, and composed of peak, or beads, or else of both interwoven together, and worked into figures, made by a nice mixture of the colors. Sometimes they wear a wreath of dyed furs; as likewise bracelets on their necks and arms. The common people go bare-headed, only sticking large shining feathers about their heads, as their fancies lead them.

"Their shoes, when they wear any, are made of an entire piece of buck-skin; except when they sew a piece to the bottom to thicken the sole. They are fastened on with running strings, the skin being drawn together like a purse on the top of the foot, and tied around the ankle.

[1] Jones's *Present State of Virginia*, p. 11.

"Aged Men of Pom-e-i-ock"

Construction of Indian Society 57

The Indian name of this kind of shoe is moccasin."[1]

"The aged men of Pom-e-i-ock are covered with a large skin which is tied upon their shoulders on one side and hangeth down beneath their knees wearing their other arm naked out of the skin, that they may be at more liberty. Those skins are dressed with the hair on, and lined with other furred skins. The young men suffer no hair at all to grow upon their faces but as soon as they grow they put them away, but when they are come to years they suffer them to grow, although, to say truth, they come up very thin. They also wear their hair bound up behind, and have a crest on their heads like the others."[2]

"Seldom any but the elder people wore the winter cloaks (which they call match-coats), till they got a supply of European goods, and now most have them of one sort or other in the cold winter weather. Figure 1 wears the proper Indian match-coat, which is made of skins, dressed with the fur on, sewed together, and worn with the fur inwards, having the edges also gashed for beauty's sake. On his feet are moccasins. By him stand some Indian cabins on the banks of the river. Figure 2 wears the Duffield match-coat, bought of the English, on his head is a coronet of peak, on his legs are stockings made of Duffields. That is, they take a length

[1] Beverley, book 3, pp. 2-3.
[2] Hariot's *Narrative*, ix.

to reach from the ankle to the knee, so broad as to wrap round the leg; this they sew together, letting the edges stand out an inch beyond the seam. When this is on, they garter below the knee, and fasten the lower end in the moccasin."[1]

We presume that the word "match-coat" is derived from the Indian word match-cores, which meant skins or garments.[2]

The next picture, which is the original of Figure 1, already given, is particularly interesting in presenting, in the background, the appearance, at a distance, of one of the Indian towns, showing the enclosing palisade, and the regularity of the corn fields surrounding it. In the first of the upper fields, on the right, is the little cabin, in which the man sat, to protect the corn from the birds and beasts which would otherwise devour it.

"The women of Se-co-tam are of reasonably good proportion. In their going they carry their hands dangling down, and are dadil[3] in a deer skin very excellently well dressed, hanging down from their navel unto the midst of their thighs, which also covereth their hinder parts. The rest of their bodies are all bare. The fore part of their hair is cut short, the rest is not over long, thin and soft, and falling down about their shoulders: They wear a wreath about their heads. Their foreheads, cheeks, chin, arms and legs are

[1] Beverley, book 3, pp. 4–5.
[2] Smith, vol. i., p. 147.
[3] Clothed with an apron.

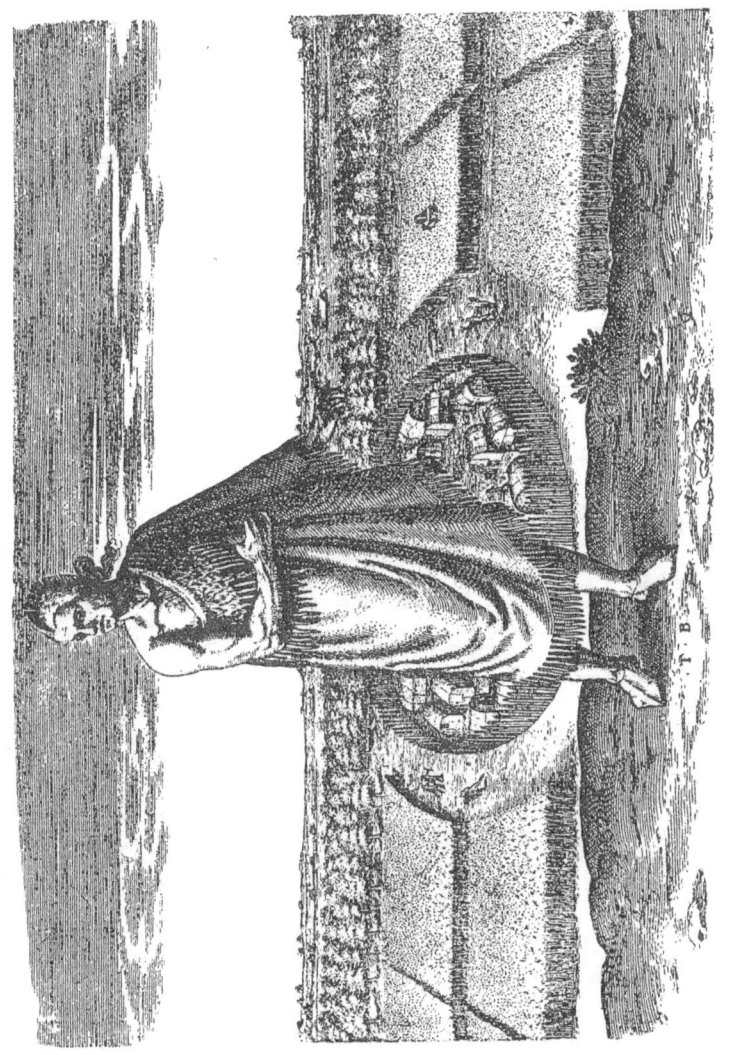
"An Aged Man in His Winter Garment"

pounced.¹ About their necks they wear a chain, either pricked or painted.

"They have small eyes, plain and flat noses, narrow foreheads, and broad mouths. For the most part they hang at their ears chains of long pearls, and of some smooth bones. Yet their nails are not long, as the women of Florida. They are also delighted with walking into the fields, and beside the rivers, to see the hunting of deer and catching of fish."²

Strachey tells us more particularly about this pouncing. He says:

"The women have their arms, breasts, thighs, shoulders, and faces, cunningly embroidered with divers works, for pouncing or searing their skins with a kind of instrument heated in the fire. They figure therein flowers and fruits of sundry lively kinds, as also snakes, serpents, eftes,³ &c., and this they do by dropping upon the seared flesh sundry colors, which, rubbed into the stamp, will never be taken away again, because it will not only be dried into the flesh, but grow therein."⁴

"The method the women have of carrying their children after they are suffered to crawl about, is very particular; they carry them at their backs in summer, taking one leg of the child in their hand over their shoulder; the other leg hanging down, and the child all the while holding fast

---

¹ Tattooed.   ² Hariot's *Narrative*, iv.
³ Small lizards.
⁴ *Historie of Travaile into Virginia*, p. 66.

with its other hand; but in winter they carry them in the hollow of their match-coat at their back, leaving nothing but the child's head out, as appears by the figure."[1]

"Men, women, and children have their several names according to the several humor of their parents. Their women (they say) are easily delivered of child, yet do they love children very dearly. To make them hardy, in the coldest mornings they wash them in the rivers, and by painting and ointments so tan their skins, that after a year or two, no weather will hurt them."[2]

"The manner of the Indians treating their young children is very strange, for instead of keeping them warm, at their first entry into the world, and wrapping them up, with I don't know how many clothes, according to our fond custom; the first thing they do, is to dip the child over head and ears in cold water,[3] and then to bind it naked to a convenient board; but they always put cotton, wool, fur, or other soft thing, for the body to rest easy on, between the child and the board. In this posture they keep it several months, till the bones begin to harden, the joints to knit, and the limbs to grow strong; and they then let it loose from the board, suffering it to crawl about except when they are feeding or playing with it.

[1] Beverley, book 3, p. 10.
[2] Smith, vol. i., p. 131.
[3] Aristotle states that this custom was in favor with many barbarians. *Politics*, book vii

The Women Carrying Their Children

Construction of Indian Society 61

"While the child is thus at the board, they either lay it flat on its back, or set it leaning on one end, or else hang it up by a string fastened to the upper end of the board for that purpose. The child and board being all this while carried about together. As our women undress their children to clean them and shift their linen, so they do theirs to wash and grease them."[1]

Spelman adds the following:

"After the mother is delivered of her child within some few days after the kinsfolk and neighbors being entreated thereunto, come unto the house: where being assembled the father takes the child in his arms: and declares that his name shall be, as he then calls him, so his name is; which done the rest of the day is spent in feasting and dancing."[2]

"About 20 miles from that Island,[3] near the lake of Pa-quip-pe,[4] there is another town called Pom-e-i-ock, hard by the sea.[5] The apparel of the chief ladies of that town differeth but little from the attire of those which live in Roanoac.[3] For they wear their hair trussed up in a knot, as the maidens do which we spoke of before, and have their skins pounced[6] in the same manner, yet they wear a chain of great pearls, or beads of copper, or smooth bones, five or six fold about

---

[1] Beverley, book 3, pp. 9-10.
[2] Spelman's *Relation of Virginia*, p. 38.
[3] Roanoke. [4] Mattamuskeet.
[5] Pamlico Sound. [6] Tattooed.

their necks, bearing one arm in the same, in the other hand they carry a gourd full of some kind of pleasant liquor. They tie deer's skin doubled about them crossing higher about their breasts, which hangs down before almost to their knees, and are almost altogether naked behind. Commonly their young daughters of seven or eight years of age do wait upon them, wearing about them a girdle of skin."[1]

"The boy wears a necklace of runtees,[2] in his right hand is an Indian rattle, and in his left, a roasting-ear of corn. Round his waist is a small string, and another brought cross through his crotch, and for decency a soft skin is fastened before."[3]

"Their elder women are cooks, barbers, and for service; the younger for dalliance. The women hang their children at their backs in summer naked, in winter under a deer skin. They are of modest behaviour. They seldom or never brawl. In entertaining a stranger, they spread a mat for him to sit down, and dance before him. They wear their nails long to flay[4] their deer: they put bow and arrows into their children's hands before they are six years old."[5]

"Virgins of good parentage are appareled altogether like the women of Secota above mentioned, saving that they wear hanging about their necks

---

[1] Hariot's *Narrative*, viii. [2] Disks of shells used as ornaments.
[3] Beverley, book 3, p. 7. [4] Strip off the skin of.
[5] Purchas, vol. v., p. 844.

"One of the Chief Ladies of Secota"

instead of a chain certain thick and round pearls, with little beads of copper, or polished bones between them. Their hair is cut with two ridges above their foreheads, the rest is trussed up on a knot behind, they have broad mouths, reasonable fair black eyes: they lay their hands often upon their shoulders, and cover their breasts in token of maidenlike modesty. The rest of their bodies are naked, as in the picture is to be seen. They delight also in seeing fish taken in the rivers."[1]

"There is notice to be taken to know married women from maids, the maids you shall always see the fore part of their head and sides shaven close, the hinder part very long, which they tie in a plait hanging down to their hips. The married women wear their hair all of a length, and it is tied of that fashion that the maids are. The women kind in this country doth pounce and rase[2] their bodies, thighs, arms and faces with a sharp iron, which makes a stamp in curious knots, and draws the proportion of fowls, fish, or beasts, then with paintings of sundry lively colors, they rub it into the stamp which will never be taken away, because it is dried into the flesh where it is sered."[3]

"The Indian damsels are full of spirit, and from thence are always inspired with mirth and good humor. They are extremely given to laugh, which they do with a grace not to be resisted.

[1] Hariot's *Narrative*, vi.   [2] Tattoo and mark.
[3] Secured. Purchas, vol. iv., p. 1689.

The excess of life and fire, which they never fail to have, makes them frolicsome, but without any real imputation to their innocence. However, this is ground enough for the English, who are not very nice in distinguishing betwixt guilt, and harmless freedom, to think them incontinent.

"The dress of the women is little different from that of the men, except in the tying of their hair. The ladies of distinction wear deep necklaces, pendants and bracelets, made of small cylinders of the conque shell, which they call peak. They likewise keep their skin clean, and shining with oil, while the men are commonly bedaubed all over with paint.

"They are remarkable for having small round breasts and so firm, that they are hardly ever observed to hang down, even in old women. They commonly go naked as far as the navel downward, and upward to the middle of the thigh, by which means they have the advantage of discovering their fine limbs, and complete shape."[1]

A sample of the way these girls sometimes did is given us in the following, which describes a dance gotten up by Pocahontas, to entertain Captain Smith, while waiting for her father to make his appearance:

"In a fair plain field they made a fire, before which he sat down upon a mat, when suddenly amongst the woods was heard such a hideous noise and shrieking, that the English betook

[1] Beverley, book 3, pp. 9, 6, 7.

A Chief Lady of Pom-e-i-ock

themselves to their arms, and seized on two or three old men by them, supposing Powhatan, with all his power, was coming to surprise them. But presently Pocahontas came, willing him to kill her, if any hurt were intended; and the beholders, which were men, women and children, satisfied the Captain that there was no such matter. Then presently they were presented with this antic; thirty young women came naked out of the woods, only covered behind and before with a few green leaves, their bodies all painted, some of one color, some of another, but all differing; their leader had a fair pair of buck's horns on her head, and an otter's skin at her girdle, and another at her arm, a quiver of arrows at her back, a bow and arrows in her hand: the next had in her hand a sword, another a club, another a potstick; all of them being horned alike: the rest were all set out with their several devices. These fiends, with most hellish shouts and cries, rushing from among the trees, cast themselves in a ring about the fire, singing and dancing with most excellent ill variety, oft falling into their infernal passions, and then solemnly betaking themselves aga n to sing and dance; having spent near an hour in this mascarado,[1] as they entered, in like manner they departed."[2]

"Their women know how to make earthen vessels with special cunning, and that so large and fine that our potters with their wheels can make no better: and then remove them from

[1] Masquerade. [2] Beverley, book 3, p. 55.

place to place as easily as we can do our brassen kettles. After they have set them upon an heap of earth to stay them from falling, they put wood under, which being kindled one of them taketh great care that the fire burn equally round about. They or their women fill the vessel with water, and then put they in fruit, flesh, and fish, and let all boil together like a galliemaufrye,[1] which the Spaniards call, *olla podrida.* Then they put it out into dishes, and set before the company, and then they make good cheer together. Yet are they moderate in their eating, whereby they avoid sickness."[2]

"The women have a great care to maintain and keep firelight still within their houses, and if at any time it go out, they take it for an evil sign, but if it be out they kindle it again presently, by chaffing a dry pointed stick in a hole of a little square piece of wood; that firing itself will so fire moss, leaves, or any such like thing that is apt quickly to burn."[3]

"After they have taken store of fish, they get them unto a place fit to dress it. There they stick up in the ground four stakes in a square room,[4] and lay four potes[5] upon them, and others over thwart the same like unto an hurdle,[6] they make a fire underneath to broil the same, not after the manner of the people in Florida, which do but schorte,[7] and harden their meat in the

---

[1] Hash. [2] Hariot's *Narrative,* xv.
[3] Strachey, *Historie of Travaile into Virginia,* p. 112.
[4] In the form of a square. [5] Sticks. [6] Gridiron. [7] Cut.

A Couple of Young Women

smoke only to reserve the same during all the winter. For this people reserving nothing for store, they do broil, and spend away all at once, and when they have further need, they roast or seethe¹ fresh, as we shall see hereafter. And when as the hurdle cannot hold all the fish, they hang the rest by the fires on sticks set up in the ground against the fire, and then they finish the rest of their cookery. They take good heed that they be not burnt. When the first are broiled they lay others on, that were newly brought, continuing the dressing of their meat in this sort, until they think they have sufficient."²

"Their cookery has nothing commendable in it, but that it is performed with little trouble. They have no other sauce but a good stomach, which they seldom want. They boil, broil or rost all the meat they eat, and it is very common with them to boil fish as well as flesh with their homony; this is Indian corn soaked, broken in a mortar, husked, and then boiled in water over a gentle fire, for ten or twelve hours, to the consistence of furmity.³ The thin of this is, what my Lord Bacon calls cream of maize, and highly commends for an excellent sort of nutriment.

"They have two ways of broiling, viz.: one by laying the meat itself upon the coals, the other by laying it upon sticks raised upon forks at some distance above the live coals, which heats

¹ Boil.   ² Hariot's *Narrative*, xiv.
³ Hulled wheat boiled in milk and seasoned.

more gently, and drys up the gravy; this they, and we also from them, call barbecuing.

"They skin and paunch[1] all sorts of quadrupeds; they draw and pluck their fowl; but their fish they dress with their scales on, without gutting; but in eating they leave the scales, entrails and bones to be thrown away.

"They never serve up different sorts of victuals in one dish; as roast and boiled fish and flesh, but always serve them up in several vessels.

"They bake their bread either in cakes before the fire, or in loaves on a warm hearth, covering the loaf first with leaves, then with warm ashes, and afterwards with coals over all. Their food is fish and flesh of all sorts, and that which participates of both, as the beaver, a small kind of turtle or terrapin, (as we call them) and several species of snakes. They likewise eat grubs, the nymphe[2] of wasps, some kinds of scarabæi,[3] cicadæ,[4] etc.

"They eat all sorts of peas, beans, and other pulse,[5] both parched and boiled. They make their bread of the Indian corn, wild oats, or the seed of the sunflower. But when they eat their bread, they eat it alone, not with their meat. They have no salt among them, but for seasoning use the ashes of hickory, stickweed,[6] or some other wood or plant affording a salt ash.

"They delight much to feed on roasting-ears;

[1] Eviscerate.   [2] Chrysalis.   [3] Beetles.   [4] Locusts.
[5] Plants cultivated as field or garden crops which can be gathered by hand without cutting.
[6] Stickseed.

Cooking their Fish.

Construction of Indian Society 69

that is, the Indian corn, gathered green and milky, before it is grown to its full bigness, and roasted before the fire, in the ear. For the sake of this diet, which they love exceedingly, they are very careful to procure all the several sorts of Indian corn before mentioned, by which means they contrive to prolong their season. And indeed this is a very sweet and pleasing food.

"They have growing near their towns, peaches, strawberries, cushaws,[1] melons, pompions,[2] matcocks,[3] &c. The cushaws and pompions they lay by, which will keep several months good after they are gathered; the peaches they save, by drying them in the sun; they have likewise several sorts of the phaseoli.[4]

"In the woods they gather chincapins, chestnuts, hiccories, and walnuts. The kernels of the hiccories they beat in a mortar with water, and make a white liquor like milk, from whence they call our milk hickory. Hazlenuts they will not meddle with, though they make a shift with acorns sometimes, and eat all the other fruits mentioned before, but they never eat any sort of herbs or leaves.

"Out of the ground they dig trubbs,[5] earthnuts, wild onions and a tuberous root they call

[1] A kind of pumpkin; a variety of crooknecked squash.
[2] Pumpkins.
[3] The same as maracock, the Indian name for the fruit of the passion flower, which they ate.
[4] Phaseoleæ, a tribe of leguminous plants.
[5] Truffles, earth nuts.

tuck-a-hoe,[1] which while crude is of a very hot and virulent quality: but they can manage it so as in case of necessity, to make bread of it, just as the East Indians and those of Egypt are said to do of colocasha. It grows like a flag in the miry marshes, having roots of the magnitude and taste of Irish potatoes, which are easy to be dug up.

"They accustom themselves to no set meals, but eat night and day, when they have plenty of provisions, or if they have got anything that is a rarity. They are very patient of hunger, when by any accident they happen to have nothing to eat; which they make more easy to them by girding up their bellies, just as the wild Arabs are said to do, in their long marches, by which means they are less sensible of the impressions of hunger.

"Among all this variety of food, nature hath not taught them the use of any other drink than water: which though they have in cool and pleasant springs every where, yet they will not drink that, if they can get pond water, or such as has been warmed by the sun and weather. Baron Lahontan tells of a sweet juice of maple, which the Indians to the northward gave him, mingled with water, but our Indians use no such drink. For their strong drink, they are altogether beholding to us, and are so greedy of it, that most of them will be drunk as often as they

---

[1] Both the Virginia wake-robin and the golden-club, both aquatics with deep fleshy and starchy rootstocks.

"Their Seething of their Meat in Earthen Pots"

Construction of Indian Society 71

find an opportunity; notwithstanding which, it is a prevailing humor among them, not to taste any strong drink[1] at all, unless they can get enough to make them quite drunk and then they go as solemnly about it, as if it were part of their religion."[2]

In discussing the food supplies of this people, Strachey says:

"They neither impale for deer, nor breed cattle nor bring up tame poultry, albeit they have great store of turkies, nor keep birds, squirrels, nor tame partridges, swan, duck, nor goose."[3]

"Their corn and, indeed, their copper, hatchets, houses, beads, pearl, and most things with them of value, according to their own estimation, they hide, one from the knowledge of another, in the ground within the woods, and so keep them all the year, or until they have fit use for them, as the Romans did their moneys and treasure in certain cellars, and when they take them forth they scarse make their women privy to the storehouse."[4]

"In March and April they live much upon their fishing-weirs; and feed on fish, turkeys and squirrels. In May and June they plant their fields, and live most off acorns, walnuts, and fish. But to amend[5] their diet, some disperse themselves in small companies and live upon fish,

---

[1] The Indians gave to alcoholic liquor the name of Fire Water, because it would burn when thrown in the fire.
[2] Beverley, bk 3, pp. 14–16.
[3] Strachey, *Historie of Travaile into Virginia*, pp. 72–3.
[4] *Ibid*, p. 113.   [5] Improve.

beasts, crabs, oysters, land tortoises, strawberries, mulberries, and such like. In June and July, and August, they feed upon the roots of Tock-nough berries, fish and green wheat. It is strange to see how their bodies alter with their diet, even as the deer and wild beasts they seem fat and lean, strong and weak. Powhatan, their great king, and some others that are provident, roast their fish and flesh upon hurdles, as before expressed, and keep it till scarce[1] times."[2]

"Oysters there be in whole banks and beds, and those of the best: I have seen some thirteen inches long. The savages use to boil oysters and mussels together, and with the broth they make a good spoon-meat, thickened with the flour of their wheat; and it is a great thrift and husbandry with them to hang the oysters upon strings (being shelled and dried) in the smoke, thereby to preserve them all the year."[3]

"The manner of baking of bread is thus: after they pound their wheat into flour with hot water, they make it into paste, and work it into round balls and cakes, then they put it into a pot of seething water, when it is sod[4] thoroughly, they lay it on a smooth stone, there they harden it as well as in an oven."[5]

"Several kinds of the creeping vines bearing fruit, the Indians planted in their gardens or fields, because they would have plenty of them

---

[1] Times of dearth. [2] Smith, vol. i., p. 129.
[3] Strachey, *Historie of Travaile into Virginia*, p. 127.
[4] Boiled. [5] Purchas, vol. iv., p. 1689.

Construction of Indian Society 73

always at hand; such as muskmelons, watermelons, pompions, cushaws, macocks and gourds."[1] They also cultivated Indian corn, peas, beans, potatoes, tobacco, peaches, nectarines, apricots, plums, cherries, and grapes.

"Cushaws are a kind of pumpkin of a bluish green color, streaked with white, when fit for use. They are larger than the pumpkins, and have a long narrow neck.

"The macocks are a lesser sort of pumpkin, of these there are a great variety, but the Indian name macock serves for all."[2]

Simlins would be included under this term.

Maracock was the fruit of the passion flower. It was an article of food which grew wild.

Spelman gives us this account of their country, and food supplies:

"The country is full of wood and in some parts water they have plentiful, they have marsh ground and small fields, for corn, and other grounds whereon their deer, goats and stags feedeth. There be in this country lions, bears, wolves, foxes, musk-cats, hares, flying-squirrels, and other squirrels being all gray like conies, great store of fowl, only peacocks and common hens wanting: fish in abundance whereon they live most part of the summer time. They have a kind of wheat called loc-a-taunce and peas and beans. Great store of walnuts growing in every place. They have no orchard fruits, only

[1] Beverley, bk. 2, pp. 26–8; bk. 4, p. 78.
[2] *Ibid.*, pp. 27–8.

two kinds of plums, the one a sweet and luscious plum long and thick, in form and likeness of a nut-palm, the other resembling a medler,[1] but somewhat sweeter, yet not eatable till they be rotten as ours are."[2]

Strachey says that they were great eaters, and that when any of them were in the employment of the English, it was necessary to allow them twice as much provisions as a white man needed.

This is in harmony with Jones's statement:

"They have no notion of providing for futurity for they eat night and day whilst their provisions last, falling to as soon as they awake, and falling asleep again as soon as they are well crammed."[3]

"Before their dinners and suppers, the better sort will do a kind of sacrifice, taking the first bit and casting it into the fire, and to it repeat certain words. I have heard Ma-chumps, at Sir Thos. Dale's table, once or twice (upon our request) repeat the said grace as it were, howbeit I forgot to take it from him in writing."[4]

"Referring now to the picture here:

No. 1. Is their pot boiling with hominy and fish in it.

No. 2. Is a bowl of corn, which they gather up with their fingers to feed themselves.

---

[1] Medlar, a small bushy tree, having a fruit like a little brown-skinned apple.

[2] Spelman's *Relation of Virginia*, pp. 28–9.

[3] Jones's *Present State of Virginia*, p. 10.

[4] Strachey, *Historie of Travaile into Virginia*, p. 94; Smith, vol. i., p. 140.

A Man and His Wife at Dinner

No. 3. The tomahawk, which he lays by at dinner.
No. 4. His pocket, which is likewise stript off, that he may be at full liberty.
No. 5. A fish. } Both ready
No. 6. A heap of roasting ears. } for dressing.
No. 7. The gourd of water.
No. 8. A cockle shell, which they sometimes use instead of a spoon.
No. 9. The mat they sit on. All other matters in this figure, are understood by the foregoing, and following descriptions.

"Their fashion of sitting at meals, is on a mat spread on the ground, with their legs out at length before them, and the dish between their legs, for which reason, they seldom or never sit more than two together, at a dish, who may with convenience mix their legs together, and have the dish stand commodiously to them both. As appears by the figure.

"The spoons which they eat with, do generally hold half a pint; and they laugh at the English for using small ones, which they must be forced to carry so often to their mouths, that their arms are in danger of being tired, before their belly."[1]

"The men bestow their times in fishing, hunting, wars, and such man-like exercises, scorning to be seen in any woman-like exercise, which is the cause that the women be very painful,[2] and the men often idle. The women and chil-

[1] Beverley, book 3, pp. 16-17.
[2] Oppressed with cares and duties.

dren do the rest of the work. They make mats, baskets, pots, morters, pound their corn, make their bread, prepare their victuals, plant their corn, gather their corn, bear all kind of burdens, and such like."[1]

"Their manner of feeding is in this wise. They lay a mat made of bents[2] on the ground, and set their meat on the midst[3] thereof, and then sit down round, the men upon one side, and the women on the other. Their meat is maize sodden,[4] in such sort as I described it in the former treatise, of very good taste, deer-flesh, or of some other beast, and fish. They are very sober in their eating, and drinking, and consequently very long lived because they do not oppress nature."[5]

Spelman's account of the manner the Indians sat at meat is not like the picture given above, which represents the man and his wife sitting opposite to each other. He says:

"They sit on mats round about the house the men by themselves and the women by themselves, the women bring to every one a dish of meat, for the better sort never eat together in one dish, when he hath eaten what he will or that which was given him, for he looks for no second course, he sets down his dish by him and mumbleth certain words to himself in manner of giving thanks. If any be left the women gather it up, and either keep it till the next meal, or give it to the poorer sort, if any be there."[6]

[1] Smith, vol. i., p. 131.   [2] Made of bent or plaited grass, etc.
[3] Center.   [4] Boiled.   [5] Hariot's *Narrative*, xvi.
[6] Spelman's *Relation of Virginia*, p. 51.

CHAPTER IV

MARRIAGE

SPELMAN gives us this account of their manner of marrying:

"The custom is to have many wives and to buy them, so it is he which has most copper and beads may have most wives, for if he taketh liking of any woman he makes love to her, and seeketh to her father or kinfolks to set what price he must pay for her, which being once agreed on the kindred meet and make good cheer, and when the sum agreed on be paid she shall be delivered to him for his wife. The ceremony is thus. The parents bring their daughter between them, if her parents be dead, then some of her kinfolks, or whom it pleaseth the king[1] to appoint (for the man goes not unto any place to be married, but the woman is brought to him where he dwelleth). At her coming to him, her father or chief friend joins the hands together, and then the father or chief friend of the man bringeth a long string of beads and measuring his arm's length thereof doth break it over the hands of

[1] It was by this title that the English designated the Wer-ó-ances, or Chiefs, of the various tribes of Indians.

those that are to be married while their hands be joined together, and gives it unto the woman's father or him that brings her, and so with much mirth and feasting they go together.

"When the king of the country will have any wives he acquaints his chief men with his purpose, who sends into all parts of the country for the fairest and comliest maids out of which the king taketh his choice, giving their parents what he pleaseth. If any of the king's wives have once a child by him, he keeps her no longer, but puts her from him giving her sufficient copper and beads to maintain her and the child while it is young, and then is taken from her and maintained by the king, it now being lawful for her being thus put away to marry with any other. The king, Powhatan, having many wives, when he goeth a hunting or to visit another king under him (for he goeth not out of his own country), he leaveth them with two old men who have the charge of them till his return."[1]

"They express their love to such women as they would make choice to live withall, by presenting them with the fruits of their labors, as by fowl, fish, or wild beasts, which by their huntings, their bows and arrows, by weirs, or otherwise, they obtain, which they bring unto the young women, as also of such summer fruits and berries which their travels abroad hath made them known readily where to gather, and those of the best kind in their season. If the young

[1] Spelman's *Relation of Virginia*, p. 32.

maiden become once to be *sororians virgo*,[1] and live under parents, the parents must allow of the suitor; and for their good will, the wooer promiseth that the daughter shall not want of such provisions, nor of deer-skins fitly dressed for to wear; besides, he promiseth to do his endeavor to procure her beads, pearl, and copper, and, for handsell,[2] gives her before them something as a kind of arrasponsalitia,[3] token of betrothing or contract of a further amity and acquaintance to be continued between them, and so after as the liking grows; and as soon as he hath provided her a house (if he hath none before) and some platters, morters, and mats, he takes her home; and the wer-ó-ances after this manner may have as many as they can obtain, howbeit all the rest whom they take after their first choice are (as it were) mercenary, hired but by covenant and condition, for a time, a year or so, after which they may put them away; but if they keep them longer than the time appointed, they must ever keep them, how deformed, diseased, or unaccompaniable soever they may prove."[4]

Courtship and marriage among the Indians is thus described by Jones:

"Courtship was short, and like their marriage unembarrassed by ceremony. If the presents of a young warrior are accepted by his

---

[1] A girl growing up with a man as his sister.
[2] The first present sent to a young woman on her wedding day.
[3] "Earnest money in ratification of the espousals."
[4] Strachey, *Historie of Travaile into Virginia*, p. 109.

mistress, she is considered as having agreed to become his wife, and without any farther explanations to her family, she goes home to his hut. The principles that are to regulate their future conduct are well understood. He agrees to perform the more laborious duties of hunting and fishing; of felling the trees, erecting the hut, constructing the canoe, and of fighting the enemies of the tribe. To her custom had assigned almost all the domestic duties; to prepare the food; to watch over the infancy of the children. The nature of their lives and circumstances added another, which with more propriety, taken in a general view, should have been exercised by the male. It belonged to the women to plant the corn, and attend all the other productions of an Indian garden or plantation. But the labour required for raising these articles was trifling, and the warriors being engaged in hunting and war, had neither leisure nor inclination to attend to objects of such inferior consideration.

"Marriage, or the union of husband and wife, stood precisely on the same footing as amongst the other American tribes. A man might keep as many wives as he could support. But in general they had but one, whom, without being obliged to assign any reason, they might at any time abandon, and immediately form a new engagement. The rights of the woman are the same with this difference, that she cannot marry again until the next annual festival.

"Nothing appears to them more repugnant to

Marriage

nature and reason than the contrary system which prevails among Christians. The Great Spirit, say they, hath created us all to be happy; and we should offend him were we to live in a perpetual state of constraint and uneasiness.

"This system agrees with what one of the Mi-am-is said to one of our missionaries. My wife and I were continually at variance; my neighbour disagreed equally with his; we have changed wives, and are all satisfied."[1]

"They punish adultery in a woman by cutting off her hair, which they fix upon a long pole without the town; which is such a disgrace that the party is obliged to fly, and becomes a victim of some enemy, a slave to some rover, or perishes in the woods."[2]

"The Indians have their solemnities of marriage, and esteem the vows made at that time, as most sacred and inviolable. Notwithstanding they allow both the man and the wife to part upon disagreement; yet so great is the disreputation of a divorce, that married people, to avoid the character of inconstant and ungenerous, very rarely let their quarrels proceed to a separation. However, when it does so happen, they reckon all the ties of matrimony dissolved, and each hath the liberty of marrying another. But infidelity is accounted the most unpardonable of all crimes in either of the parties, as long as the contract continues.

[1] Burk, vol. iii., pp. 60–1.
[2] Jones's *Present State of Virginia*, p. 16.

"In these separations, the children go, according to the affection of the parent, with the one or the other; for children are not reckoned a charge among them, but rather riches, according to the blessing of the Old Testament; and if they happen to differ about dividing their children, their method is then, to part them equally, allowing the man the first choice."[1]

"The reason which each chief patron of a family, especially wer-ó-ances, are desirous, and indeed strive for many wives, is, because they would have many children, who may, if chance be, fight for them when they are old, as also then feed and maintain them; yet sure, for the number of people inhabiting these parts, this country hath not appeared so populous here to us as elsewhere in the West Indies; and perhaps their ignorance in not finding out yet the use of many things necessary and beneficial to nature, which their country yet plentifully and naturally affords, their often wars for women (in which many hundred perish) and their immoderate use and multiplicity of women (and those often full of foul diseases) leave this country not so well stocked as other parts of the main, and as the islands have been found to be by the Spaniards; besides (under correction) it yet may be a problem in philosophy whether variety of women be a furtherance or hinderer of many births, it being clear in these countries where (as I said) so many penuries for want of knowledge yet be

[1] Beverley, book 3, p. 8.

Marriage

amongst the people, that the tired body cannot have those sensual helps (as the Turks) to hold up the immoderate desires, many women dividing the body, and the strength thereof, make it general unfit to the office of increase rather than otherwise: and so may the common people especially, for the most part, for this reason likewise be not so long lived here as elsewhere, even amongst savages where greater moderation is used, and where they keep a stricter ceremony in their kind of marriages, and have not as many women as they can buy or win by force and violence from the enemies.

"We observe that those Indians which have one, two or more women, take much [tobacco] —but such as yet have no appropriate woman take little or none at all."[1]

[1] Strachey, *Historie of Travaile into Virginia*, pp. 114, 122.

CHAPTER V

THE SEASONS AND FESTIVALS

BEVERLEY says:
"They make their account by units, tens, hundreds, &c, as we do, but they reckon the years by the winters, or co-honks, as they call them; which is a name taken from the note of the wild geese, intimating so many times of the wild geese coming to them, which is every winter. They distinguish the several parts of the year, by five seasons, viz: The budding or blossoming of the spring; the earing of the corn, or roasting ear time; the summer, or highest sun; the corn gathering, or fall of the leaf; and the winter co-honks. They count the months likewise by the moons, though not with any relation to so many in a year, as we do: but they make them return again by the same name, as the Moon of Stags, the Corn Moon, the first and second Moon of Co-honks, &c. They have no distinction of the hours of the day, but divide it only into three parts, the rise, power and lowering of the sun. And they keep their account by knots on a string, or notches on a stick, not unlike the Peruvian quippoes."[1]

[1] Beverley, book 3, pp. 43-4. A quipu was a cord about two feet long, tightly spun from variously colored threads, and having a

The Seasons and Festivals 85

"At a certain time of the year they make a great, and solemn feast, whereunto their neighbors of the towns adjoining repair from all parts, every man attired in the most strange fashion they can devise, having certain marks on the backs to declare of what place they be. The place where they meet is a broad plain, about the which are planted in the ground, certain posts carved with heads like to the faces of nuns covered with their veils. Then being set in order they dance, sing, and use the strangest gestures that they can possibly devise. Three of the fairest virgins of the company, are in the midst which embracing one another do as it were turn about in their dancing. All this is done after the sun is set, for avoiding of heat. When they are weary of dancing they go out of the circle, and come in until their dances be ended, and they go to make merry as is expressed in the figure.[1]

"Those which on each side are hopping upon their hams,[2] take that way of coming up to the ring, and, when they find an opportunity, strike in among the rest."[3]

"For their music they use a thick cane, on which they pipe as on a recorder.[4] For their

---

number of smaller threads attached to it in the form of a fringe, used among the ancient Peruvians for recording events, &c.

[1] Hariot's *Narrative*, xviii. Figure means the picture opposite the preceding page. [2] Thighs. [3] Beverley, book 3, p. 54.
[4] A musical instrument of the flageolet family having a long tube with seven holes and a mouthpiece. The compass of the instrument was about two octaves.

wars they have a great deep platter of wood. They cover the mouth thereof with a skin, at each corner they tie a walnut, which meeting on the back side near the bottom, with a small rope they twitch them together till it be taut and stiff, that they may beat upon it as upon a drum. But their chief instruments are rattles made of small gourds, or pumpeon shells. Of these they have base, tenor, countertenor,[1] mean,[2] and treble. These mingled with their voices, sometimes twenty or thirty together, make such a terrible noise as would rather affright than delight any man."[3]

"Their sports and pastimes are singing, dancing, instrumental music, and some boisterous plays, which are performed by running, catching and leaping upon one another; they have also one great diversion, to the practising of which are requisite whole handfuls of sticks or hard straws, which they know how to count as fast as they can cast their eyes upon them, and can handle with a surprising dexterity.

"Their singing is not the most charming that I have heard, it consists much in exalting the voice, and is full of slow melancholy accents. However, I must allow even this music to contain some wild notes that are agreeable.

"Their dancing is performed either by few or a great company, but without much regard either to time or figure. The first of these is by one or

---

[1] High tenor, or alto.
[2] A middle voice or voice-part.   [3] Smith, vol. i., p. 136.

Dancing at the Great Feast.

two persons, or at most by three. In the meantime, the company sit about them in a ring upon the ground, singing outrageously and shaking their rattles. The dancers sometimes sing, and sometimes look menacing and terrible, beating their feet furiously against the ground, and showing ten thousand grimaces and distortions. The other is performed by a great number of people, the dancers themselves forming a ring, and moving round a circle of carved posts, that are set up for that purpose; or else round a fire, made in a convenient part of the town; and then each has his rattle in his hand, or what other thing he fancies most, as his bow and arrows, or his tomahawk. They also dress themselves up with branches of trees, or some other strange accoutrement. Thus they proceed, dancing and singing, with all the antic postures they can invent; and he is the bravest fellow that has the most prodigious gestures. Sometimes they place three young women in the middle of the circle, as you see in the figure.[1]

"They have a fire made constantly every night, at a convenient place in the town, whither all that have a mind to be merry, at the public dance or music, resort in the evening.

"Their musical instruments are chiefly drums and rattles. Their drums are made of a skin, stretched over an earthen pot half full of water. Their rattles are the shell of a small gourd or macock of the creeping kind."[2]

[1] Picture.   [2] Beverley, book 3, pp 53-5.

88   The Forest Primeval

Spelman gives this account of their pastimes:
"When they meet at feasts or otherwise they use sports much like to ours here in England as their dancing which is like our Derbysher[1] Hornpipe, a man first and then a woman, and so through them all, hanging all in a round[2] there is one which stands in the midst with a pipe[3] and a rattle with which when he begins to make a noise all the rest gigett[4] about wringing their necks and stamping on the ground.

"They use beside football play, which women and young boys do much play at. The men never. They make their goals as ours, only they never fight nor pull one another down.

"The men play with a little ball letting it fall out of their hand and striketh it with the top of his foot, and he that can strike the ball furthest wins that they play for."[5]

"When they have escaped any great danger by sea or land, or be returned from the war, in token of joy they make a great fire about which the men and women sit together, holding a certain fruit in their hands like unto a round pompion[6] or a gourd, which after they have taken out the fruits, and the seeds, then fill with small stones or certain big kernels to make the more noise and fasten that upon a stick, and singing after their manner, they make merry: as myself observed and noted down at my being among

[1] Derbyshire, a midland county of England. [2] Circle.
[3] Flageolet or whistle. [4] Move rapidly.
[5] Spelman's *Relation of Virginia*, p. 57. [6] Pumpkin.

"Their Manner of Praying with Rattles about the Fire"

them. For it is a strange custom, and worth the observation."[1]

Kercheval gives us this explanation of the term "Indian Summer."

"This expression, like many others, has continued in general use, notwithstanding its original import has been forgotten. A backwoodsman seldom hears this expression without feeling a chill of horror, because it brings to his mind the painful recollection of its original application. Such is the force of the faculty of association in human nature.

"The reader must here be reminded, that, during the long continued Indian wars sustained by the first settlers of the west, they enjoyed no peace excepting in the winter season, when, owing to the severity of the weather, the Indians were unable to make their excursions into the settlements. The onset of winter was therefore hailed as a jubilee by the early inhabitants of the country, who throughout the spring and early part of the fall had been cooped up in their little uncomfortable forts, and subjected to all the distresses of the Indian war.

"At the approach of winter, therefore, all the farmers, excepting the owner of the fort, removed to their cabins on their farms, with the joyful feeling of a tenant of a prison, recovering his release from confinement. All was bustle and hilarity in preparing for winter, by gathering in the corn, digging potatoes, fattening hogs, and

[1] Hariot's *Narrative*, xvii.

repairing the cabins. To our forefathers the gloomy months of winter were more pleasant than the zephyrs and the flowers of May.

"It however sometimes happened, after the apparent onset of winter, the weather became warm; the smoky time commenced, and lasted for a considerable number of days. This was the Indian summer, because it afforded the Indians another opportunity of visiting the settlements with their destructive warfare. The melting of the snow saddened every countenance, and the genial warmth of the sun chilled every heart with horror. The apprehension of another visit from the Indians, and of being driven back ⁱ ⁻ᵗᵒˢᵗᵉᵈ ᶠᵒʳᵗ· was painful in the highest ⁱ ⁻⁻⁻ⁱᵒⁿ was

"Toward the latter part of February we commonly had a fine spell of open warm weather, during which the snow melted away. This was denominated the 'paw-waw-ing days,' from the supposition that the Indians were then holding their war councils, for planning off their spring campaigns into the settlements. Sad experience taught us that in this conjecture we were not often mistaken."[1]

[1] Kercheval's *History of the Valley*, p. 189.

CHAPTER VI

FISHING, HUNTING, AND AGRICULTURE

THE Indian mode of fishing, is thus described by Beverley:

"Before the arrival of the English there, the Indians had fish in such vast plenty, that the boys and girls would take a pointed stick, and strike the lesser sort, as they swam upon the flats. The larger fish, that kept in deeper water, they were put to a little more difficulty to take; but for these they made weirs, that is, a hedge of small rived[1] sticks, or reeds, of the thickness of a man's finger, these they wove together in a row, with straps of green oak, or other tough wood, so close that the small fish could not pass through. Upon high water mark,[2] they pitched[3] one end of this hedge, and the other they extended into the river, to the depth of eight or ten feet, fastening it with stakes, making cods[4] out from the hedge on one side, almost at the end, and leaving a gap for the fish to go into them,

---
[1] Split.
[2] That is when the tide was at its highest point, just before the ebb set in.   [3] Fastened into the ground.
[4] Enclosures like a pouch or bag.

which were contrived so that the fish could easily find their passage into those cods, when they were at the gap, but not see their way out again, when they were in: thus if they offered to pass through, they were taken.

"Sometimes they made such a hedge as this, quite across a creek at high-water, and at low would go into the run, so contracted into a narrow compass, and take out what fish they pleased.

"At the falls of the rivers, where the water is shallow, and the current strong, the Indians use another kind of weir, thus made: They make a dam of loose stone, whereof there is plenty at hand, quite across the river, leaving one, two, or more spaces or trunnels, for the water to pass through; at the mouth of which they set a pot of reeds, wove in form of a cone, whose base is about three feet, and perpendicular ten, into which the swiftness of the current carries the fish, and wedges them so fast, that they cannot possibly return.

"The Indian way of catching sturgeon when they came into the narrow part of the rivers, was by a man's clapping[1] a noose over their tail, and by keeping fast his hold. Thus a fish finding itself intangled, would flounce, and often pull them under water, and then that man was counted a cock-a-rouse, or brave fellow that would not let go, till with swimming, wading and diving he had tired the sturgeon, and brought it ashore.

[1] Put by a sudden movement.

Fishing, Hunting, and Agriculture 93

These sturgeon would also often leap into their canoes, in crossing the river, as many of them do still every year, into the boats of the English.

"They have also another way of fishing like those on the Euxine sea, by the help of a blazing fire at night. They make a hearth in the middle of their canoe, raising it within two inches of the edge: upon this they lay their burning lightwood, split into small shivers, each splinter whereof will blaze and burn, end for end, like a candle. 'Tis one man's work to tend this fire and keep it flaming. At each end of the canoe stands an Indian, with a gig, or pointed spear, setting the canoe forward with the butt-end of the spear, as gently as he can, by that means stealing upon the fish, without any noise, or disturbing of the water. Then they, with great dexterity, dart these spears into the fish, and so take them. Now there is a double convenience in the blaze of this fire: for it not only dazzles the eyes of the fish, which will lie still, glaring upon it, but likewise discovers the bottom of the river clearly to the fisherman, which the daylight does not."[1]

Glover, in describing this fire-fishing, says that the hearth was fixed at the head of the canoe, and in it, on a dark night, would be made a fire with sticks of pine. They would then paddle along the shore in shallow water. The fish, seeing the light, would come as thick as they could swim by each other to the head of the canoe.

[1] Beverley, book 2, pp. 32–4.

With sharpened sticks the Indians would strike through them, and lift them into the canoe.[1]

Strachey, speaking of the ingenuity of the Indians, describes their weirs as:

"Certain enclosures made of reeds, and framed in the fashion of a labyrinth or maze set a fathom deep in the water, with divers chambers or beds, out of which the entangled fish cannot return or get out, being once in. Well may a great one, by chance, break the reeds and so escape, otherwise he remains a prey to the fishermen the next low water, which they fish with a net at the end of a pole."[2]

The picture on the next page represents the Indians in a canoe, with a fire in the middle, tended by a boy and a girl. In one end is a net made of silk grass, which they use in fishing their weirs. Above is the shape of their weirs, and the manner of setting a weir-wedge across the mouth of a creek.

"Note, that in fishing their weirs, they lay the side of the canoe to the cods[3] of the weir, for the more convenient coming at them, and not with the end going into the cods, as is set down in the print. But we could not otherwise represent it here, lest we should have confounded the shape of the weir, with the canoe.

"In the air you see a fishing-hawk flying away

[1] *Account of Virginia*, pp. 23-4.
[2] *Historie of Travaile into Virginia*, p. 68.
[3] The cods of the weir are the parts forming the pouch, or bag in which the fish were entrapped.

Fishing in the Canoe

Fishing, Hunting, and Agriculture

with a fish, and a bald-eagle pursuing, to take it from him; the bald-eagle has always his head and tail white, and they carry such a lustre with them that the white thereof may be discerned as far as you can see the shape of the bird."[1]

"Their fishing is much in boats. These they make of one tree by burning and scratching away the coals with stones and shells, till they have made it in form of a trough. Some of them are an elne[2] deep, and forty or fifty feet in length, and some will bear 40 men, but the most ordinary are smaller, and will bear 10, 20, or 30, according to their bigness. Instead of oars, they use paddles and sticks, with which they will row faster than our barges. Betwixt their hands and thighs, their women use to spin the barks of trees, deer sinews or a kind of grass they call pem-me-naw, of these they make a thread very even and readily. This thread serveth for many uses. As about their housing, apparel, as also they make nets for fishing, for the quantity as formally braided[3] as ours. They also make with it lines for angles.[4] Their hooks are either a bone grated as they notch their arrows in the form of a crooked pin or fish-hook, or of the splinter of a bone tied to the clift[5] of a little stick, and with the end of the line, they tie on the bait. They use also long arrows tied in a line, wherewith they shoot at fish in the rivers. But they of Ac-caw-mack[6] use staves like

[1] Beverley, book 2, pp. 34–5. [2] The English ell, 45 inches.
[3] Interwoven. [4] Fish-hooks.
[5] Crotch or fork. [6] The Eastern Shore of Virginia.

unto javelins headed with bone. With these they dart[1] fish swimming in the water. They have also many artificial[2] weirs, in which they get abundance of fish.

"In their hunting and fishing, they take extreme pains; yet it being their ordinary exercise from their infancy, they esteem it a pleasure and are very proud to be expert therein. And by their continual ranging[3] and travel, they know all the advantages and places most frequented with deer, beasts, fish, fowl, roots and berries. At their huntings they leave their habitations, and reduce themselves into companies as the Tartars do, and go to the most desert places with their families, where they spend their time in hunting and fowling up towards the mountains, by the heads of their rivers, where there is plenty of game. For betwixt the rivers[4] the grounds are so narrow that little cometh here which they devour not. It is a marvel they can so directly pass these deserts,[5] some three or four days' journey without habitation.

"Their hunting-houses are like unto arbors covered with mats. These their women bear after them, with corn, acorns, mortars, and all bag and baggage they use. When they come to the place of exercise, every man doth his best to show his dexterity, for by their excelling in those qualities, they get their wives. Forty yards

---

[1] Transfix with a dart.   [2] Made by art or science.   [3] Hunting.
[4] Smith here refers to the peninsula between the James and the York.
[5] Forests uninhabited by man.

Fishing, Hunting, and Agriculture 97

will they shoot level, or very near the mark, and 120 is their best at random.

"At their huntings in the deserts they are commonly two or three hundred together. Having found the deer, they environ them with many fires, and betwixt the fires they place themselves. And some take their stands in the midst. The deer being thus feared by the fires, and their voices, they chase them so long within that circle, that many times they kill 6, 8, 10 or 15, at a hunting. They used also to drive them into some narrow point of land, when they find that advantage; and so force them into the river, where with their boats they have ambuscadoes to kill them. When they have shot a deer by land, they follow him like bloodhounds by the blood, and strain,[1] and often-times so take them. Hares, partridges, turkeys or eggs, fat or lean, young or old, they devour all they can catch in their power. In one of these huntings they found me in the discovery of the head of the river of Chick-a-ham-a-ni-a,[2] where they slew my men, and took me prisoner in a bogmire,[3] where I saw those exercises, and gathered these observations.

"One savage hunting alone, useth the skin of a deer slit on the one side, and so put on his arm, through the neck, so that his hand comes to the head which is stuffed, and the horns, head, eyes, ears, and every part as artificially[4] counterfeited as they can devise. Thus shrowding his body in

---
[1] A hunting term meaning the view or track of the game.
[2] The Chickahominy.   [3] Swamp or marsh.   [4] Artfully.

7

the skin by stalking,[1] he approacheth the deer, creeping on the ground from one tree to another. If the deer chance to find fault,[2] or stand at gaze, he turneth the head with his hand to his best advantage to seem like a deer, also gazing and licking himself. So watching his best advantage to approach, having shot him, he chaseth him by his blood and strain till he get him."[3]

"They have likewise a notable way to catch fish in their rivers, for whereas they lack both iron, and steel, they fasten unto their reeds or long rods, the hollow tail of a certain fish like to a sea-crab instead of a point, wherewith by night or day they strike[4] fish, and take them up into their boats. They also know how to use the prickles, and pricks of other fishes. They also make weirs, with setting up reeds or twigs in the water, which they so plant one with another, that they grow narrower, and narrower as appeareth by this figure.[5] There was never seen among us so cunning a way to take fish withal, whereof sundry sorts as they found in their rivers, unlike unto ours, which are also a very good taste. Doubtless it is a pleasant sight to see the people sometimes wading, and going sometimes sailing in those rivers, which are shallow and not deep, free from all care of heaping up riches for their posterity, content with their state, and living friendly together of those

---

[1] Approaching quietly and warily. [2] Catch scent of the hunter.
[3] Smith, vol. i., pp. 132-4. [4] Strike with a spear.
[5] The picture already given showing the Indian modes of fishing.

Fishing, Hunting, and Agriculture 99

things which God of his bounty hath given unto them, yet without giving him any thanks according to his deserts."[1]

Spelman gives this account of their hunting:

"Their manner of their hunting is this, they meet some 200 or 300 together and having their bows and arrows and every one with a fire-stick in their hand they beset a great thicket round about, which done, every one sets fire on the rank grass, which the dear feigne[2] fleeth from the fire, and the men coming in by a little and little encloseth their game in a narrow room,[3] so as with their bows and arrows they kill them at their pleasure, taking their skins which is the greatest thing they desire, and some flesh for their provision."[4]

The Indian hunting is thus more fully described by Beverley:

"The Indians had no other way of taking their water or land fowl, but by the help of bows and arrows: yet, so great was their plenty that with this weapon only, they killed what numbers they pleased. And when the water-fowl kept far from shore (as in warmer weather they sometimes did), they took their canoes, and paddled after them.

"But they had a better way of killing the elks, buffaloes, deer, and greater game, by a method which we call fire-hunting: That is, a company of them would go together back into the woods,

---

[1] Hariot's *Narrative*, xiii.   [2] Desiring to flee from.
[3] Area.   [4] Spelman's *Relation of Virginia*, p. 31.

any time in the winter, when the leaves were fallen, and so dry, that they would burn; and being come to the place designed, they would fire the woods, in a circle of five or six miles compass; and when they had completed the first round, they retreated inward, each at his due distance, and put fire to the leaves and grass afresh, to accelerate the work, which ought to be finished with the day. This they repeat, till the circle be so contracted, that they can see their game herded all together in the middle, panting and almost stifled with heat and smoke; for the poor creatures being frightened at the flame, keep running continually round, thinking to run from it, and dare not pass through the fire, by which means they are brought at last into a very narrow compass. Then the Indians let fly their arrows at them, and (which is very strange) though they stand all round quite clouded in smoke, yet they rarely shoot each other. By this means they destroy all the beasts, collected within that circle. They make all this slaughter only for the sake of the skins, leaving the carcasses to perish in the woods.

"The Indians have many pretty inventions, to discover and come up to the deer, turkeys and other game undiscerned; but that being an art, known to very few English there, I will not be so accessory[1] to the destruction of their game, as to make it public. I shall therefore only tell you, that when they go a-hunting into the outlands,[2]

[1] Aiding and abetting.   [1] Remote places.

Fishing, Hunting, and Agriculture 101

they commonly go out for the whole season, with their wives and family. At the place where they find the most game, they build up a convenient number of small cabins, wherein they live during that season. These cabins are both begun, and finished in two or three days, and after the season is over, they make no further account of them.

"This and a great deal more was the natural production of that country, which the native Indians enjoyed, without the curse of industry, their diversion alone, and not their labor, supplying their necessities. The women and children indeed, were so far provident, as to lay up some of the nuts, and fruits of the earth, in their season for their further occasions: but none of the toils of husbandry were exercised by this happy people. Except the bare planting a little corn and melons, which took up only a few days in the summer, the rest being wholly spent in the pursuit of their pleasures. And indeed all that the English have done, since their going thither, has been only to make some of these native pleasures more scarce, by an inordinate and unseasonable use of them: hardly making improvements equivalent to that damage."[1]

The cultivation of the soil was the characteristic which distinguished the Indians of this part of the world from those living in the northwestern portion of the continent, and which is the reason that they are classed as barbarous, instead of

[1] Beverley, book 2, pp. 38–40.

savage, the latter living only by fishing and hunting.

The early records abound with incidents which show what an important part this cultivation of the land played in the life of the Indians and of the first settlers. The Indians had corn. The settlers needed food. There was trading with the Indians for their corn in exchange for European commodities. They appear to have generally had enough corn for themselves and a surplus which they could sell.

The White and De Brÿ pictures represent large cornfields in close proximity to the towns, and also tobacco, pumpkins, melons, and a variety of other products.

The cultivation of these articles of food was a part of the work which custom assigned to the women. The women were aided in the work by the children.[1]

The men fished, hunted, felled trees, made canoes, bows and arrows, and fought the battles of their nation. Such work as attending to a cornfield they deemed beneath their dignity.

These cultivated tracts were called by the English, in later times, at least, "Indian Old Fields." They were very numerous, as the villages themselves were, and were regarded generally as very fertile. They were sometimes very extensive, Strachey stating that at Kecough-tan (Hampton) there were two or three thousand acres cleared.

[1] Strachey, *Historie of Travaile into Virginia*, pp. 111, 116-17.

Fishing, Hunting, and Agriculture 103

So important was this cultivation that the English found one of the most effective ways of fighting the Indians was to destroy their corn crops. This was conspicuously the case in the war with the Pa-mun-keys, in 1624, when, after a battle lasting two days against eight hundred Indian warriors, enough corn was destroyed to have sustained four thousand men for a twelve-month.

Their system of planting is thus presented to us by Spelman:

"They make most commonly a place about their houses to set their corn, which if there be much wood, in that place they cut down the great trees some half a yard above the ground, and the smaller they burn at the root, pulling a good part of bark from them, to make them die, and in this place they dig many holes which before the English brought them shovels and spades they used to make with a crooked piece of wood being scraped on both sides in fashion of a gardener's paring-iron. They put into these holes ordinarily four or five kernels of their wheat and two beans like French beans, which, when the wheat doth grow up, having a straw as big as a cane-reed, the beans run up therein like our hops on poles. The ears of the wheat[1] are of great bigness in length and compass and yet for all the greatness of it every stalk hath most commonly some four or five ears on it. Their corn is set and gathered about the time we use,[2] but their man-

[1] Indian corn.   [2] Do these things.

ner of their gathering is as we do our apples, first in a hand-basket, emptying them as they are filled into other bigger baskets, whereof some are made of the barks of trees, some of hemp, which naturally groweth there, and some of the straw whereon the wheat groweth. Now after the gathering, they lay it upon mats a good thickness in the sun to dry and every night they make a great pile of it, covering it over with mats to defend it from the dew, and when it is sufficiently weathered, they pile it up in their houses daily as occasion serveth, wringing the ears in pieces[1] between their hands, and so rubbing out their corn do put it into a great basket which taketh up the best part of some of their houses, and all this is chiefly the womens' work, for the men do hunt to get skins in winter and do tew[2] or dress them in summer.

"But, though now out of order, yet let me not altogether forget the setting of the King's corn, for which a day is appointed wherein great part of the country people meet, who, with such diligence worketh, as, for the most part, all the King's corn is set on a day; after which setting the King takes the crown which the King of England sent him,[3] being brought him by two men, and sets it on his head, which done the people goeth about the corn in manner backwards, for they going before, and the King following, their faces are

[1] Shelling the corn.
[2] To make hides into leather by soaking them after cleaning, etc.
[3] The copper crown sent over to Powhatan by King James I.

Fishing, Hunting, and Agriculture

always toward the King, expecting when he should fling some beads among them, which his custom is at that time to do, making those which had wrought, to scramble for them. But to some he favors, he bids those that carry his beads to call such and such unto him, unto whom he giveth beads into their hands, and this is the greatest courtesy he doth his people. When his corn is ripe, the country people come to him again and gather, dry and rub out all his corn for him, which is laid in houses appointed for that purpose."[1]

Tobacco, "the Indians' revenge upon the White Man," as it has been well called, is thus described by Hariot. It is interesting to read the estimation in which this weed was held, and the various virtues attributed to it, virtues, which three hundred years of use, have abundantly proved never existed.

"There is an herb which is sowed apart by itself, and is called by the inhabitants up-po-woc: in the West Indies it hath divers names, according to the several places and countries where it groweth and is used: the Spaniards generally call it tobacco. The leaves thereof being dried and brought into powder, they used to take the fume or smoke thereof, by sucking it through pipes made of clay, into their stomach and head: from whence it purgeth superflous phlegm and other gross humors, and openeth all the pores and

[1] Spelman's *Relation of Virginia*, pp. 47–50.

passages of the body; by which means the use thereof not only preserveth the body from obstructions, but also (if any be, so that they have not been of too long continuance) in short time breaketh them: whereby their bodies are notably preserved in health, and know not many grievous diseases, wherewithal we in England are often times afflicted.

"We ourselves, during the time we were there, used to suck it after their manner, as also since our return, and have found many rare and wonderful experiments of the virtues thereof: of which the relation would require a volume by itself: the use of it by so many of late, men and women of great calling, as else,[1] and some learned physicians also, is sufficient witness."[2]

The Indians' method of cultivating this plant so highly valued, is thus described by Glover:

"In the Twelve days[3] they begin to sow their seed in beds of fine mould, and when the plants be grown to the breadth of a shilling, they are fit to replant into the hills; for in their plantations they make small hills about four feet distant from each other, somewhat after the manner of our hop-yards. These hills being prepared against the plants be grown to the forementioned bigness

[1] Else, meaning besides these great personages, persons of lesser station.
[2] Hakluyt, vol. ii., p. 339.
[3] The Epiphany season, the twelfth day after Christmas, January, 6th.

(which is about the beginning of May) they then in moist weather draw the plants out of their beds, and replant them in the hills, which afterwards they keep with diligent weedings. When the plant hath put out so many leaves as the ground will nourish to a substance and largeness that will render them merchantable, then they take off the top of the plant; if the ground be very rich, they let a plant put out a dozen or sixteen leaves before they top it; if mean,[1] then not above nine or ten, and so according to the strength of their soil, the top being taken if the plant grows no higher; but afterwards it will put out suckers between their leaves, which they pluck away once a week, till the plant comes to perfection, which it doth in August. Then in dry weather, when there is a little breeze of wind, they cut down what is ripe, letting it lie about four hours on the ground, till such time as the leaves, that stood strutting out, fall down to the stalk, then they carry it on their shoulders into their tobacco-houses, where other servants taking of it, drive into the stalk of each plant a peg, and as fast as they are pegged, they hang them up by the pegs on tobacco-sticks, so nigh each other that they just touch, much after the manner they hang herrings in Yarmouth. Thus they let them hang five or six weeks, till such time as the stem in the middle of the leaf will snap in the bending of it. Then, when the air hath so moistened the leaf as that it may be handled without breaking,

[1] Average.

they strike it down, strip it off the stalk, bind it up in bundles, and pack it into hogsheads for use. "Sometimes they are forced to plant their hills twice or thrice over, by reason of an earthworm which eats the root, and when the plant is well grown they suffer damage by a worm that devours the leaf, called a horn-worm (an Eruca or Caterpillar) which is bred upon the leaf; if these worms be not carefully taken off, they will spoil the whole crop."[1]

[1] *Account of Virginia*, pp. 28-30.

CHAPTER VII

CANOE-, ARROW-, AND POTTERY-MAKING

IN describing the handicrafts of the Indians, Beverley says:

"They rubbed fire out of particular sorts of wood (as the ancients did out of the ivy and bays) by turning the end of a hard piece upon the side of a piece that is soft and dry, like a spindle on its inke,[1] by which it heats, and at length burns, to this they put sometimes also rotten wood, and dry leaves to hasten the work.

"Under the disadvantage of such tools, they made a shift to fell vast, great trees, and clear the land of wood, in places where they had occasion.

"They bring down a great tree by making a small fire round the root, and keeping the flame from running upward, until they burn away so much of the base, that the least puff of wind throws it down. When it is prostrate, they burn it off to what length they would have it, and with their stone tomahawks break off all the bark, which when the sap runs, will easily strip, and at other times also, if it be well warmed with fire. When it is brought to a due length, they raise it upon a bed to a convenient height for

[1] The socket of a mill-spindle.

their working, and they begin by gentle fires to hollow it, and with scrapers rake the trunk, and turn away the fire from one place to another, till they have deepened the belly of it to their desire. Thus also they shape the ends, till they have made it a fit vessel for crossing the water, and this they call a canoe, one of which I have seen thirty feet long.

"When they wanted any land to be cleared of the woods, they chopped a notch round the trees quite through the bark with their stone hatchets, or tomahawks, and that deadened the trees, so that they sprouted no more, but in a few years fell down. However, the ground was plantable, and would produce immediately upon the withering of the trees: but now for all these uses they employ axes, and little hatchets, which they buy of the English. The occasions aforementioned, and the building of their cabins, are still the greatest use they have for these utensils, because they trouble not themselves with any other sort of handicraft, to which such tools are necessary.

"Their household utensils are baskets, made of silk-grass; gourds, which grow to the shapes they desire them; and earthen pots, to boil victuals in, which they make of clay."[1]

In the account of Master Barlow of the first voyage to Virginia, made for Sir Walter Raleigh, in 1584, he tells us how they made their canoes. He says:

"Their boats were made of one tree, either of

[1] Beverley, book 3, pp. 60–2.

Canoe-Making and Felling Trees

pine, or of pitch-trees, a wood not commonly known to our people, nor found growing in England. They have no edge-tools to make them withal, if they have any they are very few, and those it seems they had twenty years since, which, as those two men[1] declared, was out of a wreck, which happened upon their coast of some Christian ship, being beaten that way by some storm and outrageous weather, whereof none of the people were saved; but only one ship, or some part of her being cast upon the land, out of whose sides they drew the nails and the spikes, and with those they made their best instruments. The manner of making their boats is thus; they burn down some great tree, or take such as are wind-fallen, and putting gum and rosin upon one side thereof, they set fire into it, and when it has burnt it hollow, they cut out the coal with their shells, and ever where they would burn it deeper or wider they lay on gums, which burn away the timber, and by this means they fashion very fine boats, and such as will transport twenty men. Their oars are like scoops, and many times they set[2] with long poles as the depth serves."[3]

"Their fire they kindle presently by chafing a dry pointed stick in a hole of a little square piece of wood, that firing itself, will so fire the moss, leaves, or any such like dry thing, that will quickly burn."[4]

[1] Two Indians, Man-te-o and Wan-che-se, whom Barlow took back with him to England.
[2] Propel the canoe by pushing against the bottom of the stream.
[3] *Hakluyt's Voyages*, vol. ii., pp. 282 *et seq.*   [4] Smith, vol. i., p. 131.

"Before I finish my account of the Indians, it will not be amiss to inform you, that when the English went first among them, they had no sort of iron or steel instruments: but their knives were either sharpened reeds, or shells, and their axes sharp stones bound to the end of a stick, and glued in with turpentine. By the help of these, they made their bows of the locust tree, an excessive hard wood when it is dry, but much more easily cut when it is green, of which they always took the advantage.[1] They made their arrows of reeds or small wands, which needed no other cutting, but in the length, being otherwise ready for notching, feathering and heading. They fledged their arrows with turkey-feathers, which they fastened with glue made of the velvet horns of a deer, but it has not that quality it's said to have, of holding against all weathers. They armed the heads with a white transparent stone, like that of Mexico mentioned by Peter Martyr, of which they have many rocks; they also headed them with the spurs of the wild turkey cock."[2]

Strachey says that they also made their bows out of "weech," that is, the witch-hazel; and their shields were made of the bark of trees, thick enough to keep out an arrow. Their use was not universal.[3]

The following excellently expressed remarks

---

[1] That is, cut it when it was green.
[2] Beverley, book 3, p. 60.
[3] *Historie of Travaile into Virginia*, pp. 105-6.

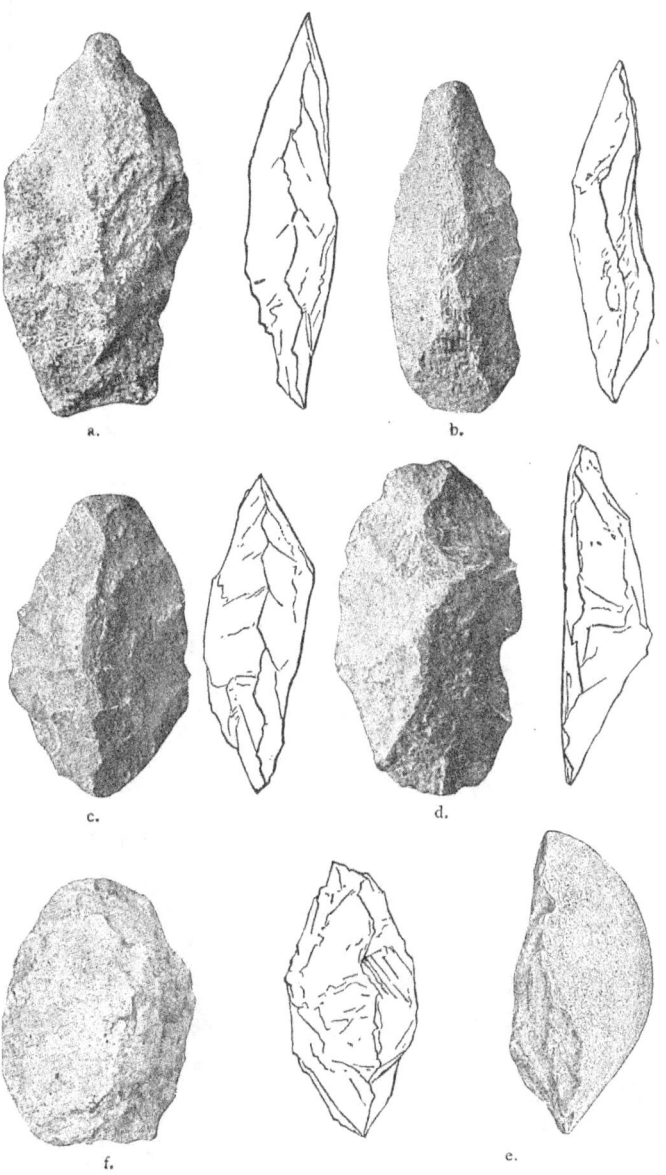

Plate I

Paleolithic Implements from the District of Columbia

From the *American Anthropologist*, Vol. 2, p. 238

on the stone implements which have been found in Denmark apply equally to those found in Virginia, and well deserve to be reproduced:

"It must excite our astonishment that any uncivilized people should be capable of producing such well-finished instruments of stone. The arrow-heads" frequently found "are so admirably formed, that at the present day, with all the advantage of our modern tools of metal, we could scarcely equal, certainly could not surpass them; and yet it is supposed the use of metals was not understood. We can easily see and understand how the arrow-head or axe was first formed and afterwards polished; for indeed in several instances the very whetstones have been found near such stone implements; we are also able to prove that the greater part of the arrow-heads are formed of flints, which the makers knew how to split out of large masses of that stone. But the manner in which they contrived by means of a stone, so to split the flint, and that too, into such long and slender pieces, is still a mystery to us; for from those uncivilized nations which still make use of stone implements no satisfactory information has yet been obtained as to the mode in which they manufacture them. Some have been of opinion that the aborigines endeavored to prevent the splitting of the stone by boiling it, or by keeping it under water while they fashioned it into the desired form. Others, on the contrary, have maintained, that such stone implements could not possibly have been so well formed by means of a stone, but must have been the work of those who were possessed of the necessary metal. Probably the truth lies between these two opinions, namely, in the supposition, that in the earliest times, when the use of metals was unknown, the stone implements were of the very simplest make, but that at a later period, when some had attained to the use of metals, they assumed a more perfect and handsome form. For it must be borne in mind that the use of instruments of stone unquestionably extended over a very long period.

"Lastly, we must not lose sight of this fact, that the weapons and instruments of stone which are found in the north, in Japan, in America, the South Sea Islands and elsewhere, have for the most part such an extraordinary resemblance to one another in point of form, that one might almost suppose the whole of them to have been the production of the same maker. The reason of this is very obvious, namely, that their form is that which first and most naturally suggests itself to the human mind."[1]

The location of some of the aboriginal workshops of the men of the Stone Age have been definitely fixed. One of these is in the District of Columbia, on the north bank of Piney Branch, near its confluence with Rock Creek, just below the Fourteenth Street bridge. An account of this is given by Mr. S. V. Proudfit:

"From the bed of the creek to the brow of the

[1] *The Primeval Antiquities of Denmark* by Worsaae, pp. 22-3.

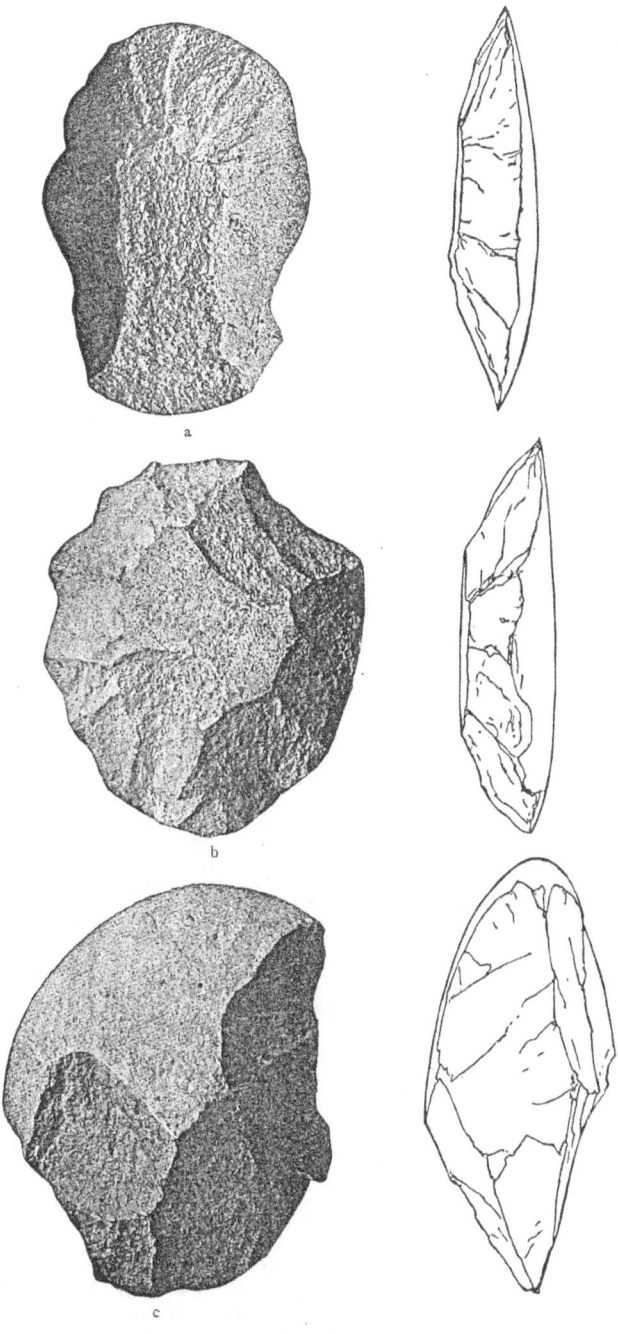

Plate II

Paleolithic Implements from the District of Columbia

From the *American Anthropologist*, Vol. 2, p. 238

Canoe-, Arrow-, and Pottery-Making

hill, and for some distance back, the ground is littered, and in many places covered to the depth of several inches, with chipped stones, chips, and flakes. Many of the stones show but slight marks of chipping, a few pieces having been struck off without materially modifying the original form. Others, however, and they may be numbered by the thousand, have been worked into definite form. The material used was the quartzite pebble, which composes to a large extent the gravel beds of the hill. The forms vary from that of the split pebble, with the outer face worked at the edges, leaving the center with its original surface untouched (see c, Plate III, and a, Plate IV), to that of the almond shape, chipped on both sides (see b, Plate IV). While these ruder forms constitute for the greater part the mass of the remains, thin knife-shaped implements of the same material are also found (see c, Plate IV). Most of these are broken, but perfect specimens occur frequently. While an occasional arrow-head has been found, not a scrap of pottery or other indication of residence marks the place.

"On the level ground at the top of the hill, the earth in places is covered with small chips and flakes, and mingled with them the butts and tips of broken knives. The comparative absence of rough material, large chips, and rude forms, noted on the hillside below, and the presence of small chips and finished forms, are at once apparent, and are not without suggestion as to the relative character of the work prosecuted in each place.

"The area covered by this workshop, embracing several acres in extent, is not confined to the north side of the branch, but includes both sides, as well as the very bed of the stream. The greater part of the work, however, was done on the north side, and any attempt to state its amount would hardly be received with credence by one who has not visited the place and made it a study.

"Similar workshops, though less in extent, are found in several places on Rock Creek below Piney Branch. In some instances these places cover but a few square yards; in others the work is scattered over the hillsides in profusion.

"My own conclusion as to the relics found at these points is that they are the resultant débris of Indian workshops, where material was roughly blocked out, to be afterward fashioned into knives, spearheads, etc.; and that no good reason is yet apparent for attributing their origin to paleolithic man.[1]

"Among the remains found on the village sites fragments of soapstone vessels and other forms of the same material frequently occur, and in sufficient quantity to establish the fact that the value of soapstone for vessels and other articles of domestic use had received substantial recognition. The material is found in many places in

[1] That is, to a race antedating the Indians of the period of the Conquest.

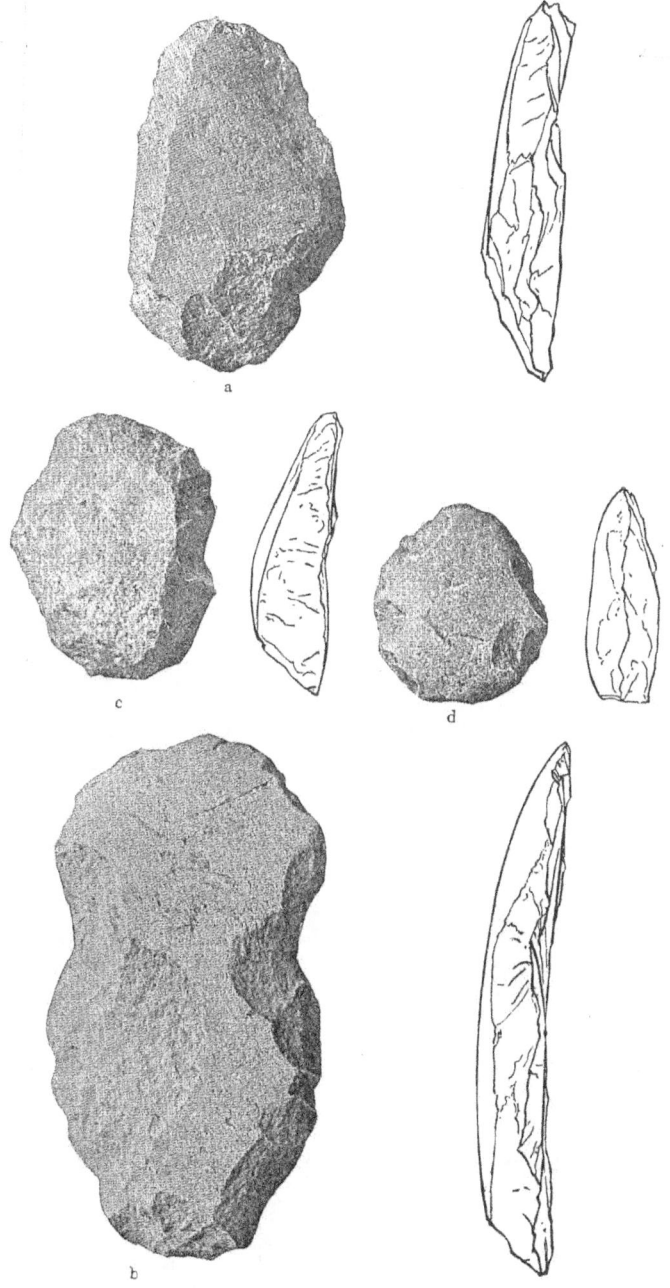

Plate III

Rude Chipped Implements from the District of Columbia

From the *American Anthropologist*, Vol. 2, p. 242

the Potomac valley, and several aboriginal quarries have been located within the limits of the District. The most notable of these is the Rose Hill quarry, about three miles north of the city and near Tenleytown, a full account of which was furnished by Doctor Reynolds in the 13th Annual Report of the Peabody Museum. An examination of the place shows extensive workings, prosecuted intelligently and with considerable success. Pits and trenches, now filled with trees and underbrush, mark the hillside on every hand, and rough fragments of broken and unfinished vessels are scattered about half buried in the forest soil that has accumulated since the abandonment of the quarry. The comparative absence of fragments would seem to indicate that the process of manufacture at this place was not carried farther than to reduce the original block to a vessel convenient in size and weight for transportation.

"At a point one mile below Falls Church, Virginia, on the old Febrey estate, I found a small but interesting soapstone workshop. It is located on a hillside overlooking Four-Mile Run and about one-fourth of a mile below a recently worked soapstone quarry. Large pieces of the unworked stone and fragments of unfinished vessels covered the ground, which occupies an area of not more than half an acre in extent. No perfect vessels were found, and the best specimen obtained was a small core worked out from the interior of a vessel in the process of its construction. Several quartz implements suited for working the stone were found mingled with the débris. The amount of material on the ground was comparatively small, when compared with that at the Rose Hill quarry, and probably it had been carried from the quarry above, where the recent operations have obliterated all traces of ancient mining, if any existed. Careful and repeated research in the neighborhood of this quarry only resulted in the discovery of a few pieces of unfinished vessels —enough, perhaps, to justify the conclusion that this quarry furnished the material used at the workshop.

"Taking the evidence of the fields of to-day, we are enabled to supplement, in some degree, the brief historic account of the early people of the Potomac. Where recorded observation has fallen short the archæologist may thus take up the study of this primitive period in the less imperishable, though unwritten, record left by this vanished people.

"Having identified a camp site by means of historical evidence, it is easy, by a study of its character, to determine the location of others of equal importance, though not mentioned by the historian, especially where the remains are so abundant and distinctive in character as they are in this region. By adding the deductions to be drawn from the comparative study of the archæologic material to the historic facts we may determine the status and rank of this

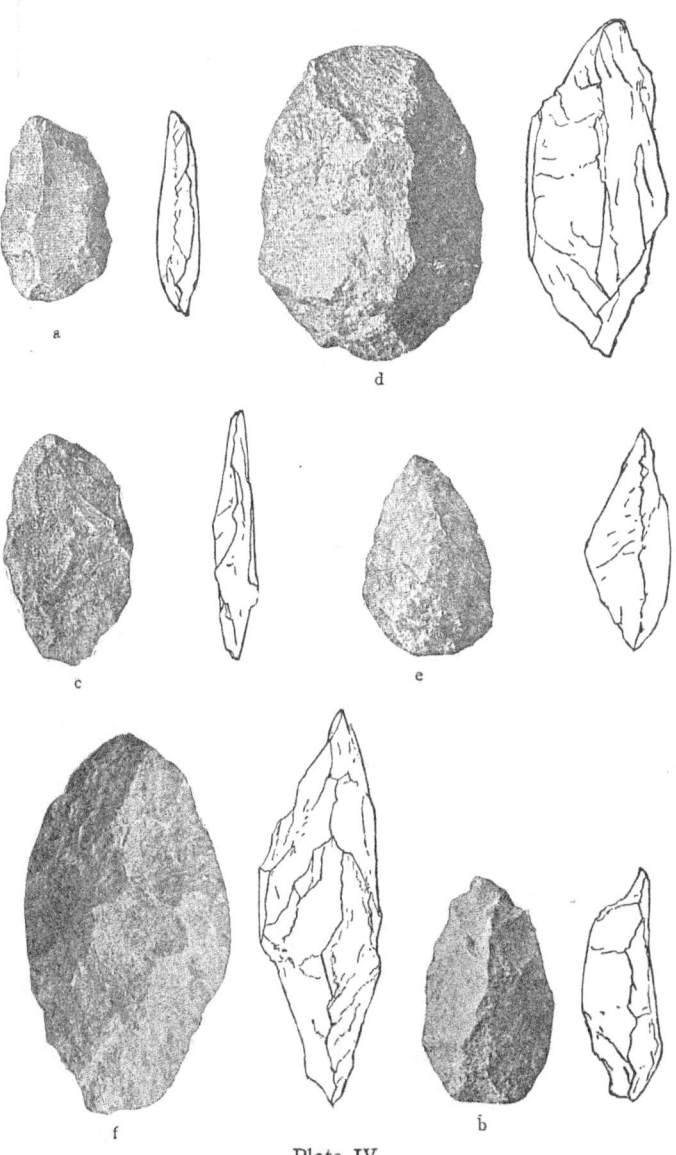

Plate IV

Rude Chipped Implements from the District of Columbia

From the *American Anthropologist*, Vol. 2, p. 244

people among the aboriginal tribes of North America."[1]

The following interesting account of the pottery of the Potomac, tide-water region, is given by Mr. W. H. Holmes:

"The manufacture of earthenware was one of the few simple arts practiced by the primitive inhabitants of the Potomac, tide-water region. Clay was employed chiefly in the construction of vessels for domestic purposes, and fragments of the fragile utensils were left upon camp sites or built into the gradually accumulating masses of kitchen refuse. These sherds constitute the chief record upon which we rely for our knowledge of the art.

"Meagre references to the use of earthen vessels by the natives are found in the writings of the first colonists, and it is known that feeble remnants of the Virginia Indians have continued to practice the art even down to our own time.

"It is difficult to say whether or not pottery was universally employed by the tribes who dwelt upon or who from time to time visited our shores, for its durability varies greatly, and the village sites that now furnish us no specimens whatever may in former times have been well supplied.

"It may further be noted that the duration of the practice of art cannot be definitely determined; for, although fragments may be found from base to summit of shell-heaps and mounds

[1] *The American Anthropologist*, vol. xi., pp. 244-6.

that must have been hundreds of years building or accumulating, we cannot as yet say that a long paleolithic epoch of occupation did not pass entirely without pottery.

"Whole vessels are rarely found, and such as we have are recovered from graves where they were deposited with especial care and at considerable depth. From camp or village sites and from all artificial deposits and accumulations where they are mere refuse they are recovered in a fragmentary state and in pieces so small and so entirely disassociated that full restorations are exceedingly difficult.

"There is enough, however, to give a pretty clear idea of the scope of the art and of the character of its products—enough, it may be added, to enable us to form a definite notion of the culture status of the pre-Columbian peoples as well as to throw considerable light upon their ethnic affinities.

"The localities represented are quite numerous and very generally distributed along the shores of rivers and bays.

"The clay employed is of varying degrees of purity and is tempered with divers ingredients. These ingredients have varied with tribes and with localities; they comprise all grades and varieties of sand and artificially pulverized rock, such as quartz, schist, steatite, etc. Pounded shell was extensively employed, but the fragments of this substance have in many cases decayed and dropped out, and are represented

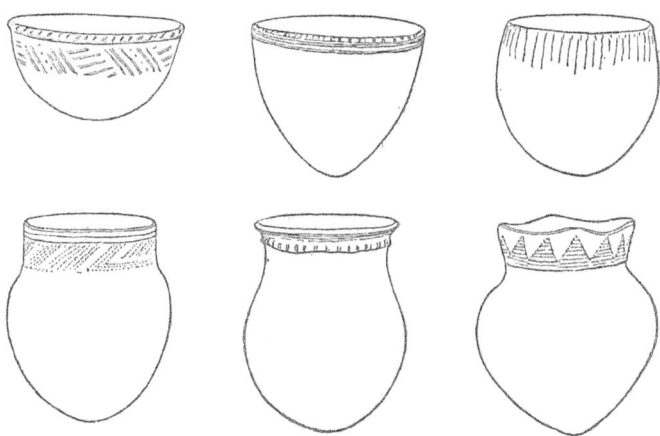

Types of form, pottery of the Potomac Valley.

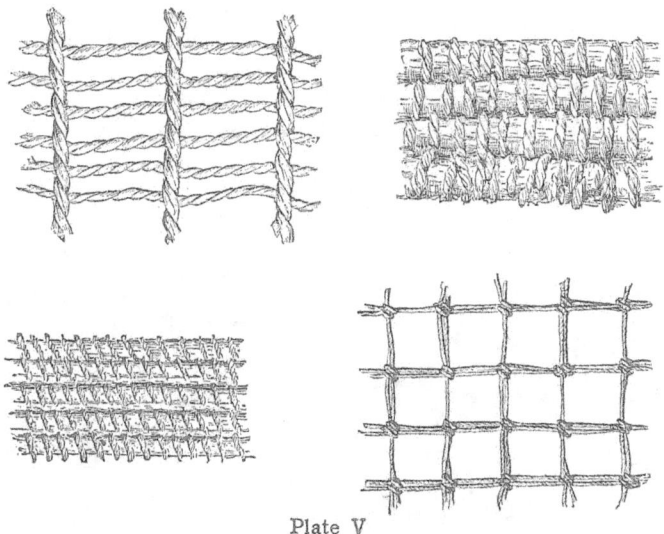

Plate V

Examples of Fabrics Impressed upon Pottery of the Potomac Valley
From the *American Anthropologist*, Vol. 2, p. 250

Canoe-, Arrow-, and Pottery-Making 121

by the irregular pits which now characterize many of the sherds.

"The percentage of these ingredients is often surprisingly great, as they constitute one-half or even, in cases, three-fourths of the mass.

"Upon what theory these tempering substances were added to the clay we are unable positively to determine. We conjecture that strength, porosity, resistance to heat, etc., were qualities especially sought, but we cannot say that superstition did not have something to do with it. The potter may have believed that the clay at hand, unmixed with ingredients from particular localities or of certain kinds, would subject the utensils made from it to the influence of malignant spirits, or from a vision or dream he may have learned that a vessel not containing a proper amount of shell material would never be well filled with chowder or with terrapin.

"Of the preparation of the clay we can say nothing, save through our knowledge of modern practices, but the relics give us many clues as to the methods of building and finishing the ware. Systematic coiling was not practiced, but the walls were in cases built up by means of more or less narrow bands of clay, which were pressed together and smoothed down by the fingers or a suitable tool. In many cases the vases break along the junction lines of the original bands.

"To what extent molds such as baskets, gourds, and the like were used we cannot clearly determine, but that they were used is pretty certain. Exterior impressions of basket-like textures are not uncommon. The surfaces were, to a limited extent, shaped and finished by the use of improvised paddles.

"The shapes of this pottery do not show a very wide range of variation, for the stamp of the preceramic[1] originals are still upon them, and the differentiation of use and office had not yet gone so far in modification and multiplication of forms as it had with the wares of the more advanced races of the West and South. The pot, with all that the name implies, was still the leading idea, and now furnishes the type of form. Its outline varies from a deep bowl, through many degrees of rim and neck constriction and expansion, to a rather wide-mouthed, sub-bottle shape. There is, however, no end of variation in detail within this narrow range of general conformation. Rims are scalloped, thickened, incurved, recurved, and otherwise modified. Necks are straight and upright, swelled out or gently or sharply constricted. Bodies are globular or oblong, and are rounded or pointed below. Illustrations of typical forms are given a, b, c, and d, Plate V. Handles, legs, knobs, and projecting ornaments are rarely met with.

"A few pipes and some round, perforated pellets—perhaps beads—are the only additional forms that I have seen.

"The size is generally medium, the capacity

[1] Prior to the development of the art of pottery.

Canoe-, Arrow-, and Pottery-Making 123

being a gallon, more or less; but minute forms, as well as very large ones, are not uncommon.

"Use was chiefly domestic and generally culinary, as the sooty surfaces and blackened paste clearly indicate; but the vessels were not infrequently diverted to sacred and ceremonial uses, as we know from historic evidence. It is instructive to note, however, that such special functions had apparently not yet, as in the West and South, given rise to especial forms.

"Surface finish was necessarily not of a very refined kind. The fingers or a polishing tool sparingly used gave all necessary evenness of surface. In many cases fabric impressions, acquired in construction or afterwards applied for effect, cover the entire exterior surface. Often these markings were afterwards smoothed down and nearly or quite obliterated, indicating that they had no important æsthetic office. Other similar impressions from fabrics or fabric-covered paddles were afterwards applied, very certainly on account of some æsthetic or superstitious office.

"Much of the ware is decorated in simple but effective ways. We cannot draw a very definite line between those features that exist through accidents of manufacture and those having æsthetic or mixed æsthetic and ideographic[1] office; but it is sufficient for our purpose to

[1] Representing ideas directly, and not through the medium of their names, as in hieroglyphic writing, etc.

classify all patterns that show evidence of design as ornament. The decorations are confined to the neck and rim of the vessel. They were impressed by means of numerous improvised stamps or were executed with the fingers or a pointed implement. The most usual method was by the employment of bits of hard-twisted or neatly-wrapped cords or thongs. If a series of short indentations was desired the cord was doubled between the thumb and finger or laid across the end of the finger and pressed sharply into the clay. Longer lines were made by laying the cord singly upon the clay and running the finger along it for the length of the desired impression. This was repeated until the pattern was finished.

"As a rule, the figures were undoubtedly suggested by textile combinations, and in many cases served simply to emphasize or carry out more fully the markings received from the basket or net-mold employed in construction. Similar effects were secured by incising, trailing, or puncturing with a pointed tool.

"It is interesting to note that the tattoo marks upon the 'foreheads, cheeks, chynne, armes, and leggs' of the 'chief ladyes' of the Chesapeake,[1] as shown in John White's illustrations of the Roanoke expedition, are identical with the figures upon the pottery now exhumed from our shell-heaps.

"It happens that a study of the textile art of

[1] Should be the town of Se-co-ta.

Canoe-, Arrow-, and Pottery-Making

the Chesapeake tribes becomes a natural appendix to that of the fictile art.

"From historic sources we know that the Virginia Indians produced a variety of textile articles, wattled[1] structures for shelter and for trapping fish, mats for coverings, hangings, and carpetings, nets for fishing, besides baskets, nets, and pouches for various ordinary uses.

"From impressions upon pottery we get additional evidence upon the subject—much more indeed upon the technique of the art than can ever be known from any other source. Casts in clay from the potsherds give us numerous restorations of the construction of such cloths, nets, and baskets as happened to be associated with the potter's art. Four examples are presented in Plate V.[2]

"That all are aboriginal in origin cannot be proved, but there is nothing in them that seems out of harmony with the known art-status of the Indian tribes. The presence of nets identical with the fish nets of the European affords the only reason for making the query.

"The condition of the æsthetic idea among our predecessors must receive a moment's attention.

"The shapes of the earthen vessels are in a great measure inherited from basketry, but they are conditioned to a considerable degree by characters imposed by material, construction, use, and the rather weak promptings of the æs-

[1] Formed of interwoven rods or twigs.
[2] See page 120.

thetic idea. As a rule they are not crude, but rather shapely and graceful.

"In decoration textile ideas inherited from basketry still held almost undisputed sway, and the timorous essays of taste did not extend beyond the shadow of the mother art.

"The impressions of nets, baskets, and other textiles employed in manipulating the clay are in many cases ornamental in effect and were probably so regarded by the archaic potter.

"We are reasonably safe in assuming that the elaboration of textile suggestions by means of stamps and pointed tools was the result to a certain extent of æsthetic promptings; but there is another element to be considered—that of the inheritance of forms and ideas from antecedent stages of art and of the conservatism of habit and superstition that tends so decidedly to retain and perpetuate them even when meaningless.

"The amount of decorative elaboration is, therefore, not a correct measure of the condition of æsthetic development, although it is a measure of the condition of that body of features in the art that become the exclusive possession of the æsthetic idea after habit and superstition loosen their hold.

"I have myself gathered potsherds of the above class all along the coast from the Chowan River, in Carolina, to the eastern shore of Nantucket, and have seen specimens from all parts of the Atlantic coastal belt. Among them all there is no hint of other ethnic conditions than those known through historic channels. All indicate an even plane of barbaric simplicity. There is fair homogeneity of character as well as correspondence in stage, indicating ethnic unity.

"Every relic of art has an ethnic value, and even these stray fragments of earthenware, when all the evidence attainable has been gathered about them, may be found useful in the determination of ethnic questions.

"In glancing at the linguistic map of the United States prepared by Major Powell and his assistants I find a general correspondence between the distribution of this family of earthenware and the area assigned to the Algonkian peoples."[1]

[1] *The American Anthropologist*, vol. xi., pp. 246-52.

The plates and articles from *The American Anthropologist* presented in this volume are reproduced with the permission of The Bureau of American Ethnology, and The Anthropological Society of Washington, D. C.

CHAPTER VIII

HOUSES AND TOWNS

PROBABLY no feature of Indian life has been more generally misunderstood than that relating to their habitations. Most persons, if asked, would say that they supposed the Indians of Virginia were roving bands, occupying tents, when they could have been said to occupy anything at all of that nature.

To be told that they lived in houses, and that all their houses were located in towns, in most instances carefully palisadoed, that around these fortified towns were cultivated fields, and that each town was ruled by a king, would strike most with surprise. But such was the fact, as shown by all the early writers.

Beverley, whom we quote from so freely and frequently, tells us that:

"The method of the Indian settlements is altogether by cohabitation, in townships, from fifty to five hundred families in a town, and each of these towns is commonly a kingdom. Sometimes one king has the command of several of these towns, when they happen to be united in his hands, by descent or conquest; but in such

Houses and Towns

cases there is always a viceregent appointed in the dependent town, who is at once governor, judge, chancellor, and has the same power and authority which the king himself has in the town where he resides. This viceroy is obliged to pay to his principal some small tribute, as an acknowledgment of his submission, as likewise to follow him to his wars, whenever he is required."[1]

This was essentially the feudal system as it existed in so many other countries.

Glover, writing in 1676, says of the size of these towns:

"At the first coming of the English divers towns had two or three thousand bowmen in them; but now, in the southern parts of Virginia, the biggest Indian town hath not above five hundred inhabitants; many towns have scarce sixty bowmen in them, and in one town there are not above twenty, and they are so universally thinned in the forementioned southern part, that I verily believe there are not above three thousand left under the whole government of Sir Will Bartlet; but in my Lord of Baltimore's territories at the head of the bay, where the English were later seated, they are more numerous, there being still in some towns about three thousand Indians. But these being in continual wars with each other, are like shortly to be reduced to as small numbers as the former."[2]

[1] Beverley, book 3, p. 10.
[2] *Account of Virginia*, p. 22.

From this it would seem that earlier accounts misrepresented the size of these towns, making them appear smaller than they really were. Possibly this was done in order not to deter settlers from coming over. The Indian population was no doubt much larger than we are accustomed to think of it.

Inside the enclosing palisade, irregularly placed, stood the houses, nine or ten feet high. Around the inside of them were banks of earth cast up to serve instead of stools and beds. The furnishings were of the simplest nature—earthen pots, wooden bowls, and mats to lie on—all made by themselves.[1]

Beverley thus described these houses:

"The manner the Indians have of building their houses, is very slight and cheap; when they would erect a wig-wam, which is the Indian name for a house, they stick saplings into the ground by one end, and bend the other at the top, fastening them together with strings made of fibrous roots, the rind of trees, or of the green wood of the white oak, which will rive[2] into thongs. The smallest sort of these cabins are conical, like a bee-hive; but the larger are built in an oblong form, and both are covered with the bark of trees, which will rive off into great flakes. Their windows are little holes left open for the passage of the light, which in bad weather they stop with shutters of the same bark, open-

---

[1] Glover's *Account of Virginia*, p. 23.
[2] Split.

ing the leeward windows for air and light. Their chimney, as among the true-born Irish, is a little hole in the top of the house, to let out the smoke, having no sort of funnel, or anything within, to confine the smoke from ranging through the whole roof of the cabins, if the vent will not let it out fast enough. The fire is always made in the middle of the cabin. Their door is a pendent mat, when they are near home; but when they go abroad, they barricado[1] it with great logs of wood set against the mat, which are sufficient to keep out wild beasts. There is never more than one room in a house, except in some houses of state or religion, where the partition is made only by mats and loose poles."

"Their houses or cabins, as we call them, are by this ill method of building, continually smoky, when they have fire in them; but to ease that inconvenience, and to make the smoke less troublesome to their eyes, they generally burn pine or lightwood (that is, the fat knots of dead pine) the smoke of which does not offend the eyes, but smuts the skin exceedingly, and is perhaps another occasion of the darkness of their complexion.

"Their seats, like those in the eastern part of the world, are the ground itself; and as the people of distinction amongst them used carpets, so cleanliness has taught the better sort of these, to spread match-coats[2] and mats to sit on.

[1] Shut in and defend.
[2] Clothes in shape like shawls.

"They take up their lodgings[1] in the sides of their cabins, upon a couch, made of board, sticks or reeds, which are raised from the ground upon forks,[2] and covered with mats or skins. Sometimes they lie upon a bearskin, or other thick pelt, dressed with the hair on, and laid upon the ground near a fire, covering themselves with their match-coats. In warm weather a single mat is their only bed, and another rolled up their pillow. In their travels a grass plat under the covert of a shady tree, is all the lodgings they require, and is as pleasant and refreshing to them, as a down-bed and fine Holland sheets are to us.

"Their fortifications consist only of a palisado,[3] of about ten or twelve feet high; and when they would make themselves very safe, they treble the pale.[4] They often encompass their whole town. But for the most part only their king's houses, and as many others as they judge sufficient to harbor all their people, when an enemy comes against them. They never fail to secure within their palisado, all their religious relics, and the remains[5] of their princes. Within this enclosure, they likewise take care to have a supply of water, and to make a place for a fire, which they frequently dance round with great solemnity."[6]

[1] Sleeping or resting places.
[2] Bifurcated branches of trees.
[3] Palisade.   [4] Encircle the town with three lines of palisades.
[5] Embalmed bodies.
[6] Beverley, book 3, pp. 11-13.

Palisadoed Indian Town with Cornfield. In the lower, right-hand corner, as an insert, is a Qui-oc-ca-san, or religious house, in which were the Mummies of the Kings, an image of O-kee, and other religious objects. Set around it are the posts with men's faces carved on them, and painted. Above it are types of houses. In the centre of the town is the fire around which they gathered every night for recreation and diversion.

"Each household knoweth their own lands, and gardens, and most live of their own labors."

Hariot has this to say of their towns, and the construction of their houses:

"Their towns are but small, and near the seacoast but few, some containing but ten or twelve houses: some 20, the greatest that we have seen hath been but of 30 houses: if they be walled, it is only done with barks of trees made fast to stakes, or else with poles only fixed upright, and close one by another.

"Their houses are made of small poles, made fast at the tops in round form after the manner as is used in many arbors in our gardens of England, in most towns covered with barks, and in some with artificial mats made of long rushes, from the tops of the houses down to the ground. The length of them is commonly double to the breadth, in some places they are but 12 and 16 yards long, and in other some we have seen of four and twenty."[1]

"By the dwellings of the savages," says Strachey, "are bay trees, wild roses, and a kind of low tree, which bears a cod like to the peas, but nothing so big; we take it to be locust."[2] This is identified as a tree very much like the European crab.

"Every small town is a petty kingdom governed by an absolute monarch, assisted and advised by his great men, selected out of the

[1] Twenty-four yards long. Hakluyt, vol. ii., p. 348.
[2] *Historie of Travaile into Virginia*, pp. 72, 130.

gravest, oldest, bravest and richest;[1] if I may allow their deerskins, peak and roanoke (black and white shells with holes, which they wear on strings about their arms and necks) to be wealth.

"They dwell in towns some twenty, some a hundred miles, and some farther from one another, each town having a particular jargon and peculiar customs; though for the most part they agree in certain signs, expressions and manners."

"They cohabit in some hundreds of families,[2] and fix upon the richest ground to build their wooden houses, which they place in a circular form, meanly defended with pales,[3] and covered with bark; the middle area (or forum) being for common use and public occasions. The women in order to plant their Indian corn and tobacco (to clear the ground of trees) cut the bark round; so that they die and don't shade the ground, and decay in time.

"Wherever we meet with an old Indian field, or place where they have lived, we are sure of the best ground. They all remove their habitation[4] for fear of their enemies, or for the sake of game and provision."[5]

"The towns in this country are in a manner like unto those which are in Florida, yet are

---

[1] A thoroughly aristocratic form of government.
[2] Live in the same town together to the number of some hundreds of families.
[3] Palisades which constituted but a weak defence.
[4] The inhabitants of the town remove together as one body.
[5] Jones's *Present State of Virginia*, pp. 8–9.

The Town of Pom-e-i-ock

Houses and Towns 135

they not so strong nor yet preserved with so great care. They are compassed about with poles stuck fast in the ground, but they are not very strong. The entrance is very narrow as may be seen by this picture, which is made according to the form of the town of Pom-e-i-ock. There are but few houses therein, save those which belong to the king and his nobles. On the one side is their temple separated from the other houses and marked with the letter A., it is builded round, and covered with skin-mats, and as it were compassed about with cortynes[1] without windows, and hath no light but the door.[2]

On the other side is the king's lodging marked with the letter B. Their dwellings are builded with certain potes[3] fastened, and covered with mats which they turn up as high as they think good, and so receive in the light and other.[4] Some are also covered with boughs of trees, as every man lusteth or liketh best. They keep their feasts and make good cheer together in the midst of the town. When the town standeth far from the water they dig a great pond noted with the letter C. where hence they fetch as much water as they need."[5]

"They eat, sleep, and dress their meat all under one roof, and in one chamber as it were."[6]

"Their towns that are not enclosed with poles

[1] Curtains.
[2] No opening for the light but the door.
[3] Sticks.   [4] Things, understood.
[5] Hariot's *Narrative*, xix.
[6] Strachey, *Historie of Travails into Virginia*, p. 71.

are commonly fairer[1] than such as are enclosed, as appeareth in this figure which lively[2] expresseth the town of Se-co-tam.[3] For the houses are scattered here and there, and they have garden expressed by the letter E. wherein groweth tobacco which the inhabitants call uppo-woc. They have also groves wherein they take deer, and fields wherein they sow their corn. In their cornfields they build as it were a scaffold, whereon they set a cottage like to a round chair, signified by F., wherein they place one to watch, for there are such number of fowls, and beasts,[4] that unless they keep the better watch, they would soon devour all their corn. For which cause the watchmen maketh continual cries and noise.

"They sow their corn with a certain distance noted by H. otherwise one stalk would choke the growth of another and the corn would not come unto its ripeness, G.[5] For the leaves thereof are large, like unto the leaves of great reeds. They have also a several[6] broad plot,[7] C. where they meet with their neighbors, to celebrate their chief solemn feasts; and a place D. where, after they have ended their feast, they make merry together. Over against this place

[1] Larger and handsomer.
[2] In a life-like manner.
[3] Generally written Se-co-ta. Se-co-tam was the name of a region of which Se-co-ta may have been the capital.
[4] Game, not domestic.
[5] G. in the picture represents the ripe corn.
[6] Separate and apart.
[7] Small piece of ground of well-defined shape.

The Unenclosed Town of Se-co-ta

Houses and Towns

they have a round plot B. where they assemble themselves to make their solemn prayers. Not far from which place there is a large building A. wherein are the tombs[1] of their kings and princes, likewise they have garden noted by the letter I, wherein they use to sow pompions.[2] Also a place marked with K. wherein they make a fire at their solemn feasts, and hard without the town a river L. from whence they fetch their water.

"This people therefore void of all covetousness live cheerfully and at their hearts' ease. But they solemnize their feasts in the night, and therefore they keep very great fires, to avoid[3] darkness, and to testify their joy."[4]

Smith's account, agreeing in the main with what has been said, and adding additional details, is as follows:

"Their buildings and habitations are, for the most part, by the rivers, or not far distant from some fresh spring. Their houses are built like our arbors, of small young sprigs[5] bowed and tied, and so close covered with mats, or the barks of trees very handsomely, that notwithstanding either wind, rain or weather, they are as warm as stoves, but very smoky, yet at the top of the house there is a hole made for the smoke to go into right over the fire.

"Against the fire they lie on little hurdles[6] of

---

[1] Receptacles for the embalmed kings.
[2] Pumpkins.   [3] Dispel.   [4] Hariot's *Narrative*, xx.
[5] Saplings.   [6] A movable frame made of interlaced sticks.

reeds covered with a mat, borne[1] from the ground a foot and more by a bundle of wood. On those round about the house they lie heads and points [2] one by the other against the fire, some covered with mats, some with skins, and some stark naked, lie on the ground, from 6 to 20 in a house.

"Their houses are in the midst of their fields or gardens, which are small plots of ground. Some 20 acres, some 40, some 100, some 200, some more, some less. In some places from 2 to 50 of these houses together, are but little separated by groves of trees. Near their habitations is little[3] small wood or old trees on the ground by reason of their burning of them for fire, so that a man may gallop a horse amongst these woods any way, but where the creeks or rivers shall hinder."[4]

It is to be observed, that the habitations of the Virginia Indians, were houses, and not tents. The popular idea on this subject is clearly erroneous. It is derived from the habits of the existing Indian tribes, inhabiting the far west, a roving collection of clans, often living in treeless regions. They have less permanency of location and their protection from the weather, is of a portable nature, made of skins and such things.

Strachey tells us that the towns of the Virginia Indians were commonly upon the rise of a hill,

[1] Supported.
[2] With the head of one opposite the feet of another lying by his side.   [3] But little.   [4] Smith, vol. i., pp. 129-31.

near some river, so that they could see whatever happened upon it. That there were not many houses in any of the towns, and that such houses as there were, were located without any regard to a street, scattered about, far and wide, and that all the houses, even the king's were alike. Every house usually had two doors, one before and a postern. The doors were hung with mats, never locked nor bolted. The houses were generally placed under the cover of large trees, for protection from bad weather, snow and rain, and from the heat of the sun in summer.

Whittaker tells us that: "they observe the limits of their own possessions."[1] That is, that the boundary lines of their several tracts of land were clearly marked out, each man owning his own piece of land. The same rule, on a larger scale, would apply to communities.

Spelman gives this account of their houses:

"Places of habitation they have but few, for the greatest towns have not above 20 or 30 houses in them. Their buildings are made like an oven with a little hole to come in at but more spacious within, having a hole in the midst of the house for smoke to go out at. The king's houses are both broader and longer than the rest, having many dark windings and turnings before any come where the king is. But in that time when they go a-hunting the women go to a place appointed before, to build houses for their husbands to lie in at night, carrying mats with

[1] Purchas, vol. iv., p. 1771.

them to cover their houses with all,[1] and as the men go further a-hunting, the women follow to make houses, always carrying their mats with them."[2]

"By their houses they have sometimes a scæna,[3] or high stage, raised like a scaffold, of small spelts,[4] reeds, or dried osiers,[5] covered with mats, which both gives a shadow and is a shelter, and serves for such a covered place where men used in old times to sit and talk for recreation or pleasure, which they called *præstega*,[6] and where, on a loft of hurdles,[7] they lay forth their corn and fish to dry.

"Round about the house on both sides are their bedsteads, which are thick, short posts stuck into the ground, a foot high and somewhat more, and for the sides small poles laid along, with a hurdle of reeds cast over, wherein they roll down a fine white mat or two (as for a bed) when they go to sleep, and the which they roll up again in the morning when they rise, as we do our pallets.

"They make a fire before them in the midst of the house, usually every night, and some one of them by agreement maintains the fire for all the night long."[8]

[1] Withal, that is, in addition.
[2] Spelman's *Relation of Virginia*, pp. 30–1.
[3] The word signified an arbor, bower or tent, and later, a stage.
[4] Split pieces of wood.
[5] Branches of the willow tree.
[6] Literally, the fore part of the deck of a ship.
[7] The floor of an attic, made in this case of a framework of sticks.
[8] Strachey, *Historie of Travaile into Virginia*, pp. 72, 130.

CHAPTER IX

THE TOWNS LOCATED

WITH reference to the map here presented, we will say that it is founded, so far as the names and position of the Indian towns are concerned, on the map known as Smith's. This map of Virginia is thus inscribed: "Discovered and Described by Captain John Smith, 1606." As the colonists never saw Virginia until 1607, the date 1606 refers to the year the expedition sailed. The map was the result no doubt of all the information gathered by the early explorers, and compiled at a later date. This map is a good one, considering the time it was made, and the inaccurate surveys it must have been based upon, but it was, of course, not perfect. The courses and distances of the rivers, while in the main correct, will be seen on comparison with any modern map of the State, to be far from accurate. In attempting therefore to project the information contained in that map upon a properly drawn chart, one is met with the impossibility of doing so, and still retaining the same relative positions of objects as presented on the old map. We have attempted to make the two as nearly harmonious as possible, measuring by the scales of the two maps, and having regard to the more important curves of the rivers. We can only claim for this map such an approximation to correctness as could be reasonably expected under these circumstances.

It gives a greater feeling of reality as to these vanished Indian towns, to meet with them by name, in the history of those times. The names of the towns are so frequently the names of the tribes which inhabited them, that when we read that one went to such a tribe, it is often equivalent to saying, that he went to the village named for that tribe. But it brings out the existence of the villages more sharply, when we see references to them purely as places. We have collected a few of the references to certain of these villages, which serve as a partial verification of the map, as the map itself helps to illuminate and verify the history.

Wer-o-wó-co-mó-co, on the north side of the York, formerly called the Pamunkey, in Gloucester County, is mentioned repeatedly in all the works on this subject. It was the favorite royal residence, and the place at which Powhatan was residing at the time of the invasion, and where Captain Smith was brought before him. It was fourteen miles from Jamestown.[1]

The exact site of this village was on the east bank of what is now known as Timberneck Bay,

[1] Smith, vol. i., p. 142.

The Towns Located

according to Campbell.[1] But it is claimed to have been on Putin, called also Poetan, that is, Powhatan Bay, and also on the estate of Rosewell, and still again at Shelly. Its exact location is therefore now in doubt. But these places are all close to each other, so its general situation is well ascertained. Incidents given in connection with Smith's arrival there which may help to locate it are given in his history.[2]

From Wer-o-wó-co-mó-co the local tradition is that there ran an Indian trail, or road, which passed near what is now Gloucester Court House; thence, it ran north, crossing the Piankatank, where it narrows, above Freeport, into Middlesex. A part of this road about ten miles long, from Wan, near the head of Ware River, to New Upton, near the Piankatank, is still known as the Indian Road, which is believed to follow exactly this Indian trail. It extended on north, through Virginia and the other States into Canada; and also, crossing the York and the James, continued to the south, into the land of the southern Indians. The tradition is that this path was only used for trade and peaceful communication, and never used for war parties.

Along the north shore of the York, and parallel to it, passing Wer-o-wó-co-mó-co, ran another trail to West Point, the land of Pamunkey. This trail is believed to be nearly coincident with the present thoroughfare known as the York River road.

[1] Campbell's *History of Virginia*, pp. 129-30.
[2] Smith, vol. i., p. 207.

Powhatan was another royal town, situated on the north side of the James, about the site of Richmond, and gave its name to the ruler of all the tribes.[1]

Powhatan sold this place, which was one of his inheritances, in September, 1609, to Captain Francis West, brother of Lord Delaware. He promptly erected a fort there, calling it West's fort, and settled there with 120 English.[2]

At Qui-yough-co-han-ock, on the south side of the James, in Surry County, some ten miles from Jamestown, they had a yearly sacrifice of children, in connection with the rite of hus-ka-naw-ing, described by Beverley.[3]

Chaw-o-po-we-an-ock, which we take to be the same as the Chaw-o-po of the map, near the above, is mentioned as a place where all the Indians ran away from the English, being so afraid of them, or so "jealous of our intents," as Smith quaintly expresses it.[4]

Pas-pa-hegh is mentioned in connection with one of Smith's early voyages in seeking to buy corn of the Indians. He says: "In my return to Pas-pa-hegh, I traded with that churlish and treacherous nation: having loaded 10 or 12 bushels of corn, they offered to take our pieces,[5] and swords, yet by stealth, but seeming to dislike it, they were ready to assault us, yet standing upon our guard in coasting the shore, divers[6]

---

[1] Smith, vol. i., p. 142.
[2] *Historie of Travaile into Virginia*, p. 48.
[3] Beverley, book 3, pp. 37–41.   [4] Smith, vol. i., p. 204.
[5] Guns.   [6] Several.

out of the woods would meet with us with corn and trade," etc.[1]

Pas-pa-hegh was the nearest village to Jamestown.

Ar-ro-ha-teck, in Henrico County, is mentioned as being near the location chosen by Sir Thomas Dale for the site of his town of Henrico.[2] The name is here spelt Ar-sa-hat-tock, but it must be meant to be the same place as Ar-ro-ha-teck.

Moy-so-nec is described as a peninsula of four miles circuit, between two rivers joined to the main land by a neck of forty or fifty yards, and being about the same distance from high water mark.

Near it were fertile corn fields, and the site of the town was described as all that could be desired. The result of these attractions, was a large population.[3]

Ap-po-cant is mentioned as the town farthest up the Chickahominy. It was in connection with making the acquaintance of this town and neighborhood, that Smith was captured by O-pe-chan-ca-nough, and dragged around the country for several weeks.[4]

Mo-hom-in-ge was a village near the Falls of the James, or near the site of Richmond. Here King James was proclaimed King by the first settlers.[5]

Cap-a-ho-wa-sick, a town on the north side of

---

[1] Smith's *True Relation*, p. 18.   [2] Smith, vol. ii., p. 10.
[3] Smith's *True Relation*, p. 22.   [4] *Ibid.*, p. 23.
[5] *Historie of Travaile into Virginia*, p. 25.

the York, in Gloucester County, about midway between Wer-o-wó-co-mó-co and Chesapeake Bay, was the place which Powhatan offered to give to Captain Smith, after his rescue by Pocahontas, and his adoption into the tribe. This was to be given him in exchange for two cannon and a grindstone.[1]

Kis-ki-ack is mentioned in connection with the journey Captain Smith took to see Powhatan, in January, 1609: "At Kis-ki-ack the frost and contrary winds forced us three or four days also (to suppress the insolency of those proud savages) to quarter in their houses, yet guard our barge, and cause them give us what we wanted."[2]

O-zi-nies, which we take to be the same as the O-ze-nick, located on the map, in James City County, is mentioned as having inhabitants who resisted the payment of the tribute of corn, and for their refusal, they were attacked by Sir George Yeardley. Their wer-ó-ance was Kis-sa-na-co-men.[3]

Ma-ma-na-hunt, on the south side of the Chickahominy, in Charles City County, is mentioned as a place whose inhabitants, also, after the departure of Sir Thomas Dale, refused to pay the tribute of corn imposed by the English. They defied Sir George Yeardley, his successor, who attacked the place, to enforce his demands. Under the wer-ó-ance, Kis-sa-na-co-men, they resisted, and a slaughter followed. During this

[1] Smith, vol. i., p. 163.
[2] *Ibid.*, p. 206.   [3] *Ibid.*, vol. ii., p. 27.

The Towns Located

fight, prisoners were taken by the English, and ransomed on the payment of one hundred barrels of corn by the Indians.

Up to this time, this people had never been a part of the Powhatan Confederacy, having been able to withstand the power of Powhatan and O-pe-chan-ca-nough. After this fight with the English, however, they acknowledged O-pe-chan-ca-nough as their King, he having made them believe that it was due to his influence with the English, that these terrible invaders made peace with them.[1]

Ches-a-ka-won, in Lancaster County, is mentioned as the place at which Captain Spelman, on board the bark *Elizabeth*, was first told by an Indian, of O-pe-chan-ca-nough's first plot to massacre the English.[2]

We-an-oack, on the north side of the James, in Charles City County, is mentioned in connection with the revenge the English took for the massacre of 1622, thus: "Shortly after, Sir George Yeardley and Captain William Powel took each of them a company of well disposed gentlemen and others to seek their enemies. Yeardley ranging the shore of We-an-ock, could see nothing but their old houses which he burnt, and went home. Powel searching another part, found them all fled but three he met by chance, whose heads he cut off, burnt their houses and so returned."[3]

[1] Smith, vol. ii., pp. 27–8.
[2] *Ibid.*, p. 78.
[3] *Ibid.*, p. 84.

Ke-cough-tan, in Elizabeth City County, near, or at, Hampton, is spoken of as being forty miles from Jamestown. The place was well known, and is often mentioned. This town is thus described by Smith. "The town containeth eighteen houses, pleasantly seated upon three acres of ground, upon a plain, half environed with a great Bay[1] of the great River,[2] the other part with a Bay of the other River[3] falling into the great Bay, with a little Isle fit for a Castle in the mouth thereof, the Town adjoining to the main[4] by a neck of land of sixty yards."[5]

The destruction of this village by Sir Thomas Gates, the Lieutenant General, in revenge for the Indians capturing, leading up into the woods, and "sacrificing" one of his men, Humfrey Blunt, is thus told us:

"The ninth of July, he prepared his forces, and early in the morning set upon a town of theirs, some four miles from Algernoone Fort,[6] called Ke-cough-tan, and had soon taken it, without loss or hurt of any of his men. The Governor and his women fled (the young king Powhatan's son not being there) but left his poor baggage and treasure to the spoil of our soldiers, which was only a few baskets of old wheat, and some other of peas and beans, a little tobacco, and some few women's girdles of silk, of the grass-silk, not

---

[1] The body of water between the mouth of Hampton Creek and Old Point.
[2] The James.
[3] Hampton Creek.
[4] Main land.
[5] Smith's *True Relation*, p. 16.
[6] Built by the English.

The Towns Located 149

without art, and much neatness finely wrought; of which I have sent divers into England, (being at the taking of the town) and would have sent your Ladyship some of them, had they been a present so worthy."[1]

Ap-po-cant, on the Chickahominy, in Hanover County, is mentioned as the place at which George Cawson was, with the most cruel tortures, put to death by the Indians.[2]

Ac-quack, in Richmond County, on the North side of the Rappahannock, is mentioned in discussing plans for subjugating the Indians, as is also O-ze-nick, in James City County, on the Chickahominy.[3]

Pis-sac-o-ack, Mat-o-ho-pick and Me-cup-pom, towns next to each other on the north side of the Rappahannock, in Richmond or Westmoreland Counties, are stated to have been situated upon high, white clay cliffs.[4]

War-ras-koy-ack, in Isle of Wight County, is often mentioned. An English settlement there was attacked, but successfully defended, in the great massacre of 1622.[5]

Nan-se-mond, in the County of that name, is frequently mentioned. One of the earliest references to it is this: "Seven or eight miles we sailed up this narrow river (the Nansemond), at last on the western shore we saw large corn-

---

[1] Purchas, vol. iv., p. 1755.
[2] *Historie of Travaile into Virginia*, p. 52.
[3] Smith, vol. ii., p. 91. [4] *Ibid.*, vol i., p. 185.
[5] *Ibid.*, vol. ii., p. 68.

fields, in the midst a little Isle; and in it was abundance of corn, the people he (an Indian of that tribe) told us were all a-hunting, but in the Isle was his house, to which he invited us with much kindness."[1]

Houses of the Chesapeake tribe are thus mentioned: "So setting sail for the southern shore (that is, from Point Comfort) we sailed up a narrow river,[2] up the country of Chisapeack; it hath a good channel, but many shoals, about the entrance. By that[3] we had sailed six or seven miles,[4] we saw two or three little garden plots with their houses, the shores overgrown with the greatest pine and fir trees we ever saw in the country. But not seeing nor hearing any people, and the river very narrow, we returned to the great river,[5] to see if we could find any of them."[6]

Nom-i-ny, on the south side of the Potomac, in Westmoreland County, where cliffs and a creek still bear this name, was visited by Smith and a party he commanded. They were conducted by two Indians "up a little bayed creek, towards Nom-i-ny, where they discovered the woods laid with ambuscadoes,[7] to the number of three or four thousand Indians, strangely grimed,[8] disguised and making a horrible shouting and yelling."[9]

[1] Smith, vol. i., p. 190.   [2] The Elizabeth.   [3] When.
[4] This would have brought them to the neighborhood of Norfolk.
[5] The James.   [6] Smith, vol. i., p. 190.
[7] Ambuscades.   [8] Painted with soot.
[9] Stith's *History of Virginia*, p. 65.

The Towns Located

Pa-taw-o-mek, in Stafford County, is mentioned frequently, once in connection with a fight with the Indians, which was terminated by Spelman's head being cut off by the Indians, and thrown down the river bank to his friends.[1]

On the other side of the Chesapeake, Tockwogh, in Kent County, Maryland, was located seven miles up the river of that name, now known as the Chester. This town was a fort, well palisadoed, and mantled with the bark of trees, an armor which would be very effective against arrows.[2]

Ma-chot, on the north side of the Mattapony, in King and Queen County, was a village belonging to O-pe-chan-ca-nough. This was his principal residence after the massacre of 1622, and, no doubt, the center of the Indian opposition until his death, soon after the second massacre brought about by him, in 1644.

"Ma-chot is supposed to be identical with Eltham, the old seat of the Bassets, in King and Queen County, and which borrows its name from an old English seat in the County of Kent." It was here that Powhatan's two sons went on board the vessel, to see their sister, Pocahontas, then in captivity. Finding her well, they advised their father to make peace, and be friends with the English.[3]

Hamor, in telling of the negotiations relating

[1] Smith, vol. ii., p. 95. [2] *Ibid.*, vol. i., pp. 120, 182.
[3] Campbell's *History of Virginia*, p. 108.

to the return of Pocahontas, after her capture, says that they were "anchored near unto the chiefest residence Powhatan had, at a town called Ma-chot," etc.[1]

This would make Ma-chot equal Wer-o-wo-como-co in dignity and importance.

Powhatan was here, when Hamor and Savage and their Indian guides came to him, to try and obtain another of his daughters for marriage to some Englishman. This embassy was unsuccessful.[2]

A-quo-han-ock, in the northern part of Northampton County; O-nan-coke, in Accomack County; Paw-tux-unt, in Calvert County, Maryland, and Mat-ta-pan-i-ent, which we take to be the same as Matt-pa-ment, located on the map, in Prince George County, Maryland, are mentioned as places visited by John Pory, Secretary of Virginia, some time about 1619.[3] May-ta-pan-i-ent is also mentioned in connection with a sham battle, which was fought on one occasion between the Indians, for the entertainment of their European guests.[4]

Or-a-pax was a hunting town and seat, lying on the upper part of Chickahominy swamp, on the north side, belonging to, and much frequented by, Powhatan, and the imperial family, on account of the abundance of game it afforded.[5]

It is described as situated "in the desert be-

---

[1] Hamor's *Discourse*, p. 9.   [2] *Ibid.*, p. 38.
[3] Smith, vol. ii., p. 61.   [4] *Ibid.*, vol. i., p. 135.
[5] Burk *History of Virginia*, vol. i., p. 107.

twixt Chick-a-ham-a-nie and Yough-ta-mund," that is, somewhere in Hanover County, very probably. It was the town to which the old Emperor Powhatan retired in order to be beyond the power of the English. Near this town he had his treasures, which were kept in reserve for his death, and for his use on his journey to the spirit land, and here he finally died, in the month of April, 1618.[1]

This town was about twelve miles northeast of Richmond, and consisted of about thirty or forty houses.[2]

The Na-cotch-ta-nok of our map, was situated on the eastern side of the Anacostia River, now in the District of Columbia. Its site is thus described by Mr. S. V. Proudfit:

"The principal part of Na-cotch-tanke seems to have been about due east of the Capitol, for the fields at this point give greater evidence of occupation than at most others, though indications of Indian occupation are to be found at nearly all points of the valley. It should be noted that the dwellings were in most cases close to the bank of the stream. A line drawn parallel with the shore and three hundred feet distant would include the greater part of the houses. Within the area thus indicated may be found to-day every variety of stone implement common to the North American Indian. Arrow-heads, spear-heads, knives, drills, perforators,

[1] Smith, vol. i., pp. 142-3; vol. ii., p. 36.
[2] Campbell's *History of Virginia*, p. 46.

scrapers, sinkers, polished axes (both grooved and ungrooved), sharpening-stones, pipes, slate tablets, pestles, mortars, cup-stones, hammerstones, as well as that rude axe-shaped implement of chipped quartzite which has yet to receive a name. Associated with these, and forming no inconsiderable part of the remains, are found partly worked implements—some broken, others worked into the first rude forms of the arrowhead or knife and then abandoned, and abounding everywhere flakes, chips, and pebbles of quartz and quartzite having but a chip or two struck from the original surface.

"These fields have been under cultivation for many years, and are regularly visited by local collectors, yet they are to-day in places, fairly strewn with the wreck of the old village life."[1]

Beverley, writing in 1705, gives this list of the then existing towns, and their conditions:

"The Indians of Virginia are almost wasted, but such towns, or people as retain their names, and live in bodies, are hereunder set down; all which together can't raise five hundred fighting men. They live poorly, and much in fear of the neighboring Indians. Each town, by the Articles of Peace in 1677,[2] pays 3 Indian arrows for their land, and 20 beaver skins for protection every year.

[1] *The American Anthropologist*, vol. xi., p. 242.
[2] The settlement of the disturbances with the Indians which brought on Bacon's Rebellion the year before.

"In Accomack are eight towns,[1] viz:

"Ma-tom-kin is much decreased of late by the smallpox, that was carried thither.

"Gin-go-teque. The few remains of this town are joined with a nation of the Maryland Indians.

"Kie-quo-tank is reduced to very few men.

"Match-o-pun-go has a small number yet living.

"Oc-ca-han-ock has a small number yet living.

"Pun-go-teque. Governed by a queen, but a small nation.

"O-a-nan-cock has but four or five families.

"Chi-con-es-sex has very few, who just keep the name.

"Nan-du-ye. A seat of the Empress. Not above twenty families, but she hath all the nations of this shore under tribute.

"In Northampton. Gan-gas-coe which is almost as numerous as all the foregoing nations put together.

"In Prince George. Wy-a-noke is almost wasted, and now gone to live among other Indians.

"In Charles City. Ap-pa-mat-tox. These live in Colonel Byrd's pasture, not being above seven families.

"In Surry. Not-ta-ways, which are about a hundred bowmen, of late a thriving and increasing people.

[1] Most of these names are still to be found on the map of this county.

"By Nan-sa-mond. Men-heer-ing, has about thirty bowmen, who keep at a stand.

"Nan-sa-mond. About thirty bowmen: They have increased much of late.

"In King William County, 2.[1] Pa-mun-kie has about forty bowmen, who decrease.

"Chick-a-hom-o-nie, which had about sixteen bowmen, but lately increased.

"In Essex. Rap-pa-han-nock is reduced to a few families, and live scattered upon the English seats.

"In Richmond. Port-Ta-ba-go has about five bowmen, but wasting.

"In Northumberland. Wic-co-com-o-co has but three men living, which yet keep up their kingdom and retain their fashion; they live by themselves, separate from all other Indians, and from the English."[2]

In 1705, when Beverley wrote this, only some twenty-odd of about one hundred and sixty counties which were formed in what was once Virginia's territory were in existence. He is therefore speaking only of those in the eastern portion of the Colony. The names he mentions are, as a rule, those of the tribes, as well as the names of the towns which they inhabited.

The Indian villages were situated at points of advantage which in many instances seem to have been recognized and adopted by the Virginians as the sites of their towns; thus, there was on the site of

[1] Two towns of the Pa-mun-key tribe.
[2] Beverley, book 3, pp. 62–3.

The Towns Located

Richmond, Powhatan;
Norfolk, Ski-co-ak;
Petersburg, Ap-pa-ma-tuck;
Alexandria, As-sa-o-meck;
Fredericksburg, Sock-o-beck;
Hampton, Ke-cough-tan;
Suffolk, Man-tough-que-me-o;
Cape Charles, Ac-cow-mack, and
Smithfield, War-ros-quy-oake.

At least, if these cities be not on the very sites of these Indian villages, they are very near them.

Many of the fine estates in Virginia also occupy such village sites. These presented the advantage of being always fertile ground from which the forest had, to some extent, been cleared away, and fields ready for further cultivation.

The first settlers on Roanoke Island mention the following Indian towns:

Ski-co-ak, mentioned as a great city. Its location on the early maps would indicate that it occupied the site of the present city of Norfolk. It will be mentioned again more fully later on in connection with the Chesapeake tribe.

Ro-a-noke, at the north end of the island of that name, a village of nine houses, built of cedar and fortified with a palisade.

Pom-e-i-ock, on Pamlico Sound, in Hyde County, east of Lake Mattamuskeet.

We know this town well, a picture of the same being given to us by John White.

Pas-que-noke, located probably at the southeast end of Camden County, on Albemarle Sound.

Chep-a-now, or Chep-a-nock, in Perquimans County, on the north shore of Albemarle Sound.

Mas-com-ing in Chowan County. The name is also written Mus-ca-mun-ge. It was probably on the site of Edenton.

War-a-tan, in the same county, a little farther up the Chowan on the east side.

Cat-o-kin-ge, farther up the same river, at the southern extremity of Gates County, at the fork of the streams.

O-hau-nook, farther up the same stream, on its west side, in Hertford County, or lower down in Bertie.

Ram-us-how-og, still farther up the Chowan, probably just north of its confluence with Kirby's Creek.

Met-pow-em, in Bertie County, lower down on the west side of the Chowan facing Albemarle Sound, and near the mouth of Roanoke River. It is also called Me-tack-wem.

Chaw-a-nook, whose lord was Po-o-nens, in Chowan County, on the east side of Chowan River, probably on the site of the present Chowan.

Tan-da-quo-muc in the same county and neighborhood, a little up the Roanoke River, on its north side.

Mor-a-tuc in the same county, a little farther up the Roanoke River.

The Towns Located

Me-quo-pen in Washington County, possibly on Mackay's Creek.

Tram-as-que-coock in Tyrrell, on the west side of Alligator River.

Das-a-mon-que-pe-uc in Dare County, on Croatan Sound, opposite the northern end of Roanoke Island.

A-gus-cog-oc in Hyde County, west of Pom-e-i-ock, on Rose Bay.

Co-tan in Hyde County on the east side of Pungo River.

Se-co-ta in Beaufort County, on the point of land between the Pamlico and Pungo rivers.

This is said to have been the southernmost town ruled by Win-gi-na.[1] We are fortunate in having also a picture of this place.

Sec-tu-o-oc in Pamlico County somewhere between the mouths of the Pamlico and Neuse rivers, on Pamlico Sound.

Pan-a-wa-i-oc in Beaufort County, on the south side of Pamlico River.

New-si-oc in Carteret County, on the south side near the mouth of the Neuse.

Gwa-rew-oc also in Carteret County, on Bogue Sound.

Hat-or-ask on the sea-coast near Loggerhead Inlet.

Pa-qui-woc on the coast, near Cape Hatteras.

Cro-a-to-an on the coast between Hatteras and O-cra-coke Inlet.

[1] Hakluyt, vol. ii., p. 283 *et seq.*

Wo-ko-kon on the coast, south of O-cra-coke Inlet.

Two names of regions are given in John White's map, by which chart the above towns have been thus attempted to be localized to some degree, Se-co-tan, which would appear to be the territory between the Pamlico River and Albemarle Sound, and We-a-pe-me-oc, which would include all from Albemarle Sound to Chesapeake Bay.

This map, which was drawn by John White, was engraved by de Brÿ, and is often spoken of as de Brÿ's map of Lane's Expedition. The map here given is based upon it.

CHAPTER X

THE FALLS OF THE JAMES

THE "Falls of the James" are so often mentioned by the early writers, that it will not be out of place to say a word about their origin. In an interesting paper Mr. W. J. McGee, after tracing the successive changes through which the eastern coast of the United States has passed, the lowering and rising of the land, sometimes below the level of the ocean, and then again above it, the advance and retreat of the ice-sheet which once covered the northern part of Virginia, he says:

"With the retreat of the great ice-sheet the land rose slowly and the waters gradually retreated until the previous configuration of the land and sea was in part restored; but the face of the emerging land was changed. Not only was the surface mantled and the valleys clogged with sediments, but the country was cleft for 300 miles by a profound break or displacement by which the lowlands were lowered and the uplands lifted. This displacement of the surface and the strata extends from the Potomac to the Hudson, and every river crosses it in a cascade;

and the displacing is yet in progress—so slowly, it is true, that man has scarcely measured its rate, but so rapidly that the ever-busy rivers are unable to keep pace with it, and either cut down their upland gorges to tide level or silt[1] up their lowland estuaries."[2]

And again:

"Through the Potomac valley passes one of the most strongly marked geologic and cultural[3] boundaries on the face of the earth. It was the shore-line during the later part of the Potomac period,[4] and again during the eons of Cretaceous[5] and early Tertiary[6] deposition; it was again a shore-line during the first ice-invasion, the deposition of the Columbia gravels[7] and brick clays, and the fashioning of the Columbia[8] terraces; and it was the line of earth-fracture by which the coastal lowlands are dropped below the Piedmont uplands. It is known to students of modern manufactures as the fall-line because along it the rivers descend as abruptly as the land; and it is even more notable as a line of deflection than as one of declivity in rivers.

[1] Fill up with sediment.
[2] An arm or inlet of the sea, particularly one which is covered with water only at high tide.
[3] Relating to mental culture.
[4] The geological period during which the Potomac River was being defined.
[5] This geologic term relates to the chalk which was a characteristic of the period.
[6] The word signified third in order of formation.
[7] A soil characteristic of the District of Columbia.
[8] This relates to the District of Columbia.

The Falls of the James

"The great waterways of the Middle Atlantic slope maintain their courses through Appalachian ranges and Piedmont hills alike; but on reaching the coastal lowlands they are turned aside literally by a sand bank little higher than their depth, and thence hug the upland margin for scores of miles before finally finding their way into the ocean. So the coastal lowlands are nearly isolated by the tidal bays and river-elbows along their inner margin. Measured along the fall-line the Hudson is barred from the Rappahannock, 300 miles southward, by only 60 miles of land and unnavigable water. This remarkable physiography[1] is now and ever has been reflected in the culture of the region.

"The pioneer settlers of the country ascended the tidal canals to the falls of the rivers, where they found, sometimes within a mile, clear, fresh water, the game of the hills and woodlands, and the fish and fowl of the estuaries, and, as the population increased, abundant water-power and excellent mill-sites, easy ferriage, and practicable bridge-sites; here the pioneer settlements and villages were located; and across the necks of the inter-estuarine peninsulas the pioneer routes of travel were extended from settlement to settlement until the entire Atlantic slope was traversed by a grand social and commercial artery stretching from New England to the Gulf States.

"As the population grew and spread, the set-

[1] Physical geography.

tlements, villages, and towns along the line of Nature's selection waxed, and many of them yet retain their early prestige; and the early stage-route has become a great metropolitan railway and telegraph route connecting North and South as they were connected of old in more primitive fashion. And just as these natural conditions influenced the white invader, so, and even more strongly, must they have influenced the migrations, settlements, industries, and character of the aboriginal monarchs of the Potomac waters and woodlands."[1]

[1] *The American Anthropologist*, July, 1889, vol. xi., pp. 231, 233-4.

CHAPTER XI

POLITICAL LAWS AND THE ART OF WAR

STRACHEY gives us the best account of the political construction of Indian society. That construction appears at once upon investigation to have been thoroughly organized and essentially aristocratic. Over all was Powhatan. The English called him an Emperor because he ruled over so many kings, for each town had its king, as the English called them. The Indians called them wer-ó-ances. They exercised despotic power over their kingdoms.

Then there was a power behind the kings—the priests and conjurers, who in many respects ruled the kings.

There was thus no lack of government in the forest, but it was of the arbitrary and tyrannical sort.

Turning to the *Historie of Travaile into Virginia*, we are told:

"The great king Powhatan hath divided his country into many provinces or shires (as it were), and over every one placed a several absolute wer-ó-ance or commander, to him contributary to govern the people, there to inhabit; and his petty wer-ó-ances, in all, may be in number about three or four and thirty, all which have their precincts and bounds, proper and commodiously appointed out, that no one intrude upon the other of several forces; and for the ground wherein each one soweth his corn, plant his ap-oke[1] and garden fruits, he tithes[2] to the great king of all the commodities growing in the same, or of what else his shire brings forth, appertaining to the lands or rivers, corn, beasts, pearl, foul, fish, hides, furs, copper, beads, by what means soever obtained, a peremptory rate."[3]

The despotic rule of Powhatan and of the lesser Indian kings, as the early settlers always called them, is thus stated by Strachey:

"Nor have they positive laws, only the law whereby he ruleth is custom; yet when he pleaseth, his will is a law, and must be obeyed, not only as a king, but as half a god, his people esteem him so; his inferior kings are tied likewise to rule by like customs, and have permitted them power of life and death over their people, as their command in that nature."[4]

"There is a civil government among them which they strictly observe, and show thereby that the law of nature dwelleth in them; for they have a rude kind of commonwealth and rough

---

[1] Tobacco. [2] Pays part as taxes.
[3] Strachey, *Historie of Travaile into Virginia*, p. 55.
[4] This probably means that their jurisdiction derived from Powhatan extended even to life and death. *Historie of Travaile into Virginia*, p. 70.

government, wherein they both honor and obey their king, parents, and governors, both greater and lesser." So wrote the Rev. Alexander Whittaker, from Henrico, in 1613.[1]

The taxes levied by the autocratic ruler of the forest were very oppressive. Describing the governmental system Strachey says:

"Every wer-ó-ance knoweth his own meeres and limits[2] to fish, foul, or hunt in (as before said), but they hold all of their great wer-ó-ance Powhatan, unto whom they pay eight parts of ten tribute of all the commodities which their country yieldeth, as of wheat, peas, beans, eight measures of ten (and these measured out in little cades or backets, which the great king appoints), of the dying-roots, eight measures of ten of all sorts of skins, and furs eight of ten; and so he robs the people, in effect, of all they have, even to the deer's skin wherewith they cover them from cold, in so much as they dare not dress it and put it on until he has seen it and refused it, for what he commandeth they dare not disobey in the least thing."[3]

"The Indians having no sort of letters among them, as has been before observed, they can have no written laws; nor did the constitution in which we found them, seem to need many. Nature and their own convenience having taught them to obey one chief, who is arbiter of all

[1] Purchas, vol. iv., p. 1771.
[2] "Meeres and limits" mean seas or waters in which to fish, and the boundaries allowed them on land for hunting.
[3] *Historie of Travaile into Virginia*, p. 81.

things among them. They claim no property in lands, but they are in common to a whole nation. Every one hunts and fishes and gathers fruits in all places. Their labor in tending corn, pompions,[1] melons, etc, is not so great, that they need quarrel for room, where the land is so fertile and where so much lies uncultivated.

"They are very severe in punishing ill-breeding, of which every wer-ó-ance is undisputed judge, who never fails to lay a rigorous penalty upon it. An example whereof I had from a gentleman who was an eye-witness; which was this:

"In the time of Bacon's Rebellion, one of these wer-ó-ances, attended by several others of his nation, was treating with the English in New Kent County, about a peace; and during the time of his speech, one of his attendants presumed to interrupt him, which he resented as the most unpardonable affront that could be offered him; and therefore he instantly took his tomahawk from his girdle, and split the fellow's head, for his presumption. The poor fellow dying immediately upon the spot, he commanded some of his men to carry him out, and went on again with his speech where he left off, as unconcerned as if nothing had happened.

"The titles of honor that I have observed among them peculiar to themselves, are only cock-a-rouse, and wer-ó-ance, besides that of the king and queen; but of late they have borrowed some titles from us, which they bestow

[1] Pumpkins.

among themselves. A cock-a-rouse is one that has the honor to be of the king or queen's council with relation to the affairs of the government, and has a great share in the administration. A wer-ó-ance is a military officer, who of course takes upon him the command of all parties, either of hunting, traveling, waring, or the like, and the word signified a war captain.

"They also have people of a rank inferior to the commons, a sort of servant among them. These are called black boys, and are attendant upon the gentry, to do their servile offices, which, in their state of nature, are not many. For they live barely up to the present relief of their necessities, and make all things easy and comfortable to themselves, by the indulgence of a kind climate, without toiling and perplexing their mind for riches, which other people often trouble themselves to provide for uncertain and ungrateful heirs. In short, they seem, as possessing nothing, and yet enjoying all things."[1]

The wer-ó-ances exercised all the highest rights of the various tribes, even extending to the alienation of the soil itself upon which they lived. In the various conveyances of territory made by the Indians as the result of treaties with the English, it is the chiefs alone who execute the deed; the subordinate members of the tribe were not recognized by them as having any say in the matter. The deed made by the chief or chiefs passed an indefeasible title to the whole.

[1] Beverley, book 3, pp. 56-9.

Strachey said: "Upon Yough-ta-mund[1] is the seat of Powhatan's three brethren whom we learn are successively to govern after Powhatan, in the same dominions which Powhatan by right of birth, as the elder brother, now holds. The rest of the countries under his command are (as they report) his conquests."[2]

"I can't think it anything but their jealousy that makes them exclude the lineal issue from succeeding immediately to the crown. Thus if a king have several legitimate children, the crown does not descend in a direct line to his children, but to his brother by the same mother, if he have any, and for want of such, to the children of his eldest sister, always respecting the descent by the female, as the surer side. But the crown goes to the male heir (if any be) in equal degree, and for want of such, to the female, preferably to any male that is more distant.

"As in the beginning of a war, they have assemblies for consultation, so upon any victory, or other great success, they have public meetings again, for processions and triumphs. I never saw one of these, but have heard that they are accompanied with all the marks of a wild and extravagant joy."[3]

With reference to the political construction of the tribes, and the offices of wer-ó-ance and sachem, we are told:

---

[1] The Pamunkey River.
[2] Strachey, *Historie of Travaile into Virginia*, p. 36.
[3] Beverley, book 3, pp. 25–6.

Political Laws and the Art of War

"The sachem amongst all the tribes was a magistrate either hereditary or elective, according to their various customs, but in all cases without tribute, revenue or authority. His duty was invariably to stay at home, whilst the war-chief, who was elected for his merit, was fighting at the head of his warriors; to preside in the great council, where he had but a single voice, and in the absence of the warriors to watch over the safety of the aged, the women and children, an office of so little estimation that amongst several of the tribes it was frequently filled by women.

"A fact in confirmation of this is related by Charlevoix. A female chief of one of the tribes of the Hurons made repeated attempts in council to procure the admission of a Christian missionary, but without success.

"Nor is it the sachem only that is without power in those singular communities. There is nothing like what we conceive of authority anywhere among them. Even the great council of the nation can do nothing but by advice or persuasion, and every individual is at liberty to refuse obedience to its decisions.

"Even in war there is no such thing as an imperative direction from a general to his soldiers: Yet notwithstanding this uncontrolled license, the advice of the chiefs is scarcely ever rejected."[1]

This statement of a later writer, with reference

[1] Burk's *History of Virginia*, vol. iii., pp. 64-5.

to the powers of the Indian rulers, is not borne out by the earlier writers, who represent them as despotic.

Spelman says: "The king is not known by any difference from others of the (better) chief sort in the country, but only when he comes to any of their houses they present him with copper beads or victual, and show much reverence to him."[1]

He further says: "Concerning their laws my years and understanding made me the less to look after because I thought that infidels[2] were lawless,[3] yet when I saw some put to death I asked the cause of their offence, for in the time I was with the Patomecks I saw 5 executed, 4 for murder of a child (*id est*) the mother and two others that did the fact with her, and a fourth for concealing it as he passed by, being bribed to hold his peace; and one for robbing a traveller of copper and beads, for to steal their neighbor's corn or copper is death, or to lie one with another's wife is death if he be taken in the manner.

"Those that be convicted of capital offences are brought into a plain place before the king's house where then he lay, which was at Pamunkey, the chiefest house he hath, where one or two

---

[1] Spelman's *Relation of Virginia*, p. 52.
[2] A favorite way of regarding the savages. This lack of belief in Christianity was often viewed as of itself justifying any course with regard to them which the English deemed proper—the infidels having practically no rights the believers were bound to respect.
[3] Had no laws.

appointed by the king did bind them hand and foot, which being done a great fire was made. Then came the officer to those that should die, and with a shell cut off their long lock, which they wear on the left side of their head, and hangeth that on a bow before the king's house. Then those for murder were beaten with staves till their bones were broken and being alive were flung into the fire; the other for robbing was knocked on the head and being dead his body was burned."[1]

This account is in harmony with the statement of the Rev. Alexander Whittaker, who says: "Murder is scarcely heard of; adultery and other offences severely punished."[2]

"When they intend any wars, the wer-ó-ances usually have the advice of their priests and conjurers, and their allies, and ancient friends, but chiefly the priests determine their resolution. Every wer-ó-ance, or some lusty fellow, they appoint captain over every nation. They seldom make war for lands or goods, but for women and children, and principally for revenge. They have many enemies, namely all their westernly countries beyond the mountains, and the heads of the rivers."[3]

"For their wars also they use targets that are

[1] Spelman's *Relation of Virginia*, pp. 43–6.
[2] Purchas, vol. iv., p. 1771.
[3] Smith, vol. i., p. 134. The enemies beyond the mountains were the Shaw-a-nees, Cher-o-kees, and others; those at the heads of the rivers were the Mon-a-cans, the Man-na-ho-acks, the Mas-sa-wo-mecks, and others.

round and made of barks of trees, and a sword of wood at their backs, but oftentimes they use for swords the horn of a deer put through a piece of wood in form of a pickaxe. Some a long stone sharpened at both ends, used in the same manner."[1]

"These men are not so simple as some have supposed them: for they are of body lusty, strong and very nimble: they are a very understanding generation, quick of apprehension, sudden in their dispatches, subtile in their dealings, exquisite in their inventions, and industrious in their labor. I suppose the world hath no better marksmen with their bows and arrows than they be; they will kill birds flying, fish swimming, and beasts running: they shoot also with marvelous strength, they shot one of our men being unarmed quite through the body, and nailed both his arms to his body with one arrow."[2]

By being unarmed, the writer means that the man did not have on armor.

Their method of summoning the warriors was very original. Strachey says: "When they would press[3] a number of soldiers to be ready by a day, an officer is dispatched away, who coming into the towns, or otherwise meeting such whom he hath order to warn,[4] to strike them over the back a sound blow with a bastinado, and bids them be ready to serve the great king, and tells

[1] Smith, vol. i., p. 132.
[2] Alexander Whittaker in Purchas, vol. iv., p. 1771.
[3] Impress. [4] Summon.

them the rendezvous, from whence they dare not at any time appointed be absent."[1]

"When they are about to undertake any war or other solemn enterprise, the king summons a convention of his great men, to assist at a grand council, which in their language is called a match-a-com-o-co. At these assemblies 'tis the custom, especially when a war is expected, for the young men to paint themselves irregularly with black, red, white, and several other motley colors, making one-half of their face red, (for instance) and the other half black or white, with great circles of a different hue, round their eyes; with monstrous mustaches, and a thousand fantastical figures, all over the rest of their body; and to make themselves appear yet more ugly and frightful, they strow feathers, down, or the hair of beasts, upon the paint while it is still moist, and capable of making those light substances stick fast on. When they are thus formidably equipped, they rush into the match-a-com-o-co, and instantly begin some very grotesque dance, holding their arrows, or tomahawks in their hands, and all the while singing the ancient glories of their nation, and especially of their own families; threatening and making signs with their tomahawk, what a dreadful havoc they intend to make amongst their enemies.

"Notwithstanding these terrible airs they give themselves, they are very timorous when they come to action, and rarely perform any open or

[1] *Historie of Travaile into Virginia*, p. 100.

bold feats; but the execution they do, is chiefly by surprise and ambuscade.

"The fearfulness of their nature makes them very jealous and implacable. Hence it is, that when they get a victory, they destroy man, woman and child, to prevent all future resentments."[1]

Spelman, an eye-witness to a battle between two of the native tribes, says:

"As for armor or discipline in war they have not any. The weapons they use for offence are bows and arrows with a weapon like a hammer and their tomahawks, for defence which are shields made of the bark of a tree and hanged on their left shoulder to cover that side as they stand forth to shoot.

"They never fight in open fields, but always either among reeds or behind trees taking their opportunity to shoot at their enemies and till they can nocke[2] another arrow they make the trees their defence.

"In the time that I was there I saw a battle fought between the Pa-to-meck and the Ma-so-meck; their place where they fought was a marsh ground full of reeds. Being in the country of the Pa-to-meck the people of Ma-so-meck were brought thither in canoes which is a kind of boat they have made in the form of a hog's trough, but somewhat more hollowed in. On both sides they scatter themselves some little

---

[1] Beverley, book 3, pp. 24-5.
[2] Fit the arrow to the string of their bow.

distance one from the other; then take they their bows and arrows and having made ready to shoot, they softly steal toward their enemies, sometimes squatting down and prying if they can spy any to shoot at, whom, if at any time he so hurteth that he cannot flee, they make haste to him to knock him on the head. And they that kill most of their enemies are held the chiefest men among them.

"Drums and trumpets they have none, but when they will gather themselves together they have a kind of howling or howbabub so differing in sound one from the other as both parts may very easily be distinguished.

"There was no great slaughter of either side, but the Ma-so-mecks having shot away most of their arrows, and wanting victual, were glad to retire."[1]

"The order and deportment of an Indian assembly would not have disgraced the gravity and dignity of a Roman senate; and the effect produced upon a spectator, who is unacquainted with their language and even prejudiced against them, is in the highest degree impressive. Nor is this effect produced by the grandeur of architecture or the splendor of dress. The council is a large square space covered with rough boards; and the councilors dirty savages wrapped in skins and coarse blankets. It arises from the patience, the temper, the animation, the regular-

[1] Spelman's *Relation of Virginia*, pp. 54–6.

ity, and even the eloquence of their action and deportment. There we witness no impatience nor contradiction; no ebullitions of passions; no bursts of rage and invective; no factious intrigues. The whole subject is fairly and honestly before them, and it is discussed with the patient judgment of sages and the animated integrity of patriots. An interruption would be considered as an unpardonable insult: perhaps it would not be too much to say that there never was any such thing known as an interruption in an Indian assembly."[1]

"They use formal embassies for treating, and very ceremonious ways in concluding of peace, or else some other memorable action, such as burying a tomahawk, and raising an heap of stones thereon, as the Hebrews did over Absalom, or of planting a tree, in token that all enmity is buried with the tomahawk, that all the desolations of war are at an end, and that friendship shall flourish among them like a tree."[2]

In the many negotiations which Virginia had with various Indian tribes and nations, our people soon learned the necessity of adopting the forms and ceremonies of the Indians, and accustomed themselves to use the highly figurative language of this people.

As far as in them lay they therefore adopted their metaphors. In the negotiations preliminary to the concluding a formal treaty, they

---

[1] Burk's *History of Virginia*, vol. iii., p. 66.
[2] Beverley, book 3, p. 27.

smoked cal-u-mets; they called the Indians brothers; they brightened the chain of friendship with them; they hoped it would be no more stained with blood, nor rusted with contention, nor broken asunder with discord, but that it would last as long as the sun, the moon, and the stars gave light.

In the progress of these treaties, strings of wam-pum, in order to emphasize the less, and belts of wam-pum to emphasize the more, important matters, were freely given by the Indians. It was customary, and so the Virginians made similar presents to emphasize and act as reminders of the propositions advanced by them. Indeed, it was absolutely necessary to make these presents, and so, at a treaty held at Shen-a-pin Town in May, 1752, it is recorded that: "The Commissioners not having any wam-pum strung, without which answers could not be returned, acquainted the Indians that they would answer their speeches in the afternoon, on which the council broke up." Having provided themselves by that time with this requisite, the negotiations were then continued.

A string of wampum was given to the Virginians to enable them to see the sun clearly, and to look upon the Indians as brothers; another to clear their voices so that they could speak clearly to the Indians; another by Queen Al-li-guip-pe to clear their way to Loggs Town; another to clear their hearts from any impression that might have been made on them by flying report, or ill news; and that they might speak their minds freely. The way being long and the day hot, a string was given them to wipe off their perspiration.

Aside from these courtesies, and expressions of wishes and hopes, all the salient features of the debate were thus marked.

The Virginians gave the Indians a string of wam-pum to receive their brethren of Virginia kindly, and so on through the various phases of the negotiation, all of which were very deliberate. No hasty replies were made by the Indians. At any time, on an important matter coming up which they had not foreseen and about which they were not agreed, the meeting would be adjourned, and time taken by the Indians for private consultation before giving their answers.

One object of such a treaty, as stated by them, was to make the road between us and the Indians clearer and wider.

Approbation to propositions of importance, emphasized thus by the gift of a string or a belt of wam-pum, was expressed on the part of the Indians by a shout, or cry, the Jo-hah, as it was called.

An illustration of the Indian love of metaphor is given in the speech of Can-as-a-tee-go, delivered on June 26, 1744, at Lancaster, Pennsylvania, during the debate on the treaty pending between Virginia, Pennsylvania, Maryland, and the Six Nations. Speaking of the affectionate regard the Indians had for the Dutch, the Indian chieftain said: "We were so well pleased with them, that we tied their ship to the bushes on the shore, and afterwards, liking them still better, the longer they stayed with us, and thinking the bushes too slender, we removed the rope, and tied it to the trees, and as the trees were liable to be blown down by high winds, or to decay of themselves, from the affection we bore them, again removed the rope, and tied it to a strong and big rock (here the interpreter said they meant the O-nei-do country); and not content with this, for its further security we removed the rope to the big mountain (here the interpreter said they meant the O-non-da-go country), and there we tied it very fast, and rolled wam-pum about it; and to make it still more secure, we stood upon it, to defend it, and to prevent any hurt coming to it, and did our best endeavors, that it might remain uninjured forever."

While endowed thus by nature with poetic forms of expression, and with traits of character admirable in many respects, the Indians of Virginia were as blood-thirsty savages as ever existed. They reflected and presented all the phases of barbarism. They scalped their enemies, when dead, and practiced upon them, when alive, such tortures as make the blood run cold when we read of them. It is noticeable, however, how little the Indians were criticized in this regard by the early writers. The explanation is found in the fact that in 1607, and for many years thereafter, torture just as bad was practiced by the highly civilized nations of Europe. The abolition of "cruel and unusual" punishments is a blessing of a comparatively recent date.

These Indians, while terrible fighters in their own way, were not capable of making long sustained sieges. If their first sudden attack on a fortified place did not carry it by assault and the defense proved vigorous, in a comparatively short time they became discouraged, and abandoned the enterprise for a more favorable opportunity.

Their method of warfare was suited to the forest in which they lived, and many of their manœuvres were adopted by our men. As they fought from behind trees and such other shields, so did the Virginians. We met them on their own ground and fought them in their own manner. In this way we won the battle of Point Pleasant, while a contrary course, and the adherence to tactics unsuited to the nature of the enemy and the battle-field, led to the dreadful slaughter and rout of Braddock's defeat.

So well did the Virginians learn the warfare of the forest, that they won from their opponents the fear and admiration involved in the name which the Indians gave them, for they called the Virginians "The Big Knives."

CHAPTER XII

THE PRIESTLY MEDICINE MAN

SPELMAN gives us this account of Indian medical views and practices:

"When any be sick among them their priest comes unto the party whom he layeth on the ground upon a mat and having a bowl of water, set between him and the sick party, and a rattle by it, the priest kneeling by the sick man's side dips his hand into the bowl, which taking up full of water, he sips into his mouth, spouting it out again, upon his own arms and breast, then takes he the rattle and with one hand shakes that, and with the other, he beats his breast, making a great noise, which having done he easily riseth, as loath to wake the sick body, first with one leg, then with the other, and being now got up, he lesiurely goeth about the sick man shaking his rattle very softly over all his body: and with his hand he stroketh the grieved parts of the sick, then doth he besprinkle him with water, mumbling certain words over him, and so for that time leaves him.

"But if he be wounded, after these ceremonies done unto him, he with a little flint stone gasheth the wound making it to run and bleed, which he, setting his mouth unto it, sucks out, and then applies a certain root beaten to powder unto the sore."[1]

"Concerning a green wound caused either by the stroke of an axe, or sword, or such sharp thing, they have present remedy for, of the juice of certain herbs; howbeit a compound wound (as the surgeons call it) where, beside the opening and cutting of the flesh, any rupture is, or bone broken, such as our small shot make upon them, they know not easily how to cure, and therefore languish in the misery of the pain thereof.

"Old ulcers likewise, and putrified hurts are seldom seen cured amongst them: howbeit, to scarify[2] a swelling, or make incision, they have a kind of instrument of some splinted stone.

"Every spring they make themselves sick with drinking the juice of a root which they call wigh-sac-an and water, whereof they take so great a quantity, that it purgeth them in a very violent manner, so that in three or four days after they scarce recover their former health.

"Sometimes they are sore troubled with dropsy, swellings, aches, and such like diseases, by reason of their uncleanness and foul feeding; for cure whereof they build a stove in the form of a dove house, with mats so close, that a few coals therein covered with a pot will make the patient sweat extremely.

[1] Spelman's *Relation of Virginia*, p. 40.
[2] To scratch, or make superficial incisions.

The Priestly Medicine Man

"For swelling, also, they use small pieces of touchwood in the form of cloves, which, pricking on the grief, they burn close to the flesh, and from thence draw the corruption with their mouth.

"They have many professed physicians, who, with their charms and rattles, with an infernal rout of words and actions, will seem to suck their inward grief from their navels, or their affected places; but concerning our chirugians[1] they are generally so conceited of them, that they believe that their plasters will heal any hurt."[2]

"The Indians are not subject to many diseases, and such as they have, generally come from excessive heats, and sudden colds, which they as suddenly get away[3] by sweating. But if the humour[4] happen to fix,[5] and make a pain in any particular joint, or limb, their general cure then is by burning, if it be in any part that will bear it; their method of doing this is by little sticks of lightwood, the coal of which will burn like a hot iron; the sharp point of this they run into the flesh, and having made a sore, keep it running till the humour be drawn off; or else they take punck (which is a sort of a soft touchwood,[6] cut out of the knots of oak or hickory trees, but the hickory affords the best), this they shape like

---

[1] Surgeons.
[2] Strachey, *Historie of Travaile into Virginia*, p. 108.
[3] Cure. [4] Bodily fluid.
[5] Settle in one place.
[6] The soft white or yellowish substance into which wood is converted by the action of certain fungi.

a cone (as the Japanese do their moxa[1] for the gout), and apply the basis of it to the place affected. They set fire to it, letting it burn out upon the part, which makes a running sore effectually.

"They use smoking frequently and scarifying[2] which, like the Mexicans, they perform with a rattle-snake's tooth. They seldom cut deeper than the epidermis, by which means they give passage to those sharp waterish humours, that lie between the two skins, and cause inflammations. Sometimes they make use of reeds for cauterizing, which they heat over the fire, till they are ready to flame, and then apply them, upon a piece of thin wet leather, to the place aggrieved, which makes the heat more piercing.

"Their priests are always physicians, and by the method of their education in the priesthood, are made very knowing in the hidden qualities of plants, and other natural things, which they count a part of their religion to conceal from everybody, but from those that are to succeed them in their holy function.

"They tell us, their God will be angry with them if they should discover that part of their knowledge; so they suffer only the rattlesnake root[3] to be known, and such other antidotes, as must be immediately applied; because their doc-

---

[1] A soft downy substance prepared from the young leaves of a plant of this name. It is used as a cautery.
[2] Scratching.
[3] A plant believed at one time to be a cure for snake-bites.

The Priestly Medicine Man 187

tors can't always be at hand to remedy those sudden misfortunes, which generally happen in their hunting or travelling.

"The physic of the Indians consists for the most part in the roots and barks of trees, they very rarely using the leaves either of herbs or trees; what they give inwardly they infuse in water, and what they apply outwardly they stamp or bruise, adding water to it, if it has not moisture enough of itself; with the thin of this they bathe the part affected, then lay on the thick, after the manner of a pultis,[1] and commonly dress round, leaving the sore place bare.

"They take great delight in sweating, and therefore in every town they have a sweating-house, and a doctor is paid by the public to attend it. They commonly use this to refresh themselves, after they have been fatigued with hunting, travel, or the like, or else when they are troubled with agues, aches, or pains in their limbs.

"Their method is thus: the doctor takes three or four large stones, which after having heated red hot, he places them in the middle of the stove, laying on them some of the inner bark of oak, beaten in a mortar, to keep them from burning. This being done, they creep in six or eight at a time, or as many as the place will hold, and then close up the mouth of the stove, which is usually made like an oven, in some bank near the water side.

[1] Poultice.

"In the meanwhile, the doctor, to raise a steam, after they have been stewing a little while, pours cold water on the stones, and now and then sprinkles the men to keep them from fainting.

"After they have sweat as long as they can well endure it, they sally out, and (tho' it be in the depth of winter) forthwith plunge themselves over head and ears in cold water, which instantly closes up the pores, and preserves them from taking cold.

"The heat being thus suddenly driven from the extreme parts of the heart, makes them a little feeble for the present, but their spirits rally again, and they instantly recover their strength, and find their joints as supple and vigorous as if they never had travelled, or been indisposed. So that I may say as Bellonius does in his observations on the Turkish bagnios,[1] all the crudities contracted in their bodies are by this means evaporated and carried off.

"The Muscovites[2] and Finlanders are said to use this way of sweating also. 'It is almost a miracle,' says Olearius, 'to see how their bodies, accustomed to, and hardened by, cold, can endure so intense a heat, and how that, when they are not able to endure it longer, they come out of the stoves as naked as they were born, both men and women, and plunge into cold water, or cause it to be poured on them.'

"The Indians also pulverize the roots of a

[1] Bath-houses. [2] Russians.

The Priestly Medicine Man 189

kind of anchuse[1] or yellow alkanet,[2] which they call puc-coon, and of a sort of wild angelica,[3] and mixing them together with bear's oil, make a yellow ointment, with which, after they have bathed, they anoint themselves capapee[4]; this supplies the skin, renders them nimble and active, and withal so closes up the pores, that they lose but few of their spirits by perspiration. Piso relates the same of the Brazilians, and my Lord Bacon asserts, that oil and fat things do no less conserve the substance of the body, than oil colors and varnish do that of the wood.

"They have also a further advantage of this ointment, for it keeps all lice, fleas, and other troublesome vermin from coming near them, which otherwise, by reason of the nastiness of their cabins, they would be very much infested with.

"Smith talks of this puc-coon, as if it only grew on the mountains, whereas it is common to all the plantations of the English, except only to those situated in very low grounds."[5]

"The Indians being a rude sort of people use no curiosity in preparing their physic; yet are they not ignorant of the nature and uses of their plants, but they use no correctives to take away the flatuous, nauseous, and other bad qualities of them. They either powder, juice, infuse, or boil them, till the decoction be very strong.

[1] A rough, hairy plant.
[2] An European plant which yields a red dye.
[3] A medicinal plant.   [4] From head to foot.
[5] Beverley, book 3, pp. 49-52.

"Their usual way of cure for most inward distempers is by decoction, which they make partly pectoral, partly sudorific; these they cause the sick to drink, the quantity of half a pint at a time, two or three times a day; but they give nothing to procure vomiting in any distempers, as a bad omen that the diseased will die; neither did I ever know them to use any ways of bleeding or cupping.

"If they have any wounds, ulcers, or fractures, they have the knowledge of curing them. I did once see an Indian whose arm had been broken, and viewing the place, I found the bones to be as smoothly consolidated, and as well reduced, as any English chirurgeon could have done it.

"All Indians carry a powder about them to cure the bites of snakes, and in almost every town this powder hath a different composition, and every composition is certainly effectual to the correcting the malignity of the venom. Neither was it ever known to us, that any Indian suffered much harm by these bites, but in a day's time he would be as well as if he had never been bitten, whereas some of the English for want of a speedy remedy have lost their lives.

"The Indians are frequently troubled with violent colics, which oftentimes terminate in palsies."[1]

[1] Glover's *Account of Virginia*, p. 27.

CHAPTER XIII

HUS–KA–NAW–ING

WE are not told by the early writers as much as we would like to know about the religious rites of these people. We are told somewhat of their conjurations, their incantations, their attempt to control the weather, their rites to heal the sick, and so on, but we are told little of their worship, or of their innermost beliefs and traditions.

The rite of Hus-ka-naw-ing, however, is fully described to us, and seems to have made quite an impression on the early writers. It was certainly very peculiar.

We owe our best account of it to Strachey. His statement is as follows:

"In some part of the country they have yearly a sacrifice of children; such a one was at Qui-yough-co-han-ock, some ten miles from Jamestown, as also at Ke-cough-tan, which Capt. George Percy was at, and observed. The manner of it was, fifteen of the properest young boys, between ten and fifteen years of age, they painted white; having brought them forth, the people spent the forenoon in dancing and singing about them with rattles.

"In the afternoon they solemnly led those children to a certain tree appointed for the same purpose; at the root whereof, round about, they made the children to sit down, and by them stood the most and the ablest of the men, and some of them the fathers of the children, as a watchful guard, every one having a bastinado in his hand of reeds, and these opened a lane between all along, through which were appointed five young men to fetch those children.

"And accordingly every one of the five took his turn and passed through the guard to fetch a child, the guard fiercely beating them the while with their bastinadoes, and showing much anger and displeasure to have the children so ravished from them; all which the young men patiently endured, receiving the blows and defending the children, with their naked bodies, from the unmerciful strokes, that paid them soundly, though the children escaped.

"All the while sat the mothers and kinswomen afar off, looking on, weeping and crying out very passionately, and some, in pretty, waymenting[1] tunes, singing (as it were) their dirge or funeral song, provided with mats, skins, moss, and dry wood by them, as things fitting their children's funerals.

"After the children were thus forcibly taken from the guard, the guard possessed (as it were) with a violent fury, entered upon the tree and tore it down, bows and branches, with such a

[1] "Probably plaintive."

terrible fierceness and strength, that they rent the very body of it, and shivered it in a hundred pieces, whereof some of them made them garlands for their heads, and some stuck of the branches and leaves in their hair, wreathing them in the same, and so went up and down as mourners, with heavy and sad downcast looks.

"What else was done with the children might not be seen by our people, further than that they were all cast on a heap in a valley, where was made a great and solemn feast for all the company; at the going whereunto, the night now approaching, the Indians desired our people that they would withdraw themselves and leave them to their further proceedings, the which they did.

"Only some of the wer-ó-ances being demanded the meaning of this sacrifice, made answer, that the children did not all of them suffer death, but that the O-ke-us did suck the blood from the left breast of the child whose chance it was to be his by lot, till he were dead, and the remainder were kept in the wilderness by the said young men till nine moons were expired, during which time they must not converse with any; and of these were made the priests and conjurers to be instructed by tradition from the elder priests.

"These sacrifices, or catharmata, they hold to be so necessary, that if they should omit them they suppose this Okeus, and all the other Qui-ough-co-sughes, which are their other gods, would let them no deer, turkeys, corn, nor fish, and yet besides he would make a great slaughter amongst them; insomuch as if ever the ancient superstitious times feared the devil's *postularia fulgura*, lightnings that signified religion of sacrifices and vows to be neglected,[1] these people are dreadfully afflicted with the terror of the like, insomuch as, I may truly say therefore, the like thunder and lightning is seldom again either seen or heard in Europe as is here."[2]

Smith gave an abbreviated account of this rite, which Beverley reproduced.[3]

Commenting upon this proceeding, Beverley says:

"How far Captain Smith might be misinformed in this account, I can't say, or whether their O-kee's sucking the breast be only a delusion or pretence of the physician (or priest, who is always a physician), to prevent all reflection on his skill, when any happened to die under his discipline.

"This I choose rather to believe, than those religious romances concerning their O-kee. For I take this story of Smith's to be only an exam-

[1] "The rendering here given by Strachey of *postularia fulgura* is evidently from Festus, though his quaint diction would mislead the reader as to the intention of the words. Festus gives the following definition of the term. 'Fulgura quae votorum aut sacrificiorum spretam religionem designant.'" Lightnings which indicate religion to be treated with contempt by reason of the neglect of vows or sacrifices.

[2] *Historie of Travaile into Virginia*, pp. 94-6.

[3] Smith, vol. i., p. 140.

Hus-ka-naw-ing

ple of hus-ka-naw-ing, which being a ceremony then altogether unknown to him, he might easily mistake some of the circumstances of it.

"The solemnity of hus-ka-naw-ing is commonly practiced once every fourteen or sixteen years, or oftener, as their young men happen to grow up. It is an institution or discipline which all young men must pass, before they can be admitted to be of the number of the great men, or cock-a-rouses of the nation; whereas by Captain Smith's relation, they were only set apart to supply the priesthood. The whole ceremony is performed after the following manner:

"The choicest and briskest young men of the town, and such only as have acquired some treasure by their travels and hunting, are chosen out of the rulers to be hus-ka-naw-ed; and whoever refuses to undergo this process, dare not remain among them.

"Several of those odd preparatory fopperies are premised in the beginning, which have been before related; but the principal part of the business is to carry them into the woods, and there keep them under confinement, and destitute of all society, for several months; giving them no other sustenance but the infusion or decoction of some poisonous, intoxicating roots.

"By virtue of which physic, and by the severity of the discipline which they undergo, they become stark, staring mad, in which raving condition they are kept eighteen or twenty days. During these extremities they are shut up night and day, in a strong enclosure, made on purpose; one of which I saw belonging to the Pa-mun-key Indians, in the year 1694. It was in shape like a sugar-loaf, and every way open like a lattice for the air to pass through.[1]

"In this cage thirteen young men had been hus-ka-naw-ed, and had not been a month set at liberty when I saw it.

"Upon this occasion it is pretended that these poor creatures drink so much of that water of Lethe, that they perfectly lose the remembrance of all former things, even of their parents, their treasure,[2] and their language.

"When the doctors find that they have drunk sufficiently of the wy-soc-can (so they call this mad potion), they gradually restore them to their senses again, by lessening the intoxication of their diet; but before they are perfectly well, they bring them back into their towns, while they are still wild and crazy, through the violence of the medicine.

"After this they are very fearful of discovering any thing of their former remembrance; for if such a thing should happen to any of them, they must immediately be hus-ka-naw-ed again; and the second time the usage is so severe, that seldom any one escapes with life.

"Thus they must pretend to have forgot the very use of their tongues, so as not to be able to

---
[1] See page 231.
[2] Their hidden treasures, held in reserve both for use in life and after death.

Hus-ka-naw-ing

speak nor understand any thing that is spoken, till they learn it again.

"Now whether this be real or counterfeit, I don't know; but certain it is, that they will not for some time take notice of any body nor any thing, with which they were before acquainted, being still under the guard of their keepers, who constantly wait upon them every where, till they have learned all things perfectly over again. Thus they unlive their former lives, and commence men, by forgetting that they ever have been boys.

"If under this exercise any one should die, I suppose the story of O-kee, mentioned by Smith, is the salvo[1] for it: For (says he) O-kee was to have such as were his by lot; and such were said to be sacrificed.

"Now this conjecture is the more probable because we know that O-kee has not a share in every hus-ka-naw-ing; for tho' two young men happened to come short home[2] in that of the Pa-mun-key Indians, which was performed in the year 1694, yet the Ap-pa-mat-tucks, formerly a great nation, though now an inconsiderable people, made an hus-ka-naw in the year 1690, and brought home the same number they carried out."[3]

[1] Excuse.
[2] That is, two never returned home.
[3] Beverley, book 3, pp. 37-41.

CHAPTER XIV

THE EMBALMED KINGS AND FUNERAL RITES

STRACHEY gives us this account of the embalming of the bodies of the kings: "Within the chancel of the temple, by the O-ke-us, are the cenotaphies or the monuments of their kings, whose bodies, so soon as they be dead, they embowel, and, scraping the flesh from off the bones, they dry the same upon hurdles[1] into ashes, which they put into little pots (like ancient urns).

"The anatomy of the bones they bind together, or case up in leather, hanging bracelets, or chains of copper, beads, pearls or such like, as they used to wear, about most of their joints and neck, and so repose the body upon a little scaffold (as upon a tomb), laying by the dead body's feet, all his riches in several baskets, his a-pook,[2] and pipe, and any one toy, which in his life he held most dear in his fancy.

"Their inwards they stuff with pearl, copper, beads, and such trash, sewed in a skin, which they overlap again very carefully in white skins one or two, and the bodies thus dressed lastly

---

[1] Frames of wood. [2] Tobacco.

Embalmed Kings and Funeral Rites

they roll in mats, as for winding sheets, and so lay them orderly one by one, as they die in their turns, upon an arch standing (as aforesaid) for the tomb, and these are all the ceremonies we yet can learn that they give unto their dead.[1]

"We hear of no sweet oils or ointments that they use to dress or chest[2] their dead bodies with; albeit they want not of the precious resin running out of the great cedar, wherewith in the old times they used to embalm dead bodies, washing them in the oil and liquor thereof.

"Only to the priests the care of these temples and holy interments are committed, and these temples are to them as solitary asseteria[3] colleges or ministers to exercise themselves in contemplation, for they are seldom out of them, and therefore often lie in them and maintain continual fire in the same, upon a hearth somewhat near the east end."[4]

Beverley's description of this same proceeding, but with interesting variations as to details, is as follows:

"The Indians are religious[5] in preserving the corpses of their kings and rulers after death, which they order in the following manner. First, they neatly flay[6] off the skin as entire as they can, slitting it only in the back; then they pick all the

[1] More ceremonies were used, as we will see later on.
[2] Place in a coffin.
[3] "Possibly misspelt from Ασσύτερος quasi 'Επασσύτερος, *i. e.*, following in a row one after another."
[4] *Historie of Travaile into Virginia*, p. 89
[5] That is, observe as a religious duty.
[6] Strip.

flesh off from the bones as clean as possible, leaving the sinews fastened to the bones, that they may preserve the joints together.

"Then they dry the bones a little in the sun, and put them into the skin again, which in the meantime has been kept from drying or shrinking; when the bones are placed right in the skin, they nicely fill up the vacuities, with a very find white sand.

"After this they sew up the skin again, and the body looks as if the flesh had not been removed. They take care to keep the skin from shrinking, by the help of a little oil or grease, which saves it also from corruption.

"The skin being thus prepared they lay it in an apartment for that purpose, upon a large shelf raised above the floor. This shelf is spread with mats, for the corpses to rest easy on, and screened with the same, to keep it from the dust.

"The flesh they lay upon hurdles[1] in the sun to dry; and when it is thoroughly dried, it is sewed up in a basket, and set at the feet of the corpse to which it belongs.

"In this place also they set up a Qui-oc-cos, or Idol, which they believe will be a guard to the corpses. Here night and day one or other of the priests must give his attendance, to take care of the dead bodies. So great an honor and veneration have these ignorant and unpolished people for their princes, even after they are dead.

[1] A movable frame made of rods crossing each other.

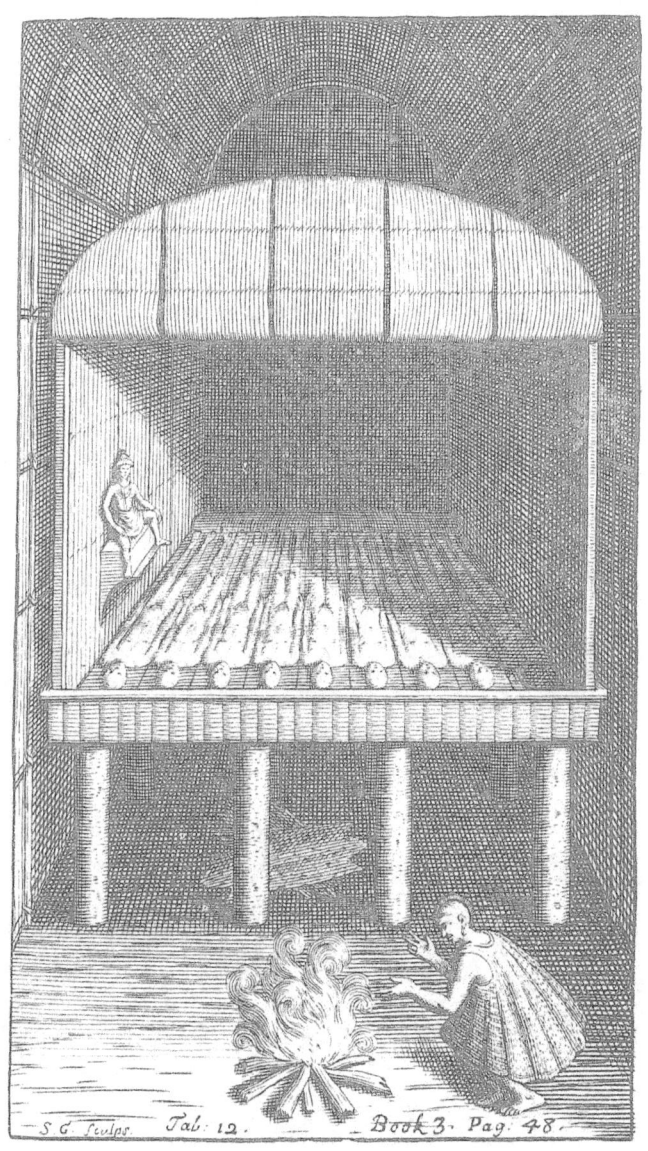

"The Burial of the Kings"

"The mat is supposed to be turned up in the figure,[1] that the inside may be viewed."[2]

Hariot tells us that the bodies lay on a scaffold nine or ten feet high, and that under this scaffold some one of the priests had his lodging, "which mumbleth his prayers night and day, and hath charge of the corpses. For his bed, he hath two deers' skins spread on the ground, if the weather be cold, he maketh a fire to warm by withal."[3]

Spelman gives us an account of the ordinary funeral customs:

"If he dies his burial is this, there is a scaffold built about three or four yards high from the ground and the dead body wrapped in a mat is brought to the place, where when he is laid thereon, the kinsfolk fall a-weeping and make great sorrow, and instead of dole[4] for him, the poorer people being got together, some of his kinsfolk fling beads[5] among them making them to scramble for them, so it happens many times divers do break their arms and legs being pressed by the company; this finished they go to the party's house[6] where they have meat given them which being eaten all the rest of the day they spend in singing and dancing, using then as much mirth as before sorrow, moreover, if any of the kindreds' bodies which have been laid on the scaffold be so consumed as nothing is left but bones they

---

[1] Picture, p. 202.   [2] Beverley, book 3, p. 47.
[3] Hariot's *Narrative*, xxii.
[4] A portion of money, food, or other things distributed in charity.
[5] Wam-pum or peak.   [6] The deceased man's home.

take those bones from the scaffold and putting them into a new mat,[1] hang them in their houses where they continue while their house falleth, and then they are buried in the ruins of the house."[2]

Strachey gives an account of another kind of burial:

"For their ordinary burials they dig a deep hole in the earth with sharp stakes, and the corpse being lapped in skins and mats with their jewels, they lay upon sticks in the ground, and so cover them with earth: the burial ended, the women, being painted all their faces with black coal and oil, do sit twenty-four hours in their houses, mourning and lamenting by turns, with such yelling and howling as may express their great passions."[3]

Still a third mode of disposing of the bodies of the dead is recorded by Glover. He says: "They burn the bodies of the dead, and sew up the ashes in mats, which they place near the cabins of their relations."[4]

With every wer-ó-ance or king was buried all his wealth, for they believed that he that died the richest, lived in another world the happiest.

In consequence of this idea, there was found by the English a great quantity of pearls stored in the "house of their sepultures," that

---

[1] Covering made of cloths or mats.
[2] Spelman's *Relation of Virginia*, pp. 40–1.
[3] *Historie of Travaile into Virginia*, p. 90.
[4] *Account of Virginia*, p. 24.

Embalmed Kings and Funeral Rites

is, the place where the embalmed bodies were preserved.

Discolored and softened by heat as they had been, having been found most probably in oysters when they were cooked, their value was not so great as it otherwise would have been.[1]

We have reason to believe that when, in pursuance of treaties or cession of land to the Virginians, the Indians withdrew from the eastern part of the State, they took all the embalmed kings with them.[2]

The honors paid to the departed, when they were personages of distinction, did not end with merely embalming their bodies. Lane tells us that it was the custom to observe a general, public mourning for a month. Such a mourning on account of the death of En-se-no-re, the father of Pem-is-a-pan, the King of the country around Roanoke Island, was made the excuse for collecting there eight hundred warriors, who were to take part in the conspiracy to exterminate the English.

[1] Brown's *Genesis of the United States*, vol. i., p. 349; A True and Sincere Declaration of the Governors and Councilors, 1609.

[2] Beverley, book 2, pp. 10-11.

CHAPTER XV

BURIAL MOUNDS

MR. JEFFERSON, in his *Notes on Virginia*, has an interesting account of an examination made by him of one of the Indian burial-places near his home. He says:

"I know of no such thing existing as an Indian monument: for I would not honour with that name arrow points, stone hatchets, stone pipes, and half shapen images. Of labour on the large scale, I think there is no remain as respectable as would be a common ditch for the draining of lands: unless indeed it would be the barrows, of which many are to be found all over this country.

"These are of different sizes, some of them constructed of earth, and some of loose stones. That they were repositories of the dead, has been obvious to all; but on what particular occasion constructed, was a matter of doubt.

"Some have thought they covered the bones of those who have fallen in battles fought on the spot of interment. Some ascribed them to the custom, said to prevail among the Indians, of collecting, at certain periods the bones of all

Burial Mounds

their dead, wheresoever deposited at the time of death. Others again supposed them the general sepulchres for towns, conjectured to have been on or near these grounds; and this opinion was supported by the quality of the lands in which they are found (those constructed of earth being generally in the softest and most fertile meadow grounds on river sides), and by a tradition, said to be handed down from the aboriginal Indians, that, when they settled in a town, the first person who died was placed erect, and earth put about him, so as to cover and support him; and when another died, a narrow passage was dug to the first, the second reclined against him, and the cover of earth replaced, and so on.

"There being one of those in my neighborhood, I wished to satisfy myself whether any, and which of these opinions were just. For this purpose I determined to open and examine it thoroughly.

"It was situated on the low grounds of the Rivanna, about two miles above its principal fork,[1] and opposite to some hills, on which had been an Indian town. It was of a spheroidical form, of about forty feet diameter at the base, and had been of about twelve feet altitude, though now reduced by the plough to seven and a half, having been under cultivation about a dozen years. Before this it was covered with trees of twelve inches diameter, and round the

---

[1] Mechum's River. The location thus described would be a point about two miles southeast of the station known as Proffit, on the Southern Railway, in Albemarle County.

base was an excavation of five feet depth and width, from whence the earth had been taken of which the hillock was formed.

"I first dug superficially in several parts of it, and came to collections of human bones, at different depths, from six inches to three feet below the surface. These were lying in the utmost confusion, some vertical, some oblique, some horizontal, and directed to every point of the compass, entangled and held together in clusters by the earth. Bones of the most distant parts were found together, as for instance, the small bones of the foot in the hollow of the skull; many skulls would sometimes be in contact, lying on the face, on the side, on the back, top or bottom, so as, on the whole, to give the idea of bones emptied promiscuously from a bag or basket, and covered over with earth, without any attention to their order.

"The bones of which the greatest numbers remained, were skulls, jaw-bones, teeth, the bones of the arms, thighs, legs, feet, and hands. A few ribs remained, some vertebræ of the neck and spine, without their processes,[1] and one instance only of the bone which serves as a base to the vertebral column.

"The skulls were so tender, that they generally fell to pieces on being touched. The other bones were stronger. There were some teeth which were judged to be smaller than those of an adult; a skull, which on a slight view, appeared to be

[1] Outgrowing parts or protuberances.

that of an infant, but it fell to pieces on being taken out, so as to prevent satisfactory examination; a rib, and a fragment of the under jaw of a person about half grown; another rib of an infant; and part of the jaw of a child, which had not cut its teeth.

"This last furnishing the most decisive proof of the burial of children here, I was particular in my attention to it. It was part of the right half of the under jaw. The processes, by which it was attenuated [1] to the temporal bones,[2] were entire, and the bone itself firm to where it had been broken off, which, as nearly as I could judge, was about the place of the eye-tooth. Its upper edge, wherein would have been the sockets of the teeth, was perfectly smooth. Measuring it with that of an adult, by placing their hinder processes together, its broken end extended to the penultimate grinder of the adult. This bone was white, all the others of a sand colour. The bones of infants being soft, they probably decay sooner, which might be the cause so few were found here.

"I proceeded then to make a perpendicular cut through the body of the barrow, that I might examine its internal structure. This passed about three feet from its centre, was opened to the former surface of the earth, and was wide enough for a man to walk through and examine its sides.

---

[1] Become thinner or smaller toward the point of connection.
[2] The complex bone situated at the side and base of the skull, in the region of the ear, whose internal organs it contains within its substance.

"At the bottom, that is, on the level of the circumjacent plain, I found bones; above these a few stones, brought from a cliff a quarter of a mile off, and from the river one-eighth of a mile off; then a large interval of earth, then a stratum of bones, and so on.

"At one end of the section were four strata of bones plainly distinguishable; at the other, three; the strata in one part not ranging with those in another: The bones nearest the surface were least decayed. No holes were discovered in any of them, as if made with bullets, arrows, or other weapons. I conjectured that in this barrow might have been a thousand skeletons.

"Every one will readily seize the circumstances above related, which militate against the opinion, that it covered the bones only of persons fallen in battle; and against the tradition also, which would make it the common sepulchre of a town, in which the bodies were placed upright, and touching each other.

"Appearances certainly indicate that it has derived both origin and growth from the accustomary collection of bones, and deposition of them together; that the first collection had been deposited on the common surface of the earth, a few stones put over it, and then a covering of earth, that the second had been laid on this, had covered more or less of it in proportion to the number of bones, and was then also covered with earth; and so on.

Burial Mounds

"The following are the particular circumstances which give it this aspect: 1. The number of bones. 2. Their confused position. 3. Their being in different strata. 4. The strata in one part having no correspondence with those in another. 5. The different states of decay in these strata, which seem to indicate a difference in the time of inhumation. 6. The existence of infant bones among them.

"But on whatever occasion they may have been made, they are of considerable notoriety among the Indians; for a party passing, about thirty years ago, through the part of the country where this barrow is, went through the woods directly to it, without any instructions or enquiry, and having staid about it some time, with expressions which were construed to be those of sorrow, they returned to the high road, which they had left about half a dozen miles to pay this visit, and pursued their journey.

"There is another barrow much resembling this, in the low grounds of the south branch of Shenandoah where it is crossed by the road leading from the Rockfish Gap to Staunton.[1] Both of these have within those dozen years, been cleared of their trees, and put under cultivation, are much reduced in their heighth, and spread in width, by the plough, and will probably disappear in time.

"There is another on a hill in the Blue Ridge

[1] This description would indicate the neighborhood of Waynesboro, in Augusta County.

of mountains, a few miles north of Wood's gap, which is made up of small stones thrown together. This has been opened and found to contain human bones, as the others do. There are also many others in other parts of the country."[1]

On the western bank of the Ohio River, at Marietta, Ohio, is a nearly perfect specimen of the barrow or mound. It was visited by the writer in the fall of 1909. The mound is appropriately surrounded by a cemetery, named Mound Cemetery. It is conical in shape, the top being reached by forty-five stone steps, and having a circumference at the base, of about three hundred and seventy-eight feet.

Surrounding the mound, for about forty feet, the earth gently slopes away from it, and then descends into a shallow moat. Around this little moat there circles a correspondingly low rampart, at a distance of sixty feet from the base of the mound. This formed the outer circle of the structure, and is about seven hundred and seventy-one feet in circumference. All of this mound, space, moat, and rampart, is covered with a well-kept lawn, and presents a beautiful and symmetrical whole.

The care with which this mound has been kept does credit to the authorities of the city where it is, although it would be still better, if certain objects now there were removed from the top as well as the stone steps which ascend it, so

[1] Jefferson's *Notes on Virginia*, p. 99 *et seq.*

The Marietta Mound

Burial Mounds 211

that the mound could be seen in its original condition.

The writer could not learn, during his short stay, whether this mound had ever been thoroughly examined, or whether the encircling moat and rampart were of recent, or of ancient construction. He was told that its excavation had been once begun, but that it was abruptly abandoned.

Further up the Ohio, on its eastern bank, in Marshall County, West Virginia, at Moundsville, stands the greatest mound in the country. This was discovered in 1772, by Joseph Tomlinson, who settled at what was then known as Grave Creek. A description of the mound given by one of its subsequent owners, Mr. A. B. Tomlinson, taken from the *American Pioneer*, is thus preserved by Howe:

"The Mammoth Mound is sixty-nine feet high, and about nine hundred feet in circumference at its base. It is a frustum of a cone, and has a flat top of about fifty feet in diameter. This flat, until lately, was slightly depressed— occasioned, it is supposed, by the falling in of two vaults below. A few years since a white oak, of about seventy feet in height, stood on the summit of the mound, which appeared to die of age. On carefully cutting the trunk transversely, the number of concentric circles showed that it was about five hundred years old.

"In 1838, Mr. Tomlinson commenced at the

level of the surrounding ground, and ran in an excavation horizontally one hundred and eleven feet, when he came to a vault that had been excavated in the earth before the mound was commenced. This vault was twelve feet long, eight wide and seven in height. It was dry as any tight room. Along each side and the two ends, stood upright timbers, which had supported transverse timbers forming the ceiling. Over the timbers had been placed unhewn stone; but the decay of the timbers occasioned the fall of the stones and the superincumbent earth, so as to nearly fill the vault."

A note here inserted by Mr. Howe states: "'At the top and bottom, where the timbers had been placed, were particles of charcoal—an evidence that fire, instead of iron had been used in severing the wood. This goes to show that the constructors of the mound were not acquainted with the use of iron; and the fact that none of that metal was found in the vault, strongly corroborates the opinion. Some of the stones were water-worn, probably from the river; others were identical with a whet-stone quarry on the Ohio side of the river, two miles north.'

"In this vault were found two skeletons, one of which was devoid of ornament—the other was surrounded by six hundred and fifty ivory beads, resembling button-moles, and an ivory ornament of about six inches in length, which is one inch and five-eighths wide in the centre, half an inch wide at the ends, and on one side

The Mound, Showing the Observatory Built on it in 1837

Burial Mounds

flat and on the other oval-shaped. A singular white exudation of animal matter overhangs the roof of this vault.

"Another excavation was commenced at the top of the mound downwards. Midway between the top and bottom, and over the vault above described, a second and similar vault was discovered, and, like that, caved in by the falling of the ceiling, timbers, stones, etc. In the upper vault was found the singular hieroglyphical stone hereafter described, one thousand seven hundred ivory beads, five hundred sea-shells of the involute species, that were worn as beads, and five copper bracelets about the wrists of the skeleton. The shells and beads were about the neck and breast of the skeleton, and there were also about one hundred and fifty pieces of isinglass strewed over the body.

"The mound is composed of the same kind of earth as that around it, being a fine loamy sand, but differs very much in color from that of the natural ground. After penetrating about eight feet with the first or horizontal excavation, blue spots began to appear in the earth of which the mound is composed. On close examination, these spots were found to contain ashes and bits of burnt bones. These spots increased as they approached the centre: at the distance of one hundred and twenty feet within, the spots were so numerous and condensed as to give the earth a clouded appearance, and excited the admiration of all who saw it. Every part of the mound presents the same appearance, except near the surface. The blue spots were probably occasioned by depositing the remains of bodies consumed by fire."

The following additional interesting information is given by Howe:

"Mr. Henry R. Colcraft (Schoolcraft), whose researches upon the Indian antiquities of the West have placed him at the head of the list of scientific inquirers upon this subject, visited Grave Creek in August, 1843, and devoted several days to the examination of the antique works of art at that place. The result of his investigations is partially given in a communication to the *New York Commercial Advertiser*, copied below. We were subsequently at Grave Creek, and obtained an impression in wax of the hieroglyphical stone to which he alludes. An accurate engraving from this impression we insert in its proper place in his article:

"'I have devoted several days to the examination of the antiquities of this place and its vicinity, and find them to be of even more interest than was anticipated. The most prominent object of curiosity is the great tumulus, of which notices have appeared in western papers; but this heavy structure of earth is not isolated. It is but one of a series of mounds and other evidences of ancient occupation at this point, of more than ordinary interest. I have visited and examined seven mounds situated within a short distance of each other. They occupy the

Burial Mounds 215

summit level of a rich alluvial plain, stretching on the left or Virginia bank of the Ohio, between the junctions of Big and Little Grave creeks with that stream. They appear to have been connected by low earthen intrenchments, of which plain traces are still visible on some parts of the commons. They included a well, stoned up in the usual manner, which is now filled with rubbish.

"'The summit of this plain is probably seventy-five feet above the present summit-level of the Ohio.

"It constitutes the second bench or rise of land above the water. It is on this summit, and one of the most elevated parts of it, that the great tumulus stands. It is in the shape of a broad cone, cut off at the apex, where it is some fifty feet across. This area is quite level, and commands a view of the entire plain, and of the river above and below, and the west shores of the Ohio in front. Any public transaction on this area would be visible to multitudes around it, and it has, in this respect, all the advantages of the Mexican and Yucatanese teocalli.[1] The circumference of the base has been stated at a little under 900 feet; the height is 69 feet.

"'The most interesting object of antiquarian inquiry is a small flat stone, inscribed with antique, alphabetic characters, which was disclosed on the opening of the mound. These characters are in the ancient rock alphabet of

---

[1] A solid, four-sided, truncated pyramid built terrace-wise, with a temple on the platform at the summit.

sixteen right and acute-angled single strokes, used by the Pelasgi[1] and other early Mediterranean nations, and which is the parent of the modern Runic[2] as well as the Bardic.[3] It is now some four or five years since the completion of the excavations, so far as they have been made, and the discovery of this relic. Several copies of it soon got abroad which differed from each other, and, it was supposed, from the original. This conjecture is true. Neither the print published in the *Cincinnati Gazette*, in 1839, nor that in the *American Pioneer*, in 1843, is correct. I have terminated this uncertainty by taking copies by a scientific process, which does not leave the lines and figures to the uncertainty of man's pencil."[4]

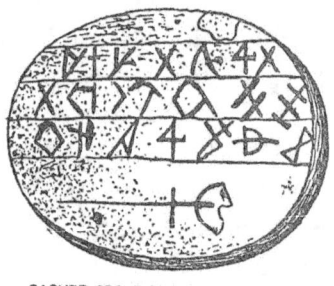

CARVED STONE FOUND IN THE MOUND

This great mound was therefore the burial-place of three distinguished persons, one alone, in the upper chamber, and two, probably a mighty warrior and his favourite wife, in the lower.

---

[1] An ancient race, widely spread over Greece and the coasts and islands of the Ægean Sea and the Mediterranean generally, in pre-historic times.
[2] The letters used by the peoples of Northern Europe from an early period to the eleventh century.
[3] The language of the bards among the ancient Celts.
[4] Howe's *Virginia, its History and Antiquities*, pp. 369-71.

Burial Mounds

It is to be observed that the bodies of the three great personages in whose special honor the mound was raised, were deposited in their chambers unburnt, while the central part of the mound is full of the remains of a large number of other corpses which had been burnt.

It was characteristic of the Stone Age in Northern Europe, to deposit bodies in such chambers as these unburnt. The chambers were then filled with earth, and the whole covered with earth. Together with the body were deposited arrow-heads, lances, chisels, and axes of flint, implements of bone, ornaments of amber or bone, and earthen vessels filled with loose earth. Around these mounds were circles of stone, often of considerable circumference.

It was characteristic of the Bronze-period to burn the bodies.

Worsaae tells us that: "At the summit and on the sides of a barrow are often found vessels of clay with burnt bones and articles of bronze, while at the base of the hill we meet with the ancient cromlechs or giants' chambers, with unburnt bodies and objects of stone. From this it is obvious that at a later time, possibly centuries after, poorer persons who had not the means to construct barrows, used the ancient tombs of the Stone-period, which they could do with the more security, since a barrow which is piled above a giant's chamber had exactly the same appearance as a barrow of the Bronze-period."[1]

[1] *Primeval Antiquities*, p. 94.

Viewing the great mound with these ideas in our mind, the facts related in connection with its opening, become more interesting and significant than ever.

It appeared that the lower vault had been excavated in the earth before the mound was commenced. This chamber was nearly filled with earth when opened. Had it been entirely filled it would have been in the same condition in which those in Europe were purposely arranged during the Stone-period. It is stated though, that in this instance this was due to the decay of the timbers, which held up the stones which formed the roof. All had fallen in. Here were two skeletons, surrounded with ivory beads and other articles.

This chamber covered with earth was probably all of the original structure.

It may have been centuries after this that another chamber was built on top of this mound. Another great man was buried. His arms were adorned with copper bracelets, and his name and his deeds were probably recorded on the hieroglyphical stone placed by his body, to give to another age a message which we are all too ignorant to decipher.

The age of Bronze now comes, and one by one, or possibly, many at a time, the bodies of the dead are burnt, and their charred remains are deposited on the sides of the tumulus, carefully covered with earth. The mound thus grows greater and greater, and becomes the cemetery of

Burial Mounds

a tribe, as well as the tomb of its most illustrious chieftains, until that tribe, like its individual members have done, itself vanishes from the face of the earth.

When seen by the writer in 1909, the condition of this mound afforded a sad contrast to that at Marietta. One was perfectly kept, the other was perfectly neglected. Around the West Virginia Mound, was no encircling space, moat, nor rampart. It uncomfortably occupied the larger part of a small city square. It was surrounded by streets which had been graded and paved, and all of the interesting outworks, such as exist at Marietta, if they ever existed here, have been utterly obliterated by a desecrating race-track, which once ran around it, and later by the grading of the streets. But there seems to be no tradition here of these circles having existed.

In fact, this great mound, after centuries of honor, had the misfortune to go through a dreary period of humiliation. The "observatory" built by Tomlinson, or some other building which succeeded it, was once used as a restaurant and dancing pavilion. Leveling the top of the mound for this house took off eleven feet of its height, which was originally ninety, reducing it to seventy-nine, according to the present local measurement. About the mound was established the Fair Grounds, and around this noble monument of antiquity, erected to the dead, was constructed the race-track over which horses ran at every county fair. The curiosity of the white man caused the two openings to be made in it, which, together with the giving away of the timbers of the two vaults, has caused the falling in of the earth through the center of the mound, although the shaft and tunnel were walled up, taking for this purpose eighty-five thousand bricks.

The top is now about 150 feet in circumference and presents the appearance of a rim of earth surrounding a cup-shaped depression, in about the center of which is a black hole. The opening on the north side, mentioned by Howe, is said to have been about seven feet wide, ten high, and ran back, gradually decreasing in size, to the center of the mound. Then the shaft was sunk through the top, met the second vault about thirty-four feet above the lower vault, and went down through the mound to the other vault. The mound being composed of loose earth, caved in.

No care having apparently been taken to prevent it, the sides are deeply marked by rains, and worn away by many foot-paths, difficult enough to ascend, and the whole lies unenclosed, liable to depredation and injury of every kind. About forty large trees, and many smaller ones, are now growing upon it, which give it the appearance of a well-wooded hill.

So great is this mound, the circumference at its base being considerably greater than the outside ring around the Marietta mound, that had it been similarly enclosed, its outlying en-

The Great Mound in 1909

Burial Mounds

circling rampart would have taken in an area equal to several squares of the town. It may have been that these very circles suggested the race-track.

The local belief is that the earth which was used to build this giant tumulus, was taken from a spot between a quarter and a half of a mile away from it, known as "The Basin," which lies on the north side of one of the principal streets, between the mound and the railroad station. This basin, enormous in area, has every appearance of having been artificially created. It breaks into the general slope of the land, its sides have not the curves of a natural hollow; and its soil is of the same character as that composing the mound. Those who dug that basin and built that mound, succeeded in accomplishing a herculean undertaking.

We are glad to say that better days are ahead. After years of work, the legislators of the State of West Virginia have been brought to partially appreciate the monument they have within their borders, and when it was in actual danger of being destroyed, or falling into utter ruin, they bought the property for the State, which will preserve it. Some work has already been done in clearing off its sides, and before long it may be put and kept in good condition, and so be properly handed down to posterity.

As this work is historical only, the interesting question of who built these mounds, whether the Indians who lived here at the time of the

English invasion, or some older race, we leave to anthropology and archæology, to which we also leave the question of whence the Indians themselves came.

Parkman gives an absorbingly interesting account of a funeral rite which existed, and was practised by the Hurons up to the time of the French occupation of Canada.[1] Every ten or twelve years, says he, the bodies of all who had died during that period were lowered from their scaffolds or lifted from their graves, and deposited in one common sepulchre. Such was no doubt the origin of the barrows which were found in Virginia, but we know of no statement by any of our early writers which would indicate that any of them were constructed during the period of the English occupation of Virginia.

But these mounds, simple in construction, do not compare in interest to this great mound at Moundsville, which, with its chambers one above the other, carries us back to the barrows of the Stone-period, the giants' chambers and cromlechs of the Stone Age of Europe.

[1] *The Jesuits in North America*, pp. 71-8.

CHAPTER XVI

PRIESTS AND CONJURERS

OF all the opponents to the English, the priests and conjurers were the most bitter. Not only did the coming of the White Man threaten political, social, and economic revolution, but one of its objects was the conversion of the heathen to Christianity. This the priests held to be an immediate attack upon them, and the whole system of which they were the exponents.

This opposition Strachey thus describes:

"Indeed their priests, being the ministers of Satan (who is very likely or visibly conversant amongst them), fear and tremble lest the knowledge of God, and of our Saviour Jesus Christ, should be taught in those parts, do now with the more vehemency persuade the people to hold on their wonted ceremonies, and every year to sacrifice still their own children to the ancient God of their fathers, and it is supposed gain double oblations this way, by reason they do at all times so absolutely govern and direct the wer-ó-ances, or lords of countries, in all their actions, and this custom he hath politically maintained, and doth yet universally, a few places excepted, over all the Indies.

"To have suffered still, therefore, me thinks, these priests of Baal or Beelzebub, were greatly offensive to the majesty of God, and most perilous for the English to inhabit within those parts; for these their qui-yough-qui-socks or prophets be they that persuade their wer-ó-ances to resist our settlement, and tell them how much their O-ke-us will be offended with them, and that he will not be appeased with a sacrifice of a thousand, nay a hecatomb of their children, if they permit a nation, despising the ancient religion of their forefathers, to inhabit among them, since their own gods have hitherto preserved them, and given them victory over their enemies, from age to age."[1]

Strachey also gives us the following account of the priests and their principal stronghold:

"Their principal temple, or place of superstition, is at Ut-ta-mus-sack, at Pa-mun-key.[2] Near unto the town, within the woods, is a chief holy house, proper to[3] Powhatan, upon the top of certain red sandy hills, and it is accompanied with two others sixty feet in length, filled with images of their kings and devils, and tombs of the predecessors. This place they count so holy as that none but the priests and kings dare come therein.

[1] *Historie of Travaile into Virginia*, pp. 83-4.
[2] The name of the region lying between the Pa-mun-key and the Mat-ta-po-nỹ Rivers.
[3] The private property of, or especially appropriated to.

"In this, as the Grecian nigromancers' psychomantie[1] did use to call up spirits, either the priests have conference, or consult, indeed, with the devil, and receive verbal answers, and so saith Acosta[2]; he spake to the βοιτη or chaplains of the West Indies, in their guacas or oratories, or at least these conjurers make the simple laity so to believe, who, therefore, so much are the people at the priests' devotion, are ready to execute any thing, how desperate soever, which they shall command. The savages dare not go up the river in boats by it, but that they solemnly cast some piece of copper, white beads, or po-chones[3] into the river, for fear that O-ke-us should be offended and revenged of them. In this place commonly are resident seven priests, the chief differing from the rest in his ornament, whilst the inferior priests can hardly be known from the common people, save that they had not (it may be, may be not have) so many holes in their ears to hang their jewels at.

"The ornaments of the chief priest were, upon his shoulders a middle-sized cloak of feathers much like the old sacrificing garment which Isodorus[4] calls cassiola, and the burlett or attire of his head was thus made: some twelve or sixteen or more snakes' sloughs or skins were

---

[1] Magicians' power over the souls of others.
[2] A Spanish Jesuit historian and archæologist.
[3] Pieces of the root puccoon, from which a red dye was made.
[4] Isodorus, a native of Charax, near the mouth of the Tigris. He was a writer of the time of Caligula.

stuffed with moss, and of weasels or other vermin were skins perhaps as many: all these were tied by the tails, so as their tails meet in the top of the head like a great tassel, and round about the tassel was circled a coronet, as it were, of feathers, the skins hanging round about his head, neck, and shoulders, and in a manner covering his face.

"The faces of all their priests are painted so ugly as they can devise; in their hands they carry every one his rattle, for the most part as a symbol of his place and profession, some base,[1] some smaller. Their devotion[2] is most in songs, which the chief priest begins and the rest follow him; sometimes he makes invocation with broken sentences, by starts and strange passions, and at every pause the rest of the priests give a short groan."[3]

The exact location of this sacred town of Ut-ta-mus-sack we can probably determine. The old maps show it to be situated on the east side of the Pamunkey River, just before it makes its sharp curves before it flows into the York. The Pamunkey Indian reservation is on the east bank of the Pamunkey just at this same point. These two locations are one and the same.

Ut-ta-mus-sack was therefore situated upon the land which has never yet been out of the possession of the Pamunkey tribe. The more we

---

[1] The large rattles would give the *base* notes, the smaller ones the treble.   [2] Religious service.
[3] *Historie of Travaile into Virginia*, p. 90.

Priests and Conjurers

think of it, the more natural this conclusion appears to be. This town was the headquarters of the priests, it was their special stronghold. The priests directed the affairs of the tribe. The tribe made peace with the Virginians, became tributary to Virginia, and had a tract of land, assigned for its own special possession. In selecting the land to be allotted to them, the priests of this tribe would naturally ask for that to which they attached the most importance, and that spot would be the one which had been held in such reverence for generations, where their temples were, and where the dead bodies of their kings had so long reposed—this St. Denis of the forest.

The conjuration of these priests is thus described by Strachey:

"They have also divers conjurations: one they made at what time they had taken Captain Smith prisoner, to know, as they reported, if any more of his countrymen would arrive there, and what they intended: the manner of it Captain Smith observed to be as followeth: first so soon as day was shut in, they kindled a fair great fire in a lone house, about which assembled seven priests, taking Captain Smith by the hand, and appointing him his seat. About the fire they made a kind of enchanted circle of meal; that done, the chiefest priest, attired as is expressed, gravely began to sing and shake his rattle, solemnly rounding and marching about the fire, the rest followed him silently until his song was done, which they all shut up with a groan. At the end of the first song the chief priest laid down certain grains of wheat, and so continued howling and invoking their O-ke-us to stand firm and powerful to them in divers varieties of songs, still counting the songs by the grains, until they had circled the fire three times, then they divided the grains by certain number with little sticks, all the while muttering some impious thing unto themselves, oftentimes looking upon Capt. Smith.

"In this manner they continued ten or twelve hours without any other ceremonies or intermission, with such violent stretching of their arms, and various passions, jestures, and symptoms, as might well seem strange to him before whom they so conjured, and who every hour expected to be the hoast[1] and one of their sacrifice. Not any meat did they eat until it was very late, and the night far spent. About the rising of the morning star they seemed to have finished their work of darkness, and then drew forth such provision as was in the said house, and feasted themselves and him with much mirth. Three or four days they continued these elvish[2] ceremonies.

"Now besides this manner of conjurations thus within doors (as we read the augurers in the old times of the like superstition, did ascend or go up into the certain towers or high places, called therefore auguracula, to divine of matters), so do they go forth, and either upon

---

[1] Host, victim offered in sacrifice.   [2] Witch-like.

Priests and Conjurers 229

some rock standing alone, or upon some desolate promontory top, or else into the midst of thick and solitary woods they call upon their o-ke-us and importune their other qui-ough-co-sughes with most impetuous and interminate clamors and howling, and with such pains and strained actions, as the neighbor places echo again of the same, and themselves are all in a sweat and over wearied."

"They have also another kind of sorcery which they use in storms, a kind of botanomantia [1] with herbs; when the waters are rough in the rivers and sea-coasts, their conjurers run to the water sides, or, passing in their quin-tans, after many hellish outcries and invocations, they cast whe-si-can,[2] tobacco, copper, po-cones, or such trash into the water, to pacify that god whom they think to be very angry in those storms."[3]

"Po-cones is a small root that groweth in the mountains, which, being dried and beat into powder, turneth red, and this they use for swellings, aches, anointing their joints, painting their heads and garments with it, for which they account it very precious and of much worth."[4]

"It could not be perceived that they keep any day as more holy than other: but only in some great distress of want, fear of enemies, times of triumph and gathering together their fruits, the whole country of men, women, and children come

---

[1] "Soothsaying from herbs."   [2] A bone.
[3] *Historie of Travaile into Virginia*, pp. 92–3.
[4] *Ibid.*, p. 121.

together to solemnities. The manner of their devotion is, sometimes to make a great fire, in the house or fields, and all to sing and dance about it with rattles and shouts together, four or five hours. Sometimes they set a man in the midst, and about him they dance and sing, he all the while clapping his hands, as if he would keep time, and after their songs and dancings ended, they go to their feasts.

"They have also certain altar-stones they call Paw-co-ran-ces, but these stand from their temples, some by their houses, others in the woods and wildernesses, where they have had any extraordinary accident or encounter. And as you travel, at those stones they will tell you the cause why they were there erected, which from age to age they instruct their children, as their best records of antiquities. Upon these they offer blood, deer-suet, and tobacco. This they do when they return from the wars, from hunting, and upon many other occasions."[1]

"The priests of the aforesaid town of Se-co-ta[2] are well stricken in years, and as it seemeth of more experience than the common sort. They wear their hair cut like a crest, on the top of their heads as others do, but the rest are cut short saving[3] those which grow above their foreheads in manner of a perriwigge.[4] They also have somewhat hanging in their ears. They wear a

[1] Smith, vol. i., p. 140.
[2] An Indian town in what is now Beaufort County, N. C.
[3] Excepting.   [4] Wig.

Priests and Conjurers

short clocke [1] made of fine hares' skins quilted with the hair outwards. The rest of their body is naked. They are notable enchanters, and for their pleasure they frequent the rivers to kill with their bows, and catch wild ducks, swans, and other fowls."

"They have commonly conjurers or jugglers which use strange gestures, and often contrary to nature in their enchantments: For they be very familiar with devils, of whom they inquire what their enemies do, or other such things. They shave all their heads saving their crest, which they wear as others do, and fasten a small black bird above one of their ears [2] as a badge of their office. They wear a bag by their side as is expressed in the figure. The inhabitants give great credit unto their speech, which oftentimes they find to be true." [3]

"I don't find that the Indians have any other distinction in their dress, or the fashion of their hair, than only what a greater degree of riches enables them to make: except it be their religious persons, who are known by the particular cut of the hair, and the unusual figure of their garments; as our clergy are distinguished by their canonical habit. [4]

"The habit of the Indian priest, is a cloak

---

[1] Cloak—a garment shaped like a bell. The word clock means bell, the sounding of the hour by a bell being its characteristic. The garment took its name from its similarity in shape to a bell.

[2] May not this be the origin of the expression—a little bird told such and such a thing?

[3] Hariot's *Narrative*, v., xi.   [4] Coat.

made in the form of a woman's petticoat, but instead of tying it about their middle, they fasten the gatherings about their neck, and tie it upon the right shoulder, always keeping one arm out to use upon occasion. This cloak hangs even at the bottom but reaches no lower than the middle of the thigh; but what is most particular in it, is, that it is constantly[1] made of a skin dressed soft, with the pelt or fur on the outside, and reversed; insomuch, that when the cloak has been a little worn, the hair falls down in flakes, and looks very shagged, and frightful.

"The cut of their hair is likewise peculiar to their function[2]; for 'tis all shaven close except a thin crest, like a cock's-comb which stands bristling up, and runs in a semicircle from the forehead up along the crown to the nape of the neck. They likewise have a border of hair over the forehead, which by its own natural strength, and by the stiffening it receives from grease and paint, will stand out like the peak[3] of a bonnet."

"He (the conjurer) as well as the priest, is commonly grimed with soot or the like; to save his modesty he hangs an otter-skin at his girdle, fastening the tail between his legs: upon his thigh hangs his pocket, which is fastened by tucking it under his girdle, the bottom of this likewise is fringed with tassels for ornament sake. In the middle between them is the hus-ka-naw-ing pen.[4]

[1] Invariably. [2] Office. [3] Projecting part.
[4] Beverley, book 3, pp. 5-6.

A Priest and a Conjurer in their Proper Habits

Priests and Conjurers 233

Spelman agrees with the above, in his account of the style of dressing the hair adopted by the priests, but adds the fact that some had beards.[1]

That these conjurers exercised a powerful control over the minds of the savages we are fully prepared to believe, when we read T. M.'s account of Bacon's rebellion, reciting events which occurred as late as the year 1676. A drought existed throughout the plantations that summer, while rain poured down every day upon Bacon and his troops in the forest. This rain was believed by the English to be due to the "pau-waw-ings," that is, the sorceries, of the Indians, who in this way obstructed the movements of Bacon's troops in his war upon them.

Beverley has this to say of them: "The priests and conjurers are also of great authority, the people having recourse to them for counsel and direction, upon all occasions; by which means, and by help of the first fruits and frequent offerings, they riot in the fat of the land, and grow rich upon the spoils of their ignorant countrymen."[2]

The Indian priests are thus described by the Rev. Mr. Whittaker, writing from Henrico in 1613: "Their priests (whom they call quick-o-soughs) are no other but such as our English witches are. They live naked in body, as if their shame of their sin deserved no covering. Their names are as naked as their body; they

[1] Spelman's *Relation of Virginia*, p. 52.
[2] Beverley, book 3, p. 57.

esteem it a virtue to lie, deceive, and steal, as their master the Devil teacheth them. . . . They (that is, all the other Indians), stand in great awe of the quick-o-soughs or priests, which are a generation of vipers, even Satan's own brood. The manner of their life is much like to the Popish hermits of our age; for they live alone in the woods, in houses sequestered from the common course of men; neither may any man be suffered to come into their house, or speak to them, but when the priest doth call them. He taketh no care of his victuals; for all such kind of things, both bread and water, etc., are brought into a place near his cottage and there left, which he fetcheth for his proper needs. If they would have rain, or have lost anything, they have recourse to him, who conjureth for them and many times prevaileth.[1] If they be sick, he is their physician; if they be wounded, he sucketh[2] them. At his command they make war and peace; neither do they anything of moment without him."[3]

"I can't understand that their women ever pretended to intermeddle with any offices that relate to the priesthood, or conjuration."[4]

This belief in the supernatural powers of the Indian priests to produce rain at will, was widely spread and seems to have been generally enter-

---

[1] The people of this period were firm believers in witchcraft, both at home and abroad.
[2] That is, sucks the blood from around the wound, to cleanse it.
[3] Purchas, vol. iv., p. 1771.   [4] Beverley, book 3, p. 47.

Priests and Conjurers

tained. Glover also mentions it. He says: "When they have great want of rain, one of their priests will go into a private cabin, and by his invocations will cause abundance to fall immediately, which they call making of rain."[1]

So deeply seated was the animosity against the Indian priests, that Strachey was evidently in favor of the "surreption" of them, that is of getting possession of them all by craft, or by stealth, if necessary. This he viewed as indispensable for the safety of the colonists and the enlargement of the plantation. He thus expresses himself:

"Yet no Spanish intention shall be entertained by us, neither hereby to root out the naturals,[2] as the Spaniards have done in Hispaniola[3] and other parts, but only to take from them these seducers, until when they [that is, until this be done the rest of the Indians] will never know God nor obey the King's majesty, and by which means we shall by degrees change their barbarous natures, make them ashamed the sooner of their savage nakedness, inform them of the true God and of the way to their salvation, and, finally, teach them obedience to the King's majesty and to his governors in those parts, declaring (in the attempt thereof) unto the several wer-ó-ances, and making the common people likewise to understand, how that his majesty hath been acquainted, that the men, women, and

[1] *Account of Virginia*, p. 24.
[2] Natives of the country.   [3] Haiti.

children of the first plantation at Roanoke were by practice and commandment of Powhatan (he himself persuaded thereunto by his priests) miserably slaughtered, without any offence given him either by the first planted[1] (who twenty and odd years[2] had peaceably lived intermixed with those savages, and were out of his territory) or by those who now are come to inhabit some part of his desert lands, and to trade with him for some commodities of ours, which he and his people stand in want of; notwithstanding, because his majesty is, of all the world, the most just and the most merciful prince, he hath given order that Powhatan himself, with the wer-ó-ances and all the people, shall be spared, and revenge only taken upon his qui-yough-qui-socks, by whose advice and persuasions was exercised that bloody cruelty."

He then proceeds to argue the benefits which would come to the Indians to be taken under the milder rule of King James instead of the tyranny they suffered under Powhatan, the better price they would receive for their commodities, etc., and then what ought to be done if all the priests could be convened when these things were discussed. He then concludes:

"This being delivered in fit terms, by some perfect interpreter, and to men that are capable enough of understanding it, may beget a fair conceit in them of us and our proceedings, and

[1] Those who were first settled or planted.
[2] Ago, or before the coming of the English to Jamestown.

leave them well satisfied; and indeed be it believed, that when so just an occasion shall offer these priests of Asmodeus [1] or the Devil into the hands of the lord general, a better time than that will not be found to perform the same acceptable service to God that Jehu, king of Israel, did, when he assembled all the priests of Baal, and slew them, to the last man, in their own temple. Of this may every vulgar sense be well assured, that seeing these monsters do offer up unto the devil their own children, and being hardened against all compassion, natural and divine, enforce their own mothers to deliver them to the executioner with their own hands, they will easily condescend unto, and assist the destruction and extirpation of all strangers, knowing or acknowledging the true God." [2]

[1] In Jewish demonology a destructive devil, lame, and often referred to as the destroyer of domestic happiness.
[2] *Historie of Travaile into Virginia*, pp. 85–86; 88–89.

CHAPTER XVII

RELIGION

THE religion of the Indians was polytheistic and idolatrous. Like most primitive nations they were strongly imbued with superstition. One of the objects of the settlement of Virginia was to Christianize the natives. Their views on religion were looked upon by the English with abhorrence, as founded on the darkest ignorance, and their priests and conjurers were regarded as representatives of Satan himself. The latter were found to be the most determined opponents of the English, who, not entirely free from superstition themselves, attributed supernatural powers to these Indian priests nearly as great as was believed to be the case by the natives.

The Indians' ideas on religion were not very easy to determine. They were reticent about them, and it was with difficulty that the English could get them to talk on this subject.

The first account we have is that given by Hariot, and is a part of his narrative written in connection with the expedition sent out by Sir Walter Raleigh in 1585. Here is what he tells us, speaking of the Indians he saw in connection with the Roanoke Island settlement, who were typical of all in that part of the world:

"The people of this country have an idol, which they call Ki-was-à: it is carved of wood in length four feet, whose head is like the heads of the people of Florida, the face is of a flesh color, the breast white, the rest is all black, the thighs are also spotted with white. He hath a chain about his neck of white beads, between which are other round beads of copper which they esteem more than gold or silver. This idol is placed in the temple of the town of Se-co-tam, as the keeper of the kings' dead corpses. Sometimes they have two of these idols in their churches, and sometimes three, but never above,[1] which they place in a dark corner where they show terrible."[2]

"They believe that there are many gods which they call Mon-to-ac, but of different sorts and degrees; one only chief and great God, which hath been from all eternity. Who as they affirm when he purposed to make the world, made first other gods of a principal order to be as means and instruments to be used in the creation and government to follow; and after the sun, moon and stars, as petty gods and the instruments of the other order more principal. First they say were made waters, out of which by the gods was made all diversity of creatures that are visible or invisible.

"For mankind they say a woman was made

[1] Above that number.   [2] Hariot's *Narrative*, xxi.

first, which by the working of one of the gods, conceived and brought forth children. And in such sort they say they had their beginning.

"But how many years or ages have passed since, they say they can make no relation, having no letters nor other such means as we keep records of the particularities of times past, but only tradition from father to son.

"They think that all the gods are of human shape, and therefore they represent them by images in the forms of men, which they call Ke-was-o-wok, one alone is called Ke-was; them they place in houses appropriate or temples which they call ma-chi-co-muck; where they worship, pray, sing, and make many times offerings unto them. In some ma-chi-co-muck we have seen but one Ke-was, in some two, and in some others three; the common sort think them to be also gods.

"They believe also the immortality of the soul, that after this life as soon as the soul is departed from the body, according to the works it hath done, it is either carried to heaven the habitacle[1] of gods, there to enjoy perpetual bliss and happiness, or else to a great pit or hole, which they think to be in the furthest parts of their part of the world towards the sunset, there to burn continually: the place they call Po-po-gus-so.

"For the confirmation of this opinion, they told me two stories of two men that had been lately dead and revived again, the one happened

[1] Dwelling-place.

Their Idol in His Tabernacle

Idol call'd. OKÈE, QUIÓCCOS, or KIWASÀ.

"The dark edging shows the sides and roof of the house, which consists of saplings and bark. The paler edging shows the mats by which they make a partition of about ten feet, at the end of the house, for the Idol's abode. The Idol is set upon his seat of mats, within his dark recess, above the people's heads, and the curtain is drawn up before him."

Religion

but few years before our coming in the country, of a wicked man which having been dead and buried, the next day the earth of the grave being seen to move, was taken up again; who made declaration where his soul had been, that is to say very near entering into Po-po-gus-so, had not one of the gods saved him and gave him leave to return again, and teach his friends what they should do to avoid that terrible place of torment.

"The other happened in the same year we were there, but in a town that was threescore miles from us, and it was told me for strange news that one being dead, buried and taken up again as the first, showed that although his body had lain dead in the grave, yet his soul was alive, and had travelled far in a long broad way, on both sides whereof grew most delicate and pleasant trees, bearing more rare and excellent fruits than ever he had seen before or was able to express, and at length came to most brave and fair[1] houses, near which he met his father, that had been dead before, who gave him great charge to go back again and show his friends what good they were to do to enjoy the pleasures of that place, which when he had done he should after come again."[2]

"Concerning the immortality of the soul, they suppose that the common people shall not live after death; but they think that their wer-ó-ances and priests, indeed whom they esteem half qui-ough-co-sughes, when their bodies are laid in

---
[1] Presenting a fine appearance.
[2] Lane's account. Hakluyt's *Voyages*, vol. ii., p.

the earth, that that which is within shall go beyond the mountains, and travel as far as where the sun sets, into most pleasant fields, grounds and pastures, where it shall do no labor; but, stuck finely with feathers, and painted with oil and po-cones, rest in all quiet and peace, and eat delicious fruits, and have store of copper, beads, and hatchets; sing, dance, and have all variety of delights and merriments till that wax old there, as the body did on earth, and then it shall dissolve and die, and be new born into the world." [1]

The belief which the Indians firmly entertained of the immortality of the soul is strikingly brought out in connection with the superstitious awe with which they regarded the white men. At first they considered them immortal, or, at least, not subject to be put to death by themselves.

Lane tells us that En-se-no-re, the father of Pe-mis-a-pan, the King of the country which included Roanoke Island, held such views, and, in the councils of his tribe, urged them upon the others.

At a time when Lane returned safely from an expedition on which certain Indians reported that he had perished, he says that En-se-no-re "renewed those his former speeches, both to the King and the rest, that we were the servants of God, and that we were not subject to be destroyed by them; but contrariwise, that they

[1] *Historie of Travaile into Virginia*, p. 96.

amongst them that sought our destruction should find their own, and not be able to work ours, and that we being dead men were able to do them more hurt, than now we could do being alive; an opinion very confidently at this day holden by the wisest amongst them, and of their old men.

"As also, that they have been in the night, being one hundred miles from any of us, in the air shot at and stroken by some men of ours, that by sickness had died among them.

"And many of them hold opinion, that we be dead men returned into the world again, and that we do not remain dead but for a certain time, and that then we return again."[1]

Smith gives us an account of an O-keè being carried by the Indians into battle. The god, made of skins, stuffed with moss, painted and hung with chains and copper, was borne before the warriors, who followed in a square order. The Indians charged the English. At the first volley from the muskets the idol fell to the ground, its bearers falling dead or wounded around it. The rest fled. Soon a priest came forward to offer peace and redeem the O-keè. Terms being offered which were satisfactory, the O-keè was restored.[2]

Beverley gives us this account of a visit to one of the O-keè's temples:

"I have been at several of the Indian towns

[1] Lane's account in Hakluyt's *Voyages*.
[2] Smith, vol. i., p. 156.

and conversed with some of the most sensible of them in that country; but I could learn little from them, it being reckoned sacrilege to divulge the principles of their religion. However, the following adventure discovered something of it. As I was ranging the woods, with some other friends, we fell upon their qui-oc-co-san (which is their house of religious worship) at a time, when the whole town was gathered together in another place, to consult about the bounds of the land given them by the English.[1]

"Thus finding ourselves masters of so fair an opportunity (because we knew the Indians were engaged) we resolved to make use of it, and to examine their qui-oc-co-san, the inside of which they never suffer any Englishman to see; and having removed about fourteen logs from the door, with which it was barricadoed, we went in, and at first found nothing but naked walls, and a fireplace in the middle. This house was about eighteen feet wide, and thirty feet long, built after the manner of their other cabins, but larger, with a hole in the middle of the roof to vent the smoke, the door being at one end. Round about the house at some distance from it, were set up posts with faces carved on them, and painted. We did not observe any window or passage for the light, except the door, and the vent of the chimney.

[1] As a part of the treaties made with the native tribes, tracts of land were assigned them, to be held as tribal property, and not subject to be patented or otherwise acquired by the white people.

"At last, we observed that at the farther end, about ten feet of the room was cut off by a partition of very close mats; and it was dismal dark behind that partition. We were at first scrupulous[1] to enter this obscure place, but at last we ventured, and groping about, we felt some posts in the middle; then reaching our hands up those posts, we found large shelves, and upon these shelves three mats, each of which was rolled up, and sewed fast. These we handed down to the light, and to save time in unlacing the seams, we made use of a knife, and ripped them, without doing any damage to the mats. In one of these we found some vast bones, which we judged to be the bones of men, particularly we measured one thigh bone, and found it two feet, nine inches long. In another mat, we found some Indian tomahawks finely graved, and painted. These resembled the wooden faulchion[1] used by the prize-fighters in England, except that they have no guard to save[3] the fingers. They were made of a rough heavy wood, and the shape of them is represented in the Tab. 10, No. 3.[4]

"Among these tomahawks was the largest that ever I saw: there was fastened to it a wild turkey's beard painted red, and two of the longest feathers of his wings hung dangling at it, by a string of about six inches long, tied to the end of the tomahawk. In the third mat there was

[1] Afraid.   [2] A short broad sword curving sharply to the point
[3] Protect.   [4] This is the picture on page 74.

something, which we took to be their idol, though of an underling[1] sort, and wanted putting together. The pieces were these, first a board three feet and a half long, with one indenture at the upper end, like a fork to fasten the head upon, from thence half way down, were half hoops nailed to the edges of the board, at about four inches distance, which were bowed out, to represent the breast and belly; on the lower half was another board of half the length of the other, fastened to it by joints or pieces of wood, which being set on each side, stood out about fourteen inches from the body, and half as high; we supposed the use of these to be for the bowing out of the knees, when the image was set up. There were packed up with these things, red and blue pieces of cotton cloath, and rolls made up for arms, thighs and legs, bent to at the knees, as is represented in the figure of their idol, which was taken by an exact drawer[2] in the country. It would be difficult to see one of these images at this day, because the Indians are extreme shy of exposing them.

"We put the cloaths upon the hoops for the body, and fastened on the arms and legs, to have a view of the representation. But the head and rich bracelets, which it is usually adorned with, were not there, or at least we did not find them.

[1] Subordinate, or lesser divinity.
[2] John White, who drew the pictures for Sir Walter Raleigh, in 1585.

"We had not leisure to make a very narrow search, for having spent about an hour in this enquiry, we feared the business of the Indians might be near over and that if we stayed longer, we might be caught offering an affront to their superstition; for this reason we wrapt up these holy materials in their several mats again, and laid them on the shelf, where we found them.

"This Image when dressed up, might look very venerable[1] in that dark place; where 'tis not possible to see it, but by the glimmering light that is let in by lifting up a piece of the matting, which we observed to be conveniently hung for that purpose; for when the light of the door and chimney glance in several directions, upon the image through that little passage, it must needs make a strange representation, which those poor people are taught to worship with a devout ignorance.

"There are other things that contribute towards carrying on this imposture; first the chief conjurer enters within the partition in the dark, and may undiscerned move the image as he pleases: secondly, a priest of authority stands in the room with the people, to keep them from being too inquisitive, under the penalty of the Deity's displeasure, and his own censure.

"Their Idol bears a several name in every nation, as O-keè, Qui-óc-cos, Ki-wa-sà. They do not look upon it, as one single being, but reckon there are many of them of the same nature; they

[1] Worthy of veneration or reverence.

likewise believe that there are tutelar deities in every town."[1]

Percy tells us that they worshiped the sun. He says:

"It is a general rule of these people when they swear by their god which is the sun, no Christian will keep their oath better upon this promise. Their people have a great reverence to the sun, above all other things at the rising and setting of the same, they set down lifting up their hands and eyes to the sun making a round circle on the ground with dried tobacco, then they began to pray making many devilish gestures with a hellish noise, foaming at the mouth, staring with their eyes, wagging their heads and hands in such a fashion and deformity as it was monstrous to behold.

"In the morning by break of day, before they eat or drink both men, women and children, that be above ten years of age run into the water, there wash themselves a good while till the sun riseth, then offer sacrifice to it, strewing tobacco on the water or land, honoring the sun as their god, likewise they do at the setting sun."[2]

"We have observed how when they would affirm any thing by much earnestness and truth, they use to bind it by a kind of oath; either by the life of the great king, or by pointing up to the sun and clapping the right hand upon the heart,

[1] Beverley, book 3, pp. 28-31.
[2] Purchas, vol. iv., p. 1690.

Kiwasà

and sometimes they have been understood to swear by the manes[1] of their dead father."[2]

Strachey says that they worshiped everything which they conceived able to do them hurt beyond their prevention. Thus, they adored the fire, water, lightning, thunder, the cannon of the English, and their horses, etc. But he says the chief object of their worship was the devil. Then he describes the whole religious system in one sentence:

"In every territory of a wer-ó-ance is a temple and a priest, peradventure two or three: yet happy doth that wer-ó-ance account himself who can detain with him a qui-yough-qui-sock, of the best, grave, lucky, well instructed in their mysteries, and beloved of their god: and such a one is no less honored than was Diana's priest at Ephesus, for whom they have their more private temples, with oratories and chancels therein, according as is the dignity and reverence of the qui-yough-qui-sock, which the wer-ó-ance will be at charge to build upon purpose, sometimes twenty feet broad and a hundred in length, fashioned arbor-wise after their building, having commonly the door opening into the east, and at the west end a spence or chancel from the body of the temple, with hollow windings and pillars, whereon stand divers black images, fashioned to the shoulders, with their faces looking down the church, and where within their wer-ó-ances, upon

[1] The deified spirit.
[2] Strachey, *Historie of Travaile into Virginia*, p. 113.

a kind of bier of reeds, lie buried; and under them, apart, in a vault low in the ground (as a more secret thing) veiled with a mat, sits their O-ke-us, an image ill-favoredly carved, all black dressed, with chains of pearl, the presentment and figure of that god (say the priests unto the laity, and who religiously believe what the priests say) which doth them all the harm they suffer, be it in their bodies or goods, within doors or abroad; and true it is many of them are divers times (especially offenders) shrewdly scratched as they walk alone in the woods, it may well be by the subtle spirit, the malicious enemy to mankind, whom, therefore, to pacify, and work to do them good (at least no harm) the priests tell them they must do these and these sacrifices unto (them), of these and these things, and thus and thus often, by which means not only their own children, but strangers, are sometimes sacrificed unto him; whilst the great God (the priests tell them) who governs all the world, and makes the sun to shine, creating the moon and stars his companions, great powers, and which dwell with him, and by whose virtues and influences the under earth is tempered, and brings forth her fruits according to her seasons, they call A-ho-ne; the good and peaceable God requires no such duties, nor needs be sacrificed unto, for he intendeth all good unto them, and will do no harm, only the displeased O-ke-us, looking into all men's actions, and examining the same according to the severe scale of justice,

Religion

punisheth them with sicknesses, beats them, and strikes their ripe corn with blastings, storms, and thunder-claps, stirs up war, and makes their women false unto them."[1]

Henry Spelman, who lived a long time with the Potomac and other Indians, gives us this account of some of their religious ideas and customs:

"For the most part they worship the Devil, which the conjurers, who are their priests, can make appear unto them at their pleasure,[2] yet nevertheless in every country they have a several image whom they call their god. As with the great Powhatan he hath an image called Cak-e-res which most commonly standeth at Yaugh-taw-noo-ne[3] or at Or-o-pikes[4] in a house for that purpose, and with him are set all the king's goods and presents that are sent him, as the corn. But the beads or crown and bed which the King of England sent him are in the god's house at Or-o-pikes, and in their houses are all the king's ancestors and kindred commonly buried. In the Patomac's country they have another god whom they call Qui-o-quas-cacke, and unto their images they offer beads and copper, if at any time they want rain or have too much, and though they observe no day to wor-

---

[1] *Historie of Travaile into Virginia*, pp. 82–3.
[2] Additional evidence of the firm belief in the power of the Indian conjurers.
[3] This place is difficult to locate, not being on the map of the towns; see page 142.
[4] A favorite town of Powhatan's, in what is now Hanover County, usually spelt Or-a-pax.

ship their god but upon necessity, yet once in the year, their priests, which are their conjurers, with the men, women and children do go into the woods, where their priests make a great circle of fire in the which after many observances in other conjurations they make offer of two or three children to be given to their god if he will appear unto them and show his mind whom he desires.

"Upon which offering they hear a noise out of the circle nominating such as he will have, whom presently they take, binding them hand and foot, and cast them into the circle of the fire, for be it the king's son he must be given if once named by their god. After the bodies which are offered are consumed in the fire and their ceremonies performed the men depart merrily, the women weeping."[1]

The Rev. Alexander Whittaker, the minister at Henrico, in 1613, has this to say of their religion: "They acknowledge that there is a great good God, but know him not, having the eyes of their understanding as yet blinded; wherefore they serve the Devil for fear, after a most base manner, sacrificing sometimes, as I have heard, their own children to him. I have sent one image of their god to the council in England, which is painted on one side of a toadstool, much like unto a deformed monster. . . . The service of their god is answerable to[2] their life, be-

[1] Spelman's *Relation of Virginia*, pp. 25–7.
[2] In conformity with.

Religion

ing performed with great fear and attention, and many strange, dumb shews used in the same, stretching forth their limbs and straining their body, much like to the counterfeit women in England, who fancy themselves bewitched or possessed of some evil spirit."[1]

Paw-co-rances in general were mentioned in the preceding chapter. It seems, however, that there was one of greater prominence and importance than all the others. This is thus described by Beverley:

"They had an altar-stone called Paw-co-rance, which, according to the account of it given by the Indians, was a solid crystal of between three or four cubic feet, upon which in their greatest solemnities, they used to sacrifice. It was at Ut-ta-mus-sack,[2] the principal temple of the country, and the metropolitan seat of the priests. They said that this stone was so clear that the grain of a man's skin might be seen through it, and so heavy that when they removed their gods and kings, not being able to carry it away, they buried it thereabouts. But the place has never yet been discovered."[3]

"They erect altars wherever they have any remarkable occasion; and because their principal devotion consists in sacrifice, they have a profound respect for these altars. They have one particular altar, to which, for some mystical

---
[1] Purchas, vol. iv., 1771.
[2] The Indian town in Pamunkey, as it was called, that is the lower part of the territory between the Pamunkey and Mattapony rivers.
[3] Beverley, bk. 2, pp. 10-11.

reason, many of their nations pay an extraordinary veneration; of this sort was the crystal cube mentioned above. The Indians call this by the name of Paw-co-rance, from whence proceeds the great reverence they have for a small bird that uses the woods, and in their note continually sound that name. The bird flies alone, and is only heard in the twilight. They say this is the soul of one of their princes; and on that score, they would not hurt it for the world. But there was once a profane Indian in the upper parts of James River, who, after abundance of fears and scruples was at last bribed to kill one of them with his gun; but the Indians say he paid dear for his presumption, for in a few days after he was taken away, and never more heard of.

"When they travel by any of these altars, they take great care to instruct their children and young people in the particular occasion and time of their erection, and recommend the respect which they ought to have for them; so that their careful observance of these traditions, proves as good a memorial of such antiquities, as any written records; especially for so long as the same people continue to inhabit in, or near the same place."[1]

A presentation of the Indian tradition of creation and an outline of their religion was obtained from Jop-as-sus, the king of the Potomac Indians, and is given to us by Strachey:

[1] Beverley, bk. 3, pp. 46-7.

"The last year 1610, about Christmas, when Captain Argal, was there trading with Jop-as-sus, the great king's brother, after many days of acquaintance with him, as the pinnace[1] rode before the town Match-o-pon-go,[2] Jop-as-sus, coming aboard and sitting, the weather being very cold, by the fire, upon a hearth in the hold, with the Captain, one of our men was reading a Bible, to which the Indian gave a very attentive care, and looked with a very wisht eye upon him, as if he desired to understand what he read, whereupon the Captain took the book, and turned to the picture of the creation of the world, in the beginning of the book, and caused a boy, one Spelman, who had lived a whole year with this Indian king, and spoke his language, to show it unto him, and to interpret it in his language, which the boy did, and which the king seemed to like well of; howbeit, he bade the boy tell the Captain if he would hear, he would tell him the manner of their beginning, which was a pretty fabulous tale indeed.

"'We have, said he, five gods in all; our chief god appears often unto us in the likeness of a mighty great Hare: the other four have no visible shape, but are indeed the four winds which keep the four corners of the earth, and then, with his hand, he seemed to quarter out the situations of

---

[1] A small vessel rigged as a schooner, generally with two masts, and capable of being propelled by oars.
[2] One of the many which are mentioned which cannot be located on the map. A town of this name was on the ocean side of Northampton County. But this town must have been on the Potomac.

the world. Our god, who takes upon him this shape of a Hare, conceived with himself how to people this great world, and with what kind of creatures, and it is true that at length he devised and made divers men and women, and made provision for them, to be kept up yet a while in a great bag. Now there were certain spirits, which he described to be like great giants, which came to the Hare's dwelling-place, being towards the rising of the sun), and had perseverance[1] of the men and women which he had put into that great bag, and they would have had them to eat, but the Godly Hare reproved those cannibal spirits, and drove them away.'

"Now if the boy had asked him of what he made those men and women, and what those spirits more particularly had been, and so had proceeded in some order, they should have made it hang together the better; but the boy was unwilling to question him so many things, lest he should offend him; only the old man went on, and said how that God-like Hare made the water, and the fish therein, and the land, and a great deer, which should feed upon the land; at which assembled the other four gods, envious hereat, from the east, the west, from the north and south, and with hunting poles killed this great deer, dressed him, and, after they had feasted with[2] him, departed again, east, west, north, and south; at which the other god, in despite for this their malice to him, took all the hairs of the slain deer,

[1] A following, or seeking after, *per sequor*.   [2] On.

and spread them upon the earth, with many powerful words and charms, whereby every hair became a deer; and then he opened the great bag, wherein the men and the women were, and placed them upon the earth, a man and a woman in one country, and a man and a woman in another country, and so the world took his[1] first beginning of mankind.

"The captain bade the boy ask him what he thought became of them after their death, to which he answered somewhat like as is expressed before of the inhabitants about us, how that after they are dead here, they go up to a top of a high tree, and there they espy a fair, plain, broad pathway, on both sides whereof doth grow all manner of pleasant fruits, as mulberries, strawberries, plums, etc. In this pleasant path they run toward the rising of the sun, where the Godly Hare's house is, and in the midway they come to a house where a woman goddess doth dwell, who hath always her doors open for hospitality, and hath at all times ready dressed green us-kat-a-ho-men and po-ka-hich-ory, (which is green corn bruised and boiled, and walnuts beaten small, then washed from the shells with a quantity of water, which makes a kind of milk, and which they esteem an extraordinary dish), together with all manner of pleasant fruits, in a readiness to entertain all such as do travel to the Great Hare's house: and when they are well refreshed, they run in this pleasant path

[1] Its.

to the rising of the sun, where they find their forefathers living in great pleasure, in a goodly field, where they do nothing but dance and sing, and feed on delicious fruits with that Great Hare, who is their great god; and when they have lived there until they be stark[1] old men, they say they die there likewise by turns, and come into the world again.

"Concerning further of the religion we have not yet learned, nor indeed shall we ever know all the certainty either of these their unhallowed mysteries, or of their further orders and policies, until we can make surprise of some of their qui-yough-qui-socks.[2]"[3]

Beverley gives us this further insight into the religious ideas of these people:

"Once in my travels, in very cold weather, I met at an Englishman's house with an Indian of whom an extraordinary character had been given me, for his ingenuity and understanding. When I saw he had no other Indian with him, I thought I might be the more free; and therefore I made much of him, seating him close by a large fire, and giving him plenty of strong cider, which I hoped would make him good company, and open-hearted.

"After I found him well warmed (for unless they be surprised some way or other, they will not talk freely of their religion) I asked him concerning their god, and what their notions of

---

[1] Strong, hale, or hearty.   [2] Priests.
[3] *Historie of Travaile into Virginia*, pp. 98-100.

him were? He freely told me, they believed God was universally beneficent, that his dwelling was in the heavens above, and that the influence of his goodness reached to the earth beneath. That he was incomprehensible in his excellence, and enjoyed all possible felicity. That his duration was eternal, his perfection boundless, and that he possessed everlasting indolence and ease.

"I told him, I had heard that they worshipped the Devil, and asked why they did not rather worship God, whom they had so high an opinion of, and who would give them all good things, and protect them from any mischief that the Devil could do them?

"To this his answer was, that, 'tis true, God is the giver of all good things, but they flow naturally and promiscuously from him; that they are showered down upon all men indifferently without distinction; that God does not trouble himself with the impertinent affairs of men, nor is concerned at what they do: but leaves them to make the most of their free will, and to secure as many as they can, of the good things that flow from him. That therefore it was to no purpose, either to fear or worship him: but, on the contrary, if they did not pacify the evil spirit and make him propitious, he would take away, or spoil all those good things that God had given, and ruin their health, their peace and their plenty, by sending war, plague and famine among them; for, said he, this Evil Spirit is always busying himself with our affairs, and frequently visiting us, being present in the air, in the thunder and in the storms. He told me farther, that he expected adoration and sacrifice from them, on pain of his displeasure; and that therefore they thought it convenient to make their court to him.

"I then asked him concerning the image which they worship in their qui-oc-ca-san; and assured him that it was a dead, insensible log, equipt with a bundle of clouts,[1] a mere helpless thing made by men, that could neither hear, see, nor speak; and that such a stupid thing could no ways hurt, or help them.

"To this he answered very unwillingly, and with much hesitation; however, he at last delivered himself in these broken and imperfect sentences; it is the priests, they make the people believe—and—here he paused a little and then repeated to me, that it was the priests—and then gave me hopes that he would have said something more, but a qualm[2] crossed his conscience, and hindered him from making any farther confession.

"The priests and conjurers have a great sway in every nation. Their words are looked upon as oracles, and consequently are of great weight among the common people. They perform their adorations and conjurations, in the general language before spoke of,[3] as the Catholics of all nations do their Mass in the Latin.

[1] Worthless pieces of cloth. [2] Scruple.
[3] That of the Oc-ca-nee-ches, mentioned in Chapter XIX. of this work.

"They teach, that the souls of men survive their bodies, and that those who have done well here, enjoy most transporting pleasures in their Elizium hereafter; that this Elizium is stored with the highest perfection of all their earthly pleasures; namely with plenty of all sorts of game, for hunting, fishing and fowling; that it is blest with the most charming women, which enjoy an eternal bloom, and have an universal desire to please. That it is delivered from excesses of cold or heat, and flourishes with an everlasting spring. But that, on the contrary, those who are wicked, and live scandalously here, are condemned to a filthy, stinking lake after death, that continually burns with flames, that never extinguish; where they are persecuted and tormented, day and night, with furies in the shape of old women."[1]

Another view entertained by the Indians on this subject is presented to us by Jones. He says:

"Upon enquiry, we have from them these their notions of the state of the dead.

"They believe that they go to Ma-hom-ny that lives beyond the sun, if they have not been wicked, nor like dogs nor wolves, that is, not unchaste, then they believe that Ma-hom-ny sends them to a plentiful country abounding with fish, flesh and fowls, the best of their kind, and easy to be caught; but if they have been naughty then he sends them to a poor, barren

[1] Beverley, book 3, pp. 32-4.

country, where be many wolves and bears, with a few nimble deer, swift fish and fowls, difficult to be taken; and when killed, being scarce anything but skin and bones."[1]

"They use many divinations and inchantments, and frequently offer burnt sacrifice to the Evil Spirit. The people annually present their first fruits of every season and kind, namely, of birds, beasts, fish, fruits, plants, roots, and of all other things, which they esteem either of profit or pleasure to themselves. They repeat their offerings as frequently as they have great successes in their wars, or their fishing, fowling or hunting."[2]

"The first deer they kill after they are in season, they lay privately on the head of a tree near the place where they killed it, and they say no good luck will befall them that year if they do not offer the first of everything."[3]

Another favorite object of sacrifice was tobacco, or up-po-woc. Hariot tells us that:

"This up-po-woc is of so precious estimation amongst them, that they think their gods are marvelously delighted therewith: whereupon sometime they make hallowed fires, and cast some of the powder therein for a sacrifice: being in a storm upon the waters, to pacify their gods, they cast some up into the air and into the water: so a weir for fish being newly set up, they

---

[1] Jones's *Present State of Virginia*, p. 16.
[2] Beverley, bk. 3, p. 34.
[3] Glover's *Account of Virginia*, p. 24.

cast some therein and into the air; also after an escape of danger, they cast some into the air likewise: but all done with strange gestures, stamping, and staring up into the heavens, uttering therewithal and chattering strange words and noises."[1]

"The Indians offer sacrifice almost upon every new occasion; as when they travel or begin a long journey, they burn tobacco instead of incense, to the sun, to bribe him to send them fair weather, and a prosperous voyage. When they cross any great water, or violent fresh or torrent, they throw tobacco, puc-coon,[2] peak,[3] or some other valuable thing, that they happen to have about them, to entreat the spirit presiding there to grant them a safe passage. It is called a fresh,[4] when after very great rains, or (as we suppose) after a great thaw of the snow and ice lying upon the mountains, to the northwest, the water descends, in such abundance into the rivers, that they overflow the banks which bound their streams at other times.

"Likewise when the Indians return from war, from hunting, from great journeys, or the like, they offer some proportion of their spoils, of their chiefest tobacco, furs and paint, as also the fat, and choice bits of their game.

"I never could learn that they had any cer-

---

[1] Hakluyt, vol. ii., p. 339.
[2] The root from which a red dye was made, the bloodroot.
[3] Money or ornament made of shells.
[4] Freshet.

tain time or set days for their solemnities: but they have appointed feasts that happen according to the several seasons. They solemnize a day for the plentiful coming of their wild fowl, such as geese, ducks, teal, etc., for the returns of their hunting seasons, and for the ripening of certain fruits: but the greatest annual feast they have is at the time of their corn-gathering, at which they revel several days together. To these they universally contribute, as they do to the gathering in the corn. On this occasion they have their greatest variety of pastimes, and more especially of their war-dances, and heroic songs; in which they boast, that their corn being now gathered, they have store enough for their women and children; and have nothing to do but to go to war, travel, and to seek out for new adventures."[1]

"The Indians have posts fixed round their qui-oc-ca-san,[2] which have men's faces carved upon them, and are painted. They are likewise set up round some of their other celebrated places, and make a circle for them to dance about, on certain solemn occasions. They very often set up pyramidical stones and pillars, which they color with puc-coon,[3] and other sorts of paint, and which they adorn with peak, roenoke,[4] etc. To these they pay all outward signs of worship and devotion; not as to God, but as they are hieroglyphicks of the permanency and

[1] Beverley, book 3, pp. 42-3.   [2] House of religious worship.
[3] The bloodroot.   [4] A kind of shell money.

immutability of the deity; because these, both for figure and substance, are, of all sublunary bodies, the least subject to decay or change; they also for the same reason keep baskets of stones in their cabins. Upon this account too, they offer sacrifice to running streams, which, by the perpetuity of their motion, typify the eternity of God."[1]

We are told by Beverley that there was near the James a flat rock upon which there was a depression resembling a gigantic footprint. This was an object of the most reverential regard by the Indians, who believed it to be an impression caused by the footstep of a god, as he passed through that country.[2]

An Indian legend is preserved in connection with a little sheet of water on the Eastern Shore of Maryland, about a mile from Betterton. It is this water from which the town of Still Pond gets its name.

The following is an account we have seen:

"This pond is so called because there has never been seen a ripple upon its surface, no matter how hard the wind blows, nor has its surface ever been coated with ice. With the mercury at six degrees below zero, not a particle of ice has been seen.

"Another interesting fact about this body of water is that, although only about twenty feet across in any direction it has never been fathomed.

[1] Beverley, bk. 3, p. 46.   [2] *Ibid.*, p. 44.

"Still Pond, one of the mysteries of the Eastern Shore, was an object of veneration among the Indians of the peninsula. So deep as never to be sounded, they believed its waters ran down in the earth to supply the happy hunting grounds of their dead. Long before the first European settler had set foot upon the shore of the Chesapeake, the Indians from all parts of the peninsula, once a year, during the full moon of September, assembled by the side of the pond to worship the Man-i-tou and to pray for the return of their mighty chief, who had, they believed, fallen into the water and sunk from their sight."

According to the beliefs of the Cher-o-kees, the Great Spirit of Evil had his throne among the peaks and precipices of Whiteside Mountain, one of the loftiest in the Co-wee[1] range, near its southern terminus. "There in a moss-grown inclosure, curved by nature to form the segment of a circle, and walled in by stupendous rocks which rise to a perpendicular height of eighteen hundred feet, he held his court; but, casting aside his state, he occasionally walked abroad upon the earth, and then, as he strode in the darkness from peak to peak, leaving upon the bald mountain tops the print of his awful footsteps, he spoke to the Red Man in the storm and in the thunder."[2]

[1] This range of mountains, a part of the southern extension of the Blue Ridge, is in the extreme western part of North Carolina, and forms the boundary between Swain and Macon, and Macon and Jackson counties.   [2] Kirke's *Rear Guard of the Revolution*, p. 18.

CHAPTER XVIII

POWHATAN AND WINGINA

AROUND the commanding figure of Powhatan centers the greatest interest, as the head and embodiment of the Indian power in Virginia, at the time of the settlement. Strachey gives us this account of his personal appearance:

"He is a goodly old man, not yet shrinking, though well beaten with many cold and stormy winters, in which he hath been patient of many necessities and attempts of fortune to make his name and family great. He is supposed to be little less than eighty years old, I dare not say how much more; others say he is of a tall stature and clean limbs, of a sad aspect, round fat visaged, with gray hair, but plain and thin, hanging upon his broad shoulders; some few hairs upon his chin, and so on his upper lip: he hath been a strong and able savage, sinewy, and of a daring spirit, vigilant, ambitious, subtle to enlarge his dominions."[1]

We are told that he was born on the north side of the James River, then known by the name

---

[1] *Historie of Travaile into Virginia*, p. 49.

of the Indian, instead of the English, king, just below the falls, near Richmond, in the country inhabited by the Powhatan tribe of Indians.

It seems that he did not naturally belong to the Algonquin race of Indians, over a portion of which he ruled. We have this interesting statement presented about his origin by Hamor, who says, "Powhatan's father was driven from the West Indies by the Spaniards."[1] Beverley says, "O-pe-chan-ca-nough was said to have been a prince of a foreign nation and came to Virginia a great way from the southwest, and by their [the Indians'] account we suppose him to have come from the Spanish Indians, somewhere near Mexico, or the mines of St. Barbe." Smith says, "O-pe-chan-ca-nough was a brother of Powhatan," which Beverley doubts.[2]

How his father, if himself a newcomer, became possessed of the rulership over this country, we do not know, but from him Powhatan inherited the sovereign power over the countries of Powhatan, Ar-ro-ha-teck, Appomattox, Pa-mun-key, Yough-ta-mund, and Mat-ta-pam-i-ent.[3]

Under Powhatan were some thirty or forty chiefs or kings, appointed by him, who had the immediate rule over separate tribes inhabiting

---

[1] Hamor's *Discourse*, p. 13.
[2] Beverley, *History of Virginia*, book 1, p. 51. This view is held by Wertenbaker in his work, *Virginia under the Stuarts*, p. 89. He says that O-pe-chan-ca-nough having been defeated by the Spaniards marched all the way from the far southwest, and united his people with the tribes under Powhatan. [3] Stith, 53.

definite areas, in which they had their towns. These tribal territories were probably about the size of the smallest of our counties. These chiefs were called wer-ó-ances.

Strachey says: "The word wer-ó-ance, which we call and conster[1] for a king, is a common word, whereby they call all commanders for they have but few words in their language, and but few occasions to use any officers more than one commander, which commonly they call wer-ó-ance."[2]

The name Powhatan was derived from the country Powhatan, wherein he was born, which is below the falls. "His own people sometimes called him Ot-tan-i-ack, sometimes Mam-a-nat-o-wick, which signifies 'great king'; but his proper right name, which they salute him with (himself in presence) is Wa-hun-sen-a-cawh."[3]

The extent of Powhatan's dominions is thus defined by Strachey:

"The greatness and bounds of whose empire, by reason of his powerfulness and ambition in his youth, hath larger limits than ever had any of his predecessors in former times, for he seems to command south and north from the Man-go-a-ges and Chaw-o-noaks bordering upon Roanoke, and the Old Virginia,[4] to Tock-wogh, a town palisadoed, standing at the north end of the bay,[5] in forty degrees or thereabouts[6]:

[1] Construe.   [2] *Historie of Travaile into Virginia*, p. 51.
[3] *Ibid.*, p. 48.   [4] The Roanoke Island settlement.
[5] The Chesapeake Bay.   [6] Of north latitude.

southwest to An-o-eg, whose houses are built as ours,[1] ten days distant from us, from whence those Wer-ó-ances sent unto him of their commodities; as We-i-nock a servant, in whom Powhatan reposed much trust, would tell our elder planters, and could repeat many words of their language he had learned among them in his employment thither for his king, and whence he often returned, full of presents, to Powhatan; west to Mon-a-has-sa-nugh, which stands at the foot of the mountains[2]; nor-west to the borders of Mas-sa-wo-meck and Boc-oo-taw-won-ough, his enemies; nor-east and by east to Ac-co-ha-nock, Ac-cow-mack, and some other petty nations, lying on the east side of our bay.[3]

"But[4] the countries Powhatan, Ar-ro-ha-tock, Ap-pa-mat-uck, Pa-mun-key, Yough-ta-mund, and Mat-ta-pam-i-ent, which are said to come unto him by inheritance, all the rest of the territories before named, and which are all adjoining to that river whereon we are seated,[5] they report (as is likewise before remembered) to have been either by force subdued unto him, or through fear yielded: cruel he hath been, and quarrelous as well with his own wer-ó-ances for trifles, and that to strike a terror and awe into them of his power and condition, as also with

---

[1] These Indians were possibly taught to build such houses by survivors of the Roanoke Island settlement.
[2] The Blue Ridge.
[3] These boundaries make Powhatan's kingdom surround the Chesapeake Bay, and include the land on the west as far as the Blue Ridge.   [4] Except.   [5] The James.

Powhatan and Wingina

his neighbors in his younger days, though now delighted in security and pleasure, and therefore stands upon reasonable conditions of peace with all the great and absolute wer-ó-ances about him, and is likewise more quietly settled amongst his own."[1]

As to his place of residence we are told:

"He hath divers seats or houses; his chief, when we came into the country, was upon Pa-mun-key River,[2] on the north side or Pembrook[3] side, called Wer-o-wó-co-mó-co, which, by interpretation, signifies kings' house; howbeit, not liking to neighbor so near us, that house being within some fifteen or sixteen miles where he saw we purposed to hold ourselves, and from whence, in six or seven hours, we were able to visit him, he removed, and ever since hath most kept at a place in the desert called Or-a-paks,[4] at the top of the river Chick-a-ham-a-ni-a, between Yough-ta-mund and Powhatan."[5]

We know several members of his family circle. Of his own generation, we find that he had four brothers, O-pit-cha-pan, afterwards called Toy-a-tan, who succeeded him in the chief power, after his retirement, and who was lame and

---

[1] *Historie of Travaile into Virginia*, pp. 48–50.   [2] The York.

[3] The first settlers took this way of naming the sides of the rivers. In this manner the north side of the James was called Popham side, in honor of Chief Justice Popham, and the south side, Salisbury side, in honor of the Earl of Salisbury.

[4] The site of this town would be in Hanover County.

[5] That is, between the Pamunkey and James rivers. *Historie of Travaile into Virginia*, p. 49.

decrepit,[1] O-pe-chan-ca-nough and Ke-ca-tough, who had villages upon the Pamunkey River, and Jop-as-sus, King of the Potomacs[2]; and two sisters, who had two daughters.[3] Whether O-pe-chan-ca-nough were really a brother is now in doubt.

As for wives, we are told that he had a large number of them. When first seen by the English, he had his "girl wives" around him. We know the name of one of his wives, O-ho-lasc, who was regent over the Tap-pa-han-nas, during the minority of her son, and the names of twelve other of his favorite wives preserved for us by Strachey, who derived his information from an Indian named Kemps. They were:

        Win-ga-us-ke;
        Ask-e-tois-ke;
        Am-a-pot-ois-ke;
        Ot-to-pom-tacks;
        At-to-so-mis-ke;
        Pon-nois-ke;
        Ap-po-mo-sis-cut;
        Ap-pim-mois-ke;
        Or-tough-nois-ke;
        O-wer-ough-wouth;
        Ot-ter-mis-ke;
        Mem-e-ough-quis-ke.

As for children, we are told that he had, living when Strachey wrote, twenty sons and ten daughters, "besides a young one by Win-gan-us-

---

[1] Stith's *History of Virginia*, p. 139.
[2] *Historie of Travaile into Virginia*, p. 98.
[3] Smith, vol. i., pp. 143, 208; Stith, pp. 154, 155.

Powhatan and Wingina 273

ke, Ma-chumps, his sister, and a great darling of the king's, and besides young Pocahontas, a daughter of his, using sometime to our fort in times past, now married to a private captain, called Ko-co-um, some two.years since.

"As he is weary of his women, he bestoweth them on those that best deserve them at his hands."[1]

Among this large number of his children, we know individually of these:

Taux-Powhatan, who has been already mentioned as the ruler over the Powhatan Indians. His name and position would indicate that he was the eldest son.

Po--chins, who has been already mentioned, as the chief of the Ke-cough-tans.

Na-mon-tack, a son who was carried over as a little boy to England, and presented to James I. He had been instructed that when he came into the presence of the King, he should not take off his hat, remaining covered on account of his own royal descent.[2]

On attempting to return to Virginia, the vessel he was in was wrecked on the Bermudas. There was another Indian among the passengers, Ma-chumps. While the shipwrecked crew were in the Bermudas, we are told that "upon some difference, Ma-chumps slew Na-mon-tack; and having made a hole to bury him, because it was too short, he cut off his legs, and laid them by

---
[1] *History of Travaile into Virginia*, pp. 53-4.
[2] Brown's *Genesis of the United States*, p. 172.

him. Neither was the murder ever discovered, before he got to Virginia."[1]

Pocahontas, which means "Bright Stream between two Hills." She is described in glowing colors by Smith, as the "Nonpareil" of her father's country.[2]

Another daughter, possibly, the one named Cle-o-pat-re, whom the English also tried to capture at the time Pocahontas was taken, and whom they wished to marry to some Englishman.

Ta-hah-coo-pe, who, as an infant, was appointed by his father chief of the Tap-pa-han-nas, his mother, O-ho-lasc, acting as regent during his minority.

Nan-ta-quaus, a son already mentioned, whom Captain Smith described as "the most manliest, comeliest, boldest spirit he ever saw in a salvage," and, lastly,

Mat-a-chan-na, a daughter, who was the wife of Tom-a-com-a.[3]

One of Powhatan's councilors, this son-in-law, named Ul-ta-mat-a-ma-kin, and often called also Tom-a-com-o, went over to England with Dale, and was a frequent guest at Master Doctor Goldstone's in 1616. Here, we are told, that, in order no doubt to entertain his host, "he sang and danced his diabolical measures and discoursed of his country and religion."[4] He is represented as being a hardened sinner.

[1] Stith's *History of Virginia*, p. 115.   [2] *True Relation*, p. 73.
[3] Stith's *History of Virginia*, p. 143.
[4] Purchas, vol. iv., p. 1774.

Powhatan and Wingina

We also know the name of one of his numerous brothers-in-law, O-pa-chis-co, he who is spoken of as the old uncle of Pocahontas, who attended her wedding. We infer that he was her mother's brother, as his name is not given among the brothers of Powhatan.

The domestic arrangements of the royal household are thus described by Captain Smith, and give us some idea of the regular arrangements which existed for comfort and safety:

"About his person ordinarily attendeth a guard of forty or fifty of the tallest men his country doth afford.

"Every night upon the four quarters of his house are four sentinels, each from other a slight shoot, and at every half-hour one from the *corps du guard* doth hollow, shaking his lips with his finger between them; unto whom every sentinel doth answer round from his stand: if any fail, they presently send forth an officer that beateth him extremely.

"A mile from Or-a-paks in a thicket of wood, he hath a house in which he keepeth his kind of treasure, as skins, copper, pearls, and beads, which he storeth up against the time of his death and burial. Here also is his store of red paint for ointment, bows, and arrows, targets and clubs. This house is fifty or sixty yards in length, frequented only by priests. At the four corners of this house stand four images as sentinels, one of a dragon, another a bear, the third like a leopard, and the fourth like a giant-like man, all made evil-favouredly,[1] according to their best workmanship.

"He hath as many women as he will, whereof when he lieth on his bed, one sitteth at his head, and another at his feet, but when he sitteth, one sitteth on his right hand and another on his left. When he dineth or suppeth, one of his women before and after meat bringeth him water in a wooden platter to wash his hands. Another waiteth with a bunch of feathers to wipe them instead of a towel, and the feathers when he hath wiped are dried again."[2]

In describing the power he exercised over the subordinate chiefs, and their obedience to, and fear of him, he says:

"They all know their several lands, and habitations, and limits, to fish, foul, or hunt in, but they hold all of their great wer-ó-ance Powhatan, unto whom they pay tribute of skins, beads, copper, pearls, deer, turkeys, wild beasts, and corn. What he commandeth they dare not disobey in the least thing. It is strange to see with what great fear and adoration all these people do obey this Powhatan, for at his feet they present whatsoever he commandeth, and at the least frown of his brow, their greatest spirits will tremble with fear: and no marvel, for he is very terrible and tyrannous in punishing such as offend him. For example, he caused certain malefactors to be bound hand and

[1] With forbidding countenances.
[2] Smith, vol. i., pp. 142–3.

foot, then having of many fires gathered great store of burning coals, they rake these coals round in the form of a cockpit, and in the midst they cast the offenders to broil to death. Sometimes he causeth the heads of them that offend him to be laid upon the altar or sacrificing stone, and one with clubs beats out their brains.

"When he would punish any notorious enemy or trespasser, he causeth him to be tied to a tree, and with mussel-shells or reeds the executioner cutteth off his joints one after another, ever casting what is cut off into the fire: then doth he proceed with shells and reeds to case[1] the skin from his head and face; after which they rip up his belly, tear out his bowels, and so burn him with the tree and all. Thus themselves reported, that they executed an Englishman, one George Cawson, whom the women enticed up from the barge unto their houses, at a place called Ap-po-cant.[2] Howbeit, his ordinary correction is to have an offender, whom he will only punish and not put to death, to be beaten with cudgels as the Turks do. We have seen a man kneeling on his knees, and, at Powhatan's command, two men have beaten him on the bare skin till the skin has been all bollen[3] and blistered and all on a goar blood,[4] and till he hath fallen senseless in a swoon, and yet never cried, com-

[1] Remove the case or skin.
[2] A town in what is now Hanover County, on the Chickahominy River.
[3] Swollen. [4] All covered with gore or blood.

plained, nor seemed to ask pardon, for that they seldom do."[1]

Strachey maintained that the proper policy for the English was to make friends and allies of the enemies of Powhatan. In discussing this he says:

"There is no man among themselves so savage, or not capable of so much sense, but that he will approve our cause, when he shall be made to understand that Powhatan hath slaughtered so many of our nation without offense given, and such as were seated far from him, and in the territory of those wer-ó-ances which did in no sort depend on him or acknowledge him; but it hath been Powhatan's great care to keep us, by all means, from the acquaintance of those nations that border and confront him, for besides his knowledge how easily and willingly his enemies will be drawn upon him by the least countenance and encouragement from us, he doth, by keeping us from trading with them, monopolize all the copper brought into Virginia by the English.

"And whereas the English are now content to receive in exchange a few measures of corn for a great deal of that metal (valuing it according to the extreme price it bears with them, not to the estimation it hath with us), Powhatan doth again vent some small quantity thereof to his neighbor nations for one hundred times the

---

[1] Smith, vol. i., pp. 143-4; *Historie of Travaile into Virginia*, p. 52.

value, reserving, notwithstanding, for himself a plentiful quantity to levy men withal when he shall find cause to use them against us; for the before-remembered wer-ó-ance of Pas-pa-hegh did once wage fourteen or fifteen wer-ó-ances to assist him in the attempt upon the fort of Jamestown, for one copper plate promised to each wer-ó-ance."[1]

Speaking of the country, and the people ruled by Powhatan, Smith says: "The land is not populous, for the men be few; their far greater number is of women and children. Within 60 miles of James Town, there are about some 5000 people, but of able men fit for their wars scarce 1500. To nourish so many together they have yet no means, because they make so small a benefit of their land, be it never so fertile. Six or seven hundred have been the most that hath been seen together when they gathered themselves to have surprised me at Pa-mun-key, having but fifteen to withstand the worst of their fury."[2]

That this estimate was far below the real state of the case, is clear from the account given by Glover, who says that at the first coming of the English, "divers towns had two or three thousand bowmen in them."[3] Any one of these larger towns, therefore, contained twice as many warriors as Smith allowed for all of them put together.

[1] *Historie of Travaile into Virginia*, pp. 103-4.
[2] Smith, vol. i., p. 129.
[3] *Account of Virginia*, p. 22.

The map of the country gives the names and locations of over one hundred of these Indian settlements. One conclusion, therefore, is, that the Indian forces, instead of one thousand five hundred, numbered many thousands of warriors.

Such were the surroundings of Powhatan. His attitude towards the English would naturally enough be that of bitter hostility, as strangers and intruders, but this feeling was heightened by a prophecy which had come to his ears. Strachey says:

"It is not long since that his priests told him how that from the Chesapeake Bay a nation should arise which should dissolve and give end to his empire, for which, not many years since (perplexed with this devilish oracle, and divers understanding thereof), according to the ancient and gentile customs, he destroyed and put to sword all such who might lie under any doubtful construction of the said prophecy, as all the inhabitants, the wer-ó-ance and his subjects of that province, and so remain all the Ches-si-o-pe-ians at this day, and for this cause, extinct.

"Some of the inhabitants, again, have not spared to give us to understand, how they have a second prophecy likewise amongst them, that twice they should give overthrow and dishearten the attempters, and such strangers as should invade their territories or labor to settle a plantation among them, but the third time they themselves should fall into their subjection, and under their conquest; and sure in the observation of our settlement, and the manner thereof hitherto, we may well suppose that this their apprehension may fully touch at us. I leave to express the particulars unto another place, albeit, let me say here, strange whispers (indeed) and secret at this hour run among these people and possess them with amazement, what may be the issue of these strange preparations landed in their coasts, and yearly supplied with fresher troops.

"Every news and blast of rumor strikes them, to which they open their ears wide, and keep their eyes waking, with good espial upon everything that stirs; the noise of our drums, of our shrill trumpets and great ordinance, terrifies them, so as they startle at the report of them, how far soever from the reach of danger. Suspicions have bred strange fears amongst them, and those fears create as strange constructions, those constructions, therefore, beget strong watch and guard, especially about their great King, who thrusts forth trusty scouts and careful sentinels, as before mentioned, which reach even from his own court down almost to our palisado gates, which answer one another duly. Many things (whilst they observe us) are suffered amiss among themselves, who were wont to be so servilly fearful to trespass against their customs, as it was a chief point of their religion not to break in any, and all this, and more than this, is thus with them, whilst the great tyrant himself nor his priests are now confident in their wonted courses."[1]

It is worthy of observation that this prophecy of the Indian priests came true. The first attempt, under Sir Walter Raleigh, failed. The second attempt, under the King, failed. It was the third attempt, at the head of which was Lord De la Warr, representing the Virginia Company, which established the Colony, and overthrew the Indian power.

The country just to the south of Virginia, where the great fact of the permanent settlement was to be finally worked out, was the scene of the first attempts to plant the English Protestant Colony in the New World.

It was in the part of the world now known as North Carolina, but then Virginia, where the attempt which failed took place. This country was presided over by Win-gi-na, who bore the same relation to it that Powhatan bore to the portion of the continent in which the settlement was ultimately established.

At the time of the arrival of the English under Captains Amadas and Barlow, he was sick, having been severely wounded in a fight with the king of the next country.

He was then at the chief town of the country, about six miles from Roanoke Island, and the first voyagers did not see him at all.

[1] *Historie of Travaile into Virginia*, p. 101.

At the time of the invasion he was in league with two other kings, Po-o-nens and Men-a-to-non, against their mortal enemies Pin-ma-cum, king of Pom-ou-ik, and the king of New-si-ok. Pom-ou-ik seems to have been a part of, if not coincident with, the territory of Se-co-tan, that is, the land between the Pamlico and Neuse rivers, while New-si-ok lay across the Neuse, to the west.

One of his brothers was Gran-ge-nim-e-o. It was this brother who the day after the first contact between the Roanoke Island settlers and the natives took place, came with his forty attendants to visit the English in their ships.

Later he visited them again, bringing his wife, daughter, and two or three children. His wife was always accompanied by forty or fifty other women.

His house is mentioned as containing nine apartments, and built of cedar.

Captain Ralph Lane tells us that Win-gi-na, upon the death of his brother Gran-ge-nim-e-o, took the name of Pem-is-a-pan. Under this name he is generally referred to in the account of the Roanoke settlement.

Like O-pe-chan-ca-nough he planned the utter and sudden extermination of the white men, and, like him, he met his death at their hands. O-pe-chan-ca-nough's two plots were partly carried out; but, Pem-is-a-pan's was nipped in the bud, and he and his followers, instead of Lane and his associates, were killed.

Powhatan, having as much as possible kept himself aloof from the white man, died a natural death. The closing scene in Pem-is-a-pan's history is that of a white man coming out of the woods with the head of the Indian king in his hand.

Though such was the tragic fate of Pem-is-a-pan, his successors succeeded in repelling the invasion and finally exterminated the first of the English; while Powhatan's kingdom passed under their dominion.

CHAPTER XIX

SOME INDIAN WORDS

ONE of the causes to which is attributed the conquest of the country inhabited by several thousand Indian warriors by the white settlers, weak and divided as they often were, was the confusion of tongues which prevailed in the forest. There was no written language. The Indians lacked the stability and expansion which that would have afforded to any leading dialect. The tribes spoke their own languages, which differed widely, so widely, it is said, that often those of one village could not understand the inhabitants of another living only a few miles away.

This was a serious impediment to concerted action to unite and crush the invaders; and to it, possibly more than to any other one thing, is due the fact that they were not destroyed. The Indians were divided by their languages, and divided they were conquered.

Beverley, says, however, that there was not entirely wanting a means of communication between them, but that there existed a sort of general language understood by the chief men of many nations, as Latin was formerly. His words are as follows:

"These Indians have no sort of letters to express their words by, but when they would communicate anything, that cannot be delivered by message, they do it by a sort of hieroglyphic, or representation of birds, beasts, or other things, showing their different meaning, by the various forms described, and by the different position of the figures.

"Their language differs very much as anciently in the several parts of Britain; so that nations, at a moderate distance, do not understand one another. However, they have a sort of general language, like what Lahontan calls the Algonkine, which is understood by the chief men of many nations, as Latin is in most parts of Europe and Lingua Franca[1] quite through the Levant.

"The general language here used is said to be that of the Oc-ca-nee-ches, though they have been but a small nation, ever since those parts were known to the English: but in what this language may differ from that of the Algonkines, I am not able to determine."[2]

In considering the language of the Indians one is apt to be struck by the length of their words and the difficulty of pronouncing them. Unbroken into syllables many are practically unpronounceable. Most of such long words as were contained in the authorities from which the list herein given is compiled, are omitted.

[1] French.   [2] Beverley, book 3, pp. 23-4.

They are often of things or abstractions of less importance and interest than the shorter or easier words, representing simpler ideas. But the Indian words in general are long. Words of one syllable, such as our language abounds in, are hardly to be met with. As the accent is not marked, the correct sounding of these words is of course uncertain, at best, but the pronunciation of such of them as are familiar to us has been the guide to the plan which has been adopted of breaking these words up into their syllables, so that an attempt at least may be made to pronounce them.

The principal authority relied upon is the dictionary of the Indian language given in Strachey's *Historie of Travaile into Virginia*.[1] We have also a short list given by Smith,[2] and other words have been gleaned from Beverley.

Glover also speaks of this diversity of language and says: "Almost every town differs in language, and yet not any of their languages copious; as may be seen by their frequent expressing their meaning to each other by signs."[3] That is, that even those who spoke the same dialect lacked words to express many of their thoughts, and had to make themselves understood by signs, there being no words in their language to express the ideas.

The great length of the Indian words, belonging as they do to a rude, primitive tongue, is in

[1] Beginning at p. 183.　　　[2] Vol. i., p. 147.
[3] *Account of Virginia*, p. 25.

harmony with a general law which obtains in the development of languages. Keightley says that: "It is a fact, well known to philologists, that the earlier the condition of a language is, the longer are its words and the more numerous its formative syllables."[1]

As there is no Indian literature, the knowledge of these words cannot be put to any practical use in reading any works in that language; and as there are no longer Indians or any one else who now uses this language, they cannot be made use of in speaking to any one. But still they have an interest and value of their own, as a part of the thought and life of a race of human beings who once lived where we now live, and who interpreted the scenes around them, and the things of life, and communicated the thoughts of the heart by the use of the words which are here recorded.

What we have here first to say, let us call

A DAY IN AN INDIAN VILLAGE

The Indian was a child of nature. His surroundings were such as he found them given by the Creator unchanged by man. His life was spent under the broad blue canopy of Heaven, and all his occupations and his pleasures were interwoven with the forest, vocal with the song of birds, and with the streams reflecting the bright rays of the sun, and teeming with all its

[1] *Mythology of Greece and Italy*, p. 15.

Some Indian Words

varied forms of life. For all these things the Indian had their several names.

Let us imagine an Indian leaving his house before daybreak, going out on a fishing expedition.

Looking upon the created universe around him, the object upon which he stood, the world itself, he called **pam-ah-saiv-uh.**

Above his head stretching out into infinity was **o-sies,** the heavens.

In contrast to it was the earth, **as-pam-u.**

As he journeys toward the place he is seeking, **kes-haw-teuh,** the light, increases; **pap-a-souh,** the sunrise, is at hand, and soon above the water, **sac-qua-han,** appears the glorious orb of day, to him an object of divine worship, **kes-kow-ghe,** the sun, shines forth in dazzling splendor.

Across the waves of the sea, **a-quas-kaw-wans,** its rays are reflected; day, **raw-co-sough,** has dispelled the darkness of night, **tap-a-coh,** and the objects of creation stand revealed.

Before him is the sea, **i-a-pam.** Around him is the air, **ra-ras-can.** Above him is the blue, **o-sa-ih,** sky, **ar-ro-koth,** in which float **mam-ma-um,** the clouds, impelled by **rowh-sun-much,** a gentle wind. Behind him is the forest, **mus-ses.**

At his feet is the sand of the shore, **ra-cauh,** and **seis-cat-u-uh,** the ebbing water. In the sand is the seaweed, **as-cax-as-qu-us.**

Toward the north, **ut-cheiks,** lies an island, **mem-nun-nah-qus,** standing out clearly in the water, **suck-a-han-na.**

Toward the west, **at-tag-was-san-na,** the land, **chep-sin,** is watered by a river, **ye-o-kan-ta,** into which flows a small creek, **me-ih-sut-ter-ask.**

On the east, **ut-chep-wo-is-sum-a,** there rises a gentle hill, **ro-mut-tun,** and beyond it a tall mountain, **pom-o-tawk.**

Winter, **pup-pa-an-noh,** with its ice, **o-re-ih,** frost, **tac-qua-cat,** and snow, **co-an,** has passed. The wild geese, the **co-honks,** and the swans, **wo-pus-so-uc,** have gone to their distant homes. The season of the year, **paw-pax-son-ghe,** is that of the balmy summer, **cow-wot-a-i-oh,** which will soon change into autumn, **pun-sa-os,** the falling of the leaf. It is hot weather, **u-nes-haw-o-can-as-sup.**

Here, **mis-ke,** is a running brook, **wous-sick-it.** Yonder, **yo-ax-u-uh,** is a place, **we-is-kis,** where the ground, **pet-a-win,** is covered with trees standing in water. It is a dreary looking place. It is a **po-co-sin.**

Making his way to near the mouth of the small creek, he and his companion proceed with the work in hand. They are going to put a fishing weir, **ne-ih-sac-an,** across the creek, to catch **nough-mass,** that is, any kind of fish.

He is supplied with his **a-quin-tain taux,** that is, a little boat or canoe; a **tse-ma-o-say,** a sail; his net, **a-us-sab;** an oar, **tshe-mac-aus; re-kas-que,** a knife; **pe-munt-naw,** a rope; **mowh-ko-han,** a fish-hook; **por-a-sap,** a bag; and **ok-tam-o-can,** a can to drink in.

Some Indian Words

While he is waiting the appropriate time for the current of the stream and the weir to do their work in entrapping the fish, a butterfly, **man-a-aug-wos,** flits by. A **moc-ca-sin** puts its head out of the water, and disappears. A crane, **us-sac,** lights upon the opposite shore, and stalks around with its long legs. With discordant note **o-ha-was,** a crow, flies across the stream frightening a wild duck, **pis-co-end** which was floating upon the surface of the water, on whom an eagle, **o-pot-e-na-i-ok** had fixed his deadly eye. A gull, **co-i-ah-guns,** floats lazily through the air, and the black back of a porpoise, **pot-a-waugh,** revolves in the deeper water beyond. A fly, **mow-ches-on,** buzzes in his ear; a gnat, **po-en-gu-uh,** stings him; and a lizard, **ut-a-cas-kis,** glides across his path.

When the weir is examined, among other captures are found a sturgeon, **cop-o-to-ne;** a turtle, **com-mo-tins;** a sea-turtle, **tuw-cup-pe-uk;** a crab, **tut-tas-cuc;** an eel, **as-cam-a-uk;** a garfish, **ta-tam-a-ho;** and a lobster, **ah-sha-ham,** and a number of fish, **nam-ma-is,** with their sharp fins, **wi-ih-cats.**

Returning, **pey-e-ugh,** to the shore, the good, **win-gan,** were taken, the rest thrown away.

Wet, **nep-pe,** but not weary, **cut-tox-een,** the Indian now puts his fish in a basket upon his back, and carries it home.

On the way to the town, **mus-sa-ran,** where he lives, he met another friend, **ne-tab,** and the three, **nuss,** proceed together, one, **ne-cut,** before, **ut-cha-rund,** the other, according to their fashion of walking.

On their way, they meet a hare, **wi-ih-cut-teis,** which scampers off into the grass, **at-tass-kuss.** A squirrel, **mous-som-ko,** runs up the rough bark of a pine tree, **a-noo-sa.** A fine deer, **ut-ta-pa-an-tam,** with long, **cun-na-i-u-uh,** horns, **wa-wi-rak,** and a little, **taux,** faun, **no-nat-te-uh,** fled upon hearing, **aump-su-uk,** the Indians coming.

They passed a village, **ka-a-sun,** also on their way, and noticed a circle, **mus-set-a-qua-i-oh,** of old women, **u-tump-seis,** around a boy, **mar-o-wan-ches-so,** who lay there dead, **tse-pa-ih** of a snake-bite, **u-tag-wo-ong.** They were making preparations for his burial, **pa-i-am-a-suw.**

Passing on, they saw a great, **man-go-i-te,** owl, **quang-at-a-rask,** in the top of a walnut tree, **as-sun-no-in-e-ind-ge.** From the next, **u-tak-i-ik,** tree, **me-ih-tucs,** a hickory of considerable height, **man-ge-ker,** a flying squirrel, **a-i-os-sa-pan-i-ik,** came out of his hole, **wo-or,** flew down, lit upon the dead leaves, **mo-in-cam-in-ge,** and disappeared in the reeds, **nis-sa-kan.**

Arrived at length at home, it was found that all, **che-isk,** were well. These were the old man, **raw-e-run-nu-uh,** his father, **now-se;** his mother, **kick-e-was;** his wife, **no-un-gas-se;** his elder, **nus-sa-andg,** brother, **ke-mot-te;** his sister, **cur-si-ne;** his aunt, **ar-i-quos-sac,** and her husband, **wi-o-wah;** his younger, **we-saws,** daughter, **am-o-sens;** and his other child, **nech-a-un,** who was a little boy, **us-ca-pess**. The baby, **pap-poose**, was fat, **wir-a-o-hawk**, and was now strapped to a board, **cut-sot-ah-wooc**, hanging from the branch of a cedar tree, **mo-ro-ke**. It was not awake, **au-mau-mer**. It was a girl, **us-qua-se-ins**.

His father, **now-se**, a strong, **to-wauh**, man yet, was busily engaged in putting his arms in order. By his side was his bow, **at-taup**; to which he had just fitted a new bowstring, **au-peis**. He was now at work on an arrow, **at-tonce**. Its head, **rap-ut-tak**, and feathers, **as-sa-cun-sauh** were being fastened on with the glue, **up-pe-in-sa-man**, used for this purpose. Leaning against a tree were his sword, **mon-a-cooke**, his shield, **au-mough-hough**, and his hatchet, **tom-a-hack**. In his belt was his knife, **dam-i-sac**, which could give a dangerous stab, **wap-in**, or cut, **wap-e-uh**. But these weapons were not equal to the lead, **wind-scup**, from the gun, **po-ko-sack**, of the English, **Tas-san-tas-ses**, protected in their coats of mail, **a-qua-hus-sun**, even though their arrows were sharp, **ken-e-i-wuh**.

His brother, **ke-mot-te**, who was rather weak, **kes-she-manc**, was engaged in fashioning from some leather, **ut-to-ca-is**, a match-coat for the coming winter.

His aunt's husband, who was lame, **nep-a-wir-o-nough**, was very bright, **mus-caus-sum**, and calm, **coh-quiv-uh**. He was engaged in making a pair of shoes, **mock-a-sins**.

His daughter, **am-o-sens,** was a fine young woman, **cren-e-po,** very much alive, **ke-kewh,** and greatly admired by the young men of the town. Her **maw-chick cham-may,** that is, her best of friends, was a young **wer-ó-ance,** war chief, who had lately distinguished himself by killing the worst of the enemies, **kas-ka-pow,** of the tribe, one of the man-eaters, **mus-sa-an-ge-gwah.**

His wife, **no-un-gas-se,** was busily occupied in preparing the meal, which was to consist of bread, **op-pones; suc-co-tash,** corn and beans; **hominy; ra-pan-ta,** venison; a little salt, **saw-wo-ne;** and milk made of walnuts, **po-co-hi-qua-ra.**

Other usual articles of food were **pec-cat-o-as,** beans; chickens, **ca-wah-che-ims;** caviare or the roe of sturgeon, **wo-ock;** oo-tun, cheese; eggs, **o-waugh;** bread made either of flour, **rouh-se-uh,** or meal, **rouh-cat;** broth, **no-ump-qua-am; cau-wa-ih,** oysters; hasty pudding, **as-a-pan;** dewberries, **ac-coon-dews;** grapes, **mar-ra-kim-mins;** and strawberries, **mus-kef-kim-mins.**

There had formerly lived with them a man **nem-a-rough,** who was a bachelor, **ma-taw-i-o-wijh,** straight, **ma-jauh,** as an arrow, **at-tonce,** but on one of the war-parties he was lost, **now-wan-us.**

The inside of the house, **yo-hac-an,** was rather dark, **pah-cun-na-i-oh,** as it seemed, as one entered through the low, **ma-chess,** doorway.

But the light, **kes-kaw-teuh**, from the hole in the roof enables the contents to be seen. Here then appear in their proper places, the bed, **tussan**, which was hard, **es-e-pan-nu-uh**, enough. On the ground lies a mat, **a-nan-son**. There is the frying-pan, **amp-ko-ne**; a dish, **o-ut-a-can**; the kettle, **au-cog-wins**; a basket, **man-o-te**; **paw-pe-co-ne**, a pipe; **an-ca-gwins**, a pot; **ham-ko-ne**, a ladle; a pot to drink in, **ke-quas-son**; a mat made of reeds, **a-nan-se-coon**; linen, **ma-tas-sa-ih**; a stool, **tau-o-sin**; and **oh-tam-o-can**, a barrel. The mat was torn, **tut-tas-cuh**.

In the middle of the chamber, **ut-she-com-muc**, there are some ashes, **pun-guy**, left from the last fire, **po-kat-a-wer**. Dust, **ne-pen-sum**, is on some of the articles, and above our heads, cobwebs, **mut-tass-a-pec**. In the corner was a rat, **a-o-tauk**.

Outside the house, by the well, **oh-ca-wooc**, is a rose bush, **pus-sa-quem-bun**; some wood, **mus-keis**; a gate, **cup-pe-nauk**, opening into the vegetable garden, **o-ron-o-cah**.

Scup-per-nong grapes were here, but no pear, **as-sen-ta-men**; nor apple, **mar-a-cah**; the walnut, **as-sim-nim**, was here; and **o-pom-mins**, the chestnut; **musk-mu-ims**, the mulberry; and **per-sim-mons**, with their numerous seeds, **a-men-a-ca-cac**. This fruit was as yet unripe, **us-can-ne-uh**, and no bird would care to plunge its beak, **meh-ke-uk**, in it. A field of corn, **po-ket-a-wes**, which the English often called wheat, and West Indians, maize, was growing here.

The meal being ended, the aunt's husband, who had once been taken over to England in a big ship, **mus-so-wux-uc,** began to teach the Indian language to a little white, **o-paiv-uh,** boy, one of the English, who had been exchanged for one of the Indian king's sons, who was to learn the English language. The first part of the lesson was devoted to teaching him to count: **ne-cut,** one; **ningh,** two; **nuss,** three; **yough,** four; **pa-rans-ke,** five; **com-o-tinck,** six; **top-pa-woss,** seven; **nuss-wash,** eight; **kek-a-towgh,** nine; **kas-ke-ke,** ten.

After this the count was by tens, but the words he taught were so long and barbarous sounding that we dare not attempt to repeat them.

He, **yoo-wah,** learned these, **youghs,** first ten, quickly, **hus-que.** The Indian then began to teach him the meaning of some verbs. By means of signs, gestures, action, and expression, and such other means as were available, he tried to teach the little Pale Face, that **pas-sah-i-ca-an** meant to clap one's hands.

Catch-cah-mun mu-she meant to chop wood.

Ah-coh-kin-ne-mun meant to carry upon one's shoulders.

Pa-tow was to bring again.

Taw-a-tut-te-ner meant to yawn or gap.

Ne-igh-se-un was to cry.

Mo-undg meant to cut the hair of a man's head.

Rick-e-uh, to divide a thing in half.

Some Indian Words

A-was-sew meant to fly.
Am-maw-skin was to fall.
Pa-atch-ah meant to give.
Quan-ta-mun was to swallow.
Paw-paw-me-ar meant to walk.
Pas-pe-ne was to walk about.
Num-mawh was to weep.
Zanc-ko-ne meant to sneeze.
Cut-to-undg meant to bark.
Am-in meant to bite.
Toos-ke-an meant to swim.
Po-kin was to dive under water.
Tchij-ma-oc meant to row.
Ke-se-i-quan meant to wash the face.
Cus-purn was to tie or make fast anything.
Nep-o-mot-a-men meant to shoot.
Ke-kut-tun was to say.
Sak-a-ho-can meant to write.
No-ha-i-u-uh meant to have.
Com-mo-to-ouh meant to steal.
Me-cher was to eat.[1]
U-ne-kish-e-mu meant to cut anything.
O-nas-can-da-men meant to catch in the mouth, as dogs do.
Ah-cou-she was to climb a tree.
Ket-a-rowk-su-mah meant to break all in pieces.
Pe-rew was to be broken or cracked.
O-tas-sap-nar meant to call one.

---

[1] This is close to our word *munch*, a word which is similar to others with the same meaning in a number of languages, for example Latin, *manduco;* French, *manger;* Spanish, *mascar;* etc.

Now-wun-ta-men meant to hear.
Kes-she-kis-sun was to laugh.
Tse-pa-an-ta-men meant to kiss.
Cant-e-cant-e was to sing or dance.
Ne-tus-pus was to leap as men leap in dancing or otherwise.
Hus-pis-sa-an meant to leap.
A-pows-saw meant to roast.
Num-me-cax-ut-te-nax was to fight at fisticuffs.
Num-mach-a meant to go home.
Ma-ent-cha-tem-a-y-o-ac was the word to express the idea—gone.
Mach-e-ne-caw-wun was to lie down to sleep.
Bah-tan-o-mun meant to warm one.
Nep-a-um was to sleep.
U-na-mun meant to awaken.
Na-ha-puc meant to dwell.
Noun-gat was to do.
Mus-kem was to run.
I-reh meant to go.
I-reh as-su-min-ge was to go and run quickly.
Pe-in-tik-er meant to come in.
Cau-mor-o-wath meant to come, being spoken familiarly or hard by.
Pi-jah meant to come, being spoken afar off to one.
Mas-ki-ha-an was to be melancholy.
A-ro-um-mos-south meant to be sick.
U-nan-na-tas-sun meant to stand.
Ud-a-pung-war-en was to open one's eyes.

Naw-wi-o-wash-im meant to carry a thing up and down.
Ne-cus-sa-guns meant to carry a thing between two.
Ah-gu-ur meant to cover one.
Waw-a-pun-nah meant to hang one.
Cut-ta-quo-cum meant to pull one down.
U-un-a-mum was to see.
Mon-as-cun-ne-mu meant to cleanse the ground and make it fit for seed.
Nut-tas-pin meant to sow wheat.

Fair progress having been made in this lesson, the man then took the boy through the town to see the people and further explain his language.

Close at hand, near enough to have heard them, sitting upon a stone, scha-quo-ho-can, was a short, tack-qua-i-sun, bald, pa-atch-kis-caw, deaf, cup-po-taw, beggar, cut-tas-sam-a-is. He was nearly naked, ne-pow-wer; a stranger, ut-tas-san-tas-so-wa-ih; without friends, ne-top-pew; and alone, a-pop-a-quat-e-cus.

It was decided to give, pa-atch-ah, him, something to eat, me-cher, so maize, corn; bread made of the hot-tasting root tuck-a-hoe; a lot of chin-ka-pins; and me-tucs-mar-a-kim-mins, a bunch of grapes, were given to him.

The town was surrounded by a palisade, inside of which were about twenty houses, the houses being scattered about irregularly, following roughly the circle of the palisade, and leaving an open space in the midst. In the center of this was now to take place a show, **mach-e-que-o.**

One of the enemies, **mar-ra-pough,** of the tribe had been captured, and now all friends, **chesk-cham-ay,** of the tribe had been summoned to enjoy the pleasure of seeing him tortured. A fire, **po-kat-a-wer,** was burning. The captive was stripped naked, **ne-paw-wer,** and ordered to sit down near the fire, and the Indians beat him with their fists and sticks. A post about fifteen feet high had been set firmly in the ground, and piles of hickory poles lay a few yards from it. The captive's hands, **metm-ge,** were tied behind his back.

A rope, **pe-munt-naw,** was produced, one end was tied to the post, and the other to the cord, **pem-a-nat-a-on,** which fastened his wrists together. The rope was long enough to permit him to walk around the stake several times and then return. They then cut off his ears, **me-tawke,** and the blood, **saw-we-ho-ne,** streamed down each side of his face, **us-ca-en-tur.** The warriors then shot charges of powder into his naked body, commencing with the calves of his leg, **mes-kott,** and continuing to his neck, **nus-quo-ik.** Three or four, by turns, would take up one of the burning pieces of wood, and apply the burning end to his body. These tormentors presented themselves on every side of him, so that whichever way he ran around the post they met him with the burning brands. Some of the squaws took broad pieces of bark, upon which they could

Some Indian Words

carry a quantity of coals of fire, **mah-ca-to-is**, and threw them on him, so that in a short time his feet, **mes-setts**, had nothing but coals of fire and hot ashes to walk upon. This ordeal had now lasted two hours; the prisoner was much exhausted, and his nerves had lost much of their sensibility. He no longer shrank from the firebrands with which his tormentors incessantly touched him. At length he sank, fainting, upon his face. Instantly an Indian sprang upon his back, knelt lightly upon one knee, made a circular incision with his knife, **re-kas-que**, upon the crown of his head, **menda-buc-cah**, and clapping his knife between his teeth, **me-pit**, taking hold of the hair, **mer-ersc**, with both hands, tore off the scalp. As soon as this was done, an old woman, **u-tump-seis**, approached with a piece of bark full of coals of fire, **mah-cat-o-is**, and poured them upon the crown of his head, now laid bare to the bone, **wos-kan**.

The wretched victim rose once more, and slowly walked around the stake. At length nature could endure no more. He fell for the last time and his soul, **net-shet-sunk**, escaped from his tormentors.[1]

Other captives were then produced. The nails, **me-kon-se**, of their fingers and toes were pulled out. Their forefingers, **num-meis-sut-**

---

[1] This account is taken from an actual case, that of Col. Wm. Crawford, who was thus put to death. Peyton's *History of Augusta County*, pp. 191–2.

te-ing-wah, were cut off. The tongue, **max-at-sno** cut out. The nose, **mes-kew,** slit. The lips, **nus-sha-ih,** cut off. The thigh, **ap-o-me,** and the arm, **me-se,** stuck full of burning pieces of lightwood. The mouth, **met-to-ne,** filled full of hot ashes. The elbows, **me-is-quan,** broken. The forehead, **mus-kan,** torn off. The beard, **mes-se-ton-a-ance,** plucked out. The veins, **a-bes-cur,** opened. The skin taken off the flesh, **wegh-shau-ghes.** The throat, **ve-gwan-ta-ak,** cut open, and the eyes, **mus-kins,** gouged out with burning sticks.

The gathering which had witnessed these scenes included the **sach-em,** the magistrate, who presided over the great councils of state, and who looked after the aged, and the women and children; a "woman queen," **wir-o-naus-qua,** from an adjoining tribe; several **cock-a-rouses,** members of the King's Council, or those otherwise distinguished for bravery; and all the **cro-nock-o-es,** that is, men of prominence in the town. The **mam-a-nat-o-wick,** the Great King, of the tribe was present, and a **ver-o-a-nee,** King or great man, from each neighboring tribe.

After these proceedings were finished they held **match-a-com-o-co,** that is, a great council of state; discussed public affairs, and smoked the **cal-u-met,** the pipe of peace.

As an appropriate conclusion to the festivities of torturing the enemies of the tribe, a dance, **kan-to-kan,** was gotten up, by the young warriors, while the bodies of the victims were thrown into a common grave, **our-car,** where they slept their last sleep, **kaw-win.**

Passing out of the town, to get a better, **win-gut-sca-ho,** view of the country around, they pass over, **os-keitch,** a stream, **tsa-quo-moi,** that is, deep to the middle of a man. A little farther down, **no-us-o-mon,** it was **nut-tah-ca-am,** that is, deep over the head. The water was cold, **nons-sa-mats,** and the stream crooked, **o-ho-rin-ne.** In it were swimming an otter, **cut-tack,** and a beaver, **poh-kev-uh.**

Behind, **ta-an-go-quaijk,** the town, was a body of woods, full of leaves, **ma-an-qui-pac-us,** which tempted them to enter it. Here was seen the root from which the red dye of the Indians was obtained, the **puc-coon,** called by the English, the bloodroot, and the **mus-quas-pen,** another root, **ut-chap-poc,** from which a dye was derived. By the marsh at the edge of the woods was the cranberry, **raw-co-mens,** growing wild. Here also was the grass from which they made threads, **pem-me-now.**

In the wood they picked up the acorns, **an-as ko-mens,** and ate them raw, **as-cun-me-uh.** A large vine, **wap-a-pam-mdge,** full of ripe, **win-gat-e-uh,** grapes, spread its branches abroad, **us-cound.** Beneath, **ut-shem-a-ijn,** it, there grew a great deal, **moow-chick,** of weeds, **at-tas-qu-us.** When, **ta-noo chinck,** they turned from it, they saw an adder, **ke-ih-tas-co-oc,** curled up under it, and killed it with a cane, **nis-a-ke.**

The bark of a dog, **at-to-mois**, attracted them. To the same tree he had tracked two curious looking animals, a **rac-coon** and an **o-pos-sum**. Other animals which had been hunted in that wood were the fox, **as-sim-o-est**; the bear, **mo-mon-sac-que-o**, and the wolf, **na-an-tam**.

A robin redbreast, **che-a-wan-ta**, a pretty bird, **tshe-hip**, left its nest, **wap-ches-a-o**, when they appeared, and, with interrupted motion of wing, **ut-to-can-nuc**, sought safety elsewhere. Here, too, were seen a turkey cock, **os-pan-no**; a turkey, **mon-y-naugh**; a wood pigeon, **qua-no-ats**; a pigeon, **tow-ac-quo-ins**; and a parrot, **mas-ko-whin-ge**.

The season being well advanced, the leaves of the gum trees have turned red, purple, **our-cre-uh**, and yellow, **ous-sa-wack**.

It was now the afternoon, **aun-she-cap-a**, and being sufficiently refreshed with this communion with nature, they reënter the town and notice a great many things, among others, the clothing, **match-co-res**, worn by those they see. It being warm weather, the inhabitants have on but little. Here come two fine young women wearing only aprons, **mat-a-heigh ca-tom-mo-ik**, before and behind. Being ladies of distinction, on their heads are coronets of **peak**; and around their necks were necklaces or chains formed of long links of copper, which ornament they called **tap-o-an-tam-nais**; but they had no use now of stockings, **caw-que-a-wans**; garters, **kis-pur-ra-caut-a-pus**; shoes, **mawh-ca-sins**, nor gloves, o-tein-gas. They were on their way to the river, to see the men fish.

A conjurer comes next on his way to give some young men medicine, wis-oc-can, for the husk-a-naw-ing pen. He had in his hand, made out of a gourd full of small stones, a rattle, chmgaw-won-auk, which he was going to use in his conjurations. Fastened to his girdle, pok-on-tats, is his tobacco-bag, re-con-ack. With him was the priest, dressed in a cloak of feathers, called put-ta-wus. He was on his way to the O-kee's temple, qui-oc-co-san, and allowed the Indian and the boy to join him. He was about to begin a pau-waw-ing, or conjuration, in order to make it rain again to-morrow, ra-i-ab, as he had made it do, as he claimed, yesterday, o-sa-i-oh.

The names and designations which he had for the Deity were numerous. Ra-wot-ton-emd meant God, but a more general word for gods was Mon-to-ac. For the images of gods in the form of men, he used the word Ke-was-o-wok. One of such images alone he called Ke-was. O-kee was another name for a god, and A-ho-ne still another. Petty gods and their affinities he called Qui-yough-co-soughs. Qui-oc-cos was the idol which dwelt in the temple already called qui-oc-co-san, but which had also another name, mach-i-co-muck. Ma-hom-ny was the name of the deity who lived beyond the sun, and who decided the fate of men after death, and sent them to a place of happiness or misery.

Ri-o-ko-sick was one of their names for the Devil, another form of which was Ri-a-poke. Mo-un-sha-quat-u-uh was their name for Heaven, while Po-po-gus-so was that for the hole in the remotest west where the souls of the evil burnt continually. It may have been that the red glow of the sunset was the origin of this belief.

The priest was going to offer a prayer, mau-no-mom-ma-on, to the sun, kes-kow-ghe, before proceeding to sacrifice, ut-tak-a-er. The war chief, wer-ó-ance, accompanied by several followers, passes by. Three feathers, ah-pe-uk, adorn his head. He has just called one of his attendants, a married man, now-i-ow-i-ih wi-o-wah, a fool, win-tuc, for selling a chain, rar-e-naw; a copper kettle, au-cut-ga-quas-san; a coat, mant-choor; a mortar, tac-ca-hooc, and pestle, poc-o-ha-ac; a bodkin, po-co-hack; a comb, rick-a-ho-ne; a needle, poc-o-ha-oc; a block, tac-ca-hooc, and a spade, aa-ix-ke-hak-e, most of which he had gotten from the English, for only ten yards of peak.

This word, sometimes spelled peag, was the name given to beads made from the ends of shells, rubbed down into a cylindrical shape, polished and strung into belts or necklaces. These were valued according to their length and the perfection of their workmanship, and were used as money or ornament. One of the pictures shows a man with a coronet of peak upon his head. Black or purple peak was worth twice as much, length for length, as white peak.

Wam-pum was the special name given to this more valuable, dark peak. Its full designation was wampum peak.

Roanoke was another kind of money made of the cockle shell. It was of less value than peak.

Runtees was still another name for the disks of shells, used as ornaments, as in the form of necklaces, etc.

The chief could not bear to have this man, who was a mariner, or seaman, **che-ik-sew**, sell his goods so cheaply, and he told him how he had had to give a whole boat, **quin-tan,** load of **maize,** corn, for a pickaxe, **tock-a-hack;** a pair of shears, **ac-cow-prets;** a ball, **a-i-towh,** made of copper, **mat-tas-sin;** a bell, **mau-ca-quins,** made of some white metal, **us-sa-was-sin;** a stool, **tau-o-sin,** and some shining brass, **os-a-was,** which a great ship, **a-quin-tay-ne mang-goy,** had just brought in.

Then he told him of a chest, **pac-us,** and a bottle, **po-he-euh,** with a dram, **ah-quo-hooc,** in it, which he had gotten from another ship **mus-so-wux-uc,** in exchange for some pearl, **ma-kat-e-weigh.**

Young men are seen at various amusements or occupations, and, as the day is now well advanced, the women come in from gathering the corn and other fruits of the soil which they have tilled and cared for, to prepare the evening meal.

The day has been not only hot, but sultry, and a great wind, **mah-qua-ih,** now comes up. In the west, piles of black clouds tower up in the sky, and advance, threatening and terrible. The Indians believe that this is a sign that the Deity is offended. They have done wrong in torturing and killing those prisoners. The Sun is obscured by the thick clouds. The priest and the conjurer offer sacrifice to it. The tobacco thrown into the air is strewn over the land by the hurricane, **toh-tum-mo-cun-num,** which is now sweeping over them. The rain, **cam-zo-wan,** falls in torrents. A flash of lightning, **ke-cut-tan-no-was,** shatters a giant oak, **po-aw-a-mingd** which falls to the ground with a crash, **pe-nim,** while the thunder, **pet-tack-queth,** shakes the world. **Righ-com-ou-ghe,** Death, is in the air.

At last the wind, **ras-so-um,** subsides. A beautiful, **mus-ca-i-u-uh,** rainbow, **quan-na-cut,** shines forth against the black, **ma-cat-a-wa-i-u-uh,** clouds. The Deity is propitiated, and the storm is over.

Sunset, **qu-un-se-uh,** was now at hand. In the western horizon hangs the moon, **ne-paw-wesh-ough,** which was now a new moon, **suc-kim-ma.**

Smoke, **kek-e-pem-quah,** rises in the air from many open fires, the last meal of the day is being prepared, so our observers go back to their house, a spark of fire, **ac-ce-cow,** lights the wood, and a fish is baked whole, **bar-be-cued.**

They then attended the social gathering

which took place nightly in the centre of the town. The company amused itself until a late hour with singing and dancing.

When all was over, the day brought to a close, they retired by the light of a pine knot, **o-san-in-tak,** which served as a candle.

Outside all was dark. Profound quiet reigned, except for the wind which sighed as it passed through the pine trees, while overhead the silent stars, **pum-ma-humps,** stood sentinel.

THE LOVER'S QUARREL

He: **Ken-cut-te-maum,** Good-morning. **Ne-tap,** my dear friend.
She: **Cham-ah wing-gap-o.** Welcome, my beloved friend.
He: **Pas-pas-a-at.** The morning is fair.
She: **Chin-gis-sum.** It is very warm weather.
He: **Tan-a-o-wa-am?** Where have you been?
She: **Yo-ax-u-uh.** Far away.
He: **Nu-me-roth-e-qui-er?** Your companion?
She: **Mah-maindg-no-hai-u-uh.** I have none.
He: **Mat-ta-que-nat-o-rath.** I understand you not.
She: **Mum-mas-cus-hen-e-po.** I have been asleep.
He: **Kick-e-ten qui-er.** Tell me.
She: **Ma-tush.** I will not.
He: **Ne-tab.** I am your friend.
She: **Ken-ne-hau-tows.** I understand well.
He: **Near-now-wan.** I have been.

She: War-nat. Enough.
He: Net-a-peuh. I am at your command.
She: Win-gan-ou-se. Very good.
   (He gives her a necklace of wampum.)
He: Thaig-wen-um-mer-a-an. I give it you gratis.
She: Ke-nah. I thank you.
He: Kaw-ko-pen qui-er. I drink to you.
She: Tang-go. Let me see it.
He: Jough-que-me wath. Let us go away.
She: Nec-qu-ris-saw. I dare not.
He: Me-ish-mi-co-an ches-soy-ouk. Give this to the child.
   (Gives her a rattle.)
She: Nu-wam-at-a-men. I love it.
He: Cum-meish yoo-wah. Give it him.
She: Mal-a-com-me-ir. I will not give it.
He: Hus-que-que-nat-o-ra. Now I understand you.
   Tah-moc-as-se-uh. He hath none.
She: Mon-i-naw. The cock crows.
   Up-pou-shun. The ships go home.
He: Ca-cut-tew-indg? What is my name?
She: Ca-iv-uh. I cannot tell.
   No-e-wa-nath-soun. I have forgotten.
He: Ke-ar! You!
She: Cup-peh. Yes.
He: Pas-ko-rath. The gold sparkles in the sand.
She: Num-mas-kat-a-men. I care not for it.
He: Koup-path-e. Yea, truly?
She: Oi-ac-pi-jaun. We will come again.

Some Indian Words

He: **Tan-oo chick?** When?
She: **Ra-i-ab.** To-morrow.
He: **Kes-so-hi-ke-ar.** Shut the door.
She: **Na-hay-hough.** I have it.
He: **Noun-ma-is.** I love you.
She: **Ne-trap-per kup-per.** Sit further.
He: **Hus-que.** By and by.
She: **Mut-tack.** No.
He: **Nim.** Yes.
She: **Ough-rath.** Far off.
He: **Com-mo-mais?** Do you love?
She: **Mat-tan-a-hay-yough.** I have it not.
(Turning to the door.)
Hat-ac-quo-ear. Hold it aside.
Num-ma? Will you go home?
He: **Kan-i-ough.** I know not.
Kutt-chaw-e. I am offended.
She: **No-raugh to-an.** Put on your hat.[1]
He: **Num-ma-cha.** I will go home.
She: **Wam-at-tuwh.** It is well.
Un-tough. Take it.
(Hands him his hat, **pat-tih-qua-pis-son.**)
He: **Ah-ath.** Farewell.
She: **Ke-ij.** Get you gone!
(Throws after him a ring, **nek-e-rein-skeps,** which he had given her.)

---

[1] Of course, the primitive Indians wore no hats. Where this man got this hat, we cannot say—possibly from some Englishman whom he had tomahawked.

THE TROUBLESOME TRAVELER

Host: **Que-quoy-ter-nis qui-re?** What is your name?
Traveler: **Pi-pis-co.**
Host: **Ke-is?** How many?
Traveler: **Na-an-tu-cah ne-cut.** Only one, I myself, ne-ar,
Host: **Ough.** It is well.
Traveler: **Ro-o-ke-uh co-an.** It snoweth.
Cur-cie ne-i-re. I am cold.
O-ram-i-ath south. I am sick.
How-ghu-eih ta-kon ne-i-re. I am hungry.
Host: (To Attendant.) **Noc-mcha-min-o bok-e-taw.** Mend up the fire.
(To Traveler.) **Me-ih-tus-suc.** Eat with me.
Traveler: **Ka-pes-se-map-a-an-gum.** Give me a little piece.
Host: **Min-chin qui-re.** Eat thou.
Traveler: **Que-quoy?** What is this?
Host: **Nec-o-on-dam-en.** It is good meat.
Traveler: **Me-ish-nah-me-cher.** Give me some meat.
Me-cho-cusk. I will eat by and by.
U-gau-co-pes-sum. I would drink.
Mam-ma-he suc-qua-hum. Give me some water.
Host: **Um-doth.** Take it.
Traveler: **Nuts-se-qua-cup.** I will drink no more.

Some Indian Words

	Pa-atch nah nun-gan. Give me some butter to spread on my bread.
	Pas-e-me up-po-oke. Give me some tobacco.
Host:	**Win-gut-see up-o-oc.** The tobacco is good.
	Bmser-an ap-o-ok. Fill the pipe with tobacco.
Traveler:	**O-pot-e-yough.** The pipe is stopped.
	Kesh-e-ma-ic po-oc. The tobacco is naught.
	Tawks ne-ge-isp. No more. I am full.
Host:	**Tas-ho-ac.** All is out.
Traveler:	**O-wan-ough.** Who hath this?
Host:	**May-an-se.** I have it not.
	Daw-ba-son-qui-re. Warm yourself.
Traveler:	**Ot-a-wi-a-ac bac-a-taw.** The fire is out.
Host:	**Mat-a-ches-a.** It is not lighted.
Traveler:	**Pow-tow-ho-ne bok-e-tan.** Blow the fire with your mouth.
Host:	**As-sen-tew-ca-i-ah.** It shineth.
Traveler:	**Win-gan outs-sem-et-sum-ne-ic.** My foot is well.
	U-ne-gap-a-mut-ta men-ne-tat-a-ki-i. My legs ache.
	Mat-a-mau-ca-sun-ne-ih. I have no shoes.
	Ken-o-rock-o-no-rem qui-re. Come look at my head.

	Ah-kij. It hurts me.
Host:	Ne-hap-per. Sit down.
	Num-pe-nam-un. Let me see it.
Traveler:	Ne-pun-che-ne-ir. I am dead.

THE QUARRELSOME CHIEFS

" Mow-chick way-a-ugh taugh ne-o-ragh ka-que-re me-cher. I am very hungry, what shall I eat?

" Taw-nor ne-hiegh Powhatan? Where dwells Powhatan?

" Mach-e, ne-hiegh you-rough Or-a-paks. Now he dwells a great way hence at Or-a-paks.

" Vit-ta-pitch-e-way-ne an-pech-itchs ne-haw-per Wer-o-wo-co-mo-co. You lie, he staid ever at Wer-o-wo-co-mo-co.

" Ka-tor ne-hiegh mat-tagh ne-er ut-ta-pitch-e-way-ne. Truly he is there, I do not lie.

" Spaugh-tyn-e-re ke-ragh wer-ó-wance Maw-mar-i-nough kek-a-te-waugh pey-a-qua-ugh. Run you then to the King Maw-mar-i-nough and bid him come hither.

"Ut-te-ke e-pey-a-wey-ack wigh-whip. Get you gone, and come again quickly.

" Kek-a-ten Po-ka-hon-tas pat-i-a-quah ni-ugh tanks ma-not-yens neer mow-chick raw-re-nock au-dough. Bid Pokahontas bring hither two little baskets and I will give her white beads to make her a chain." [1]

[1] Smith, vol. i., pp. 147-8.

Some Indian Words

The meaning of a few of their names of places and persons has been preserved. We can well wish that we knew more of them.

Pocahontas means bright stream between two hills.

Wer-o-wo-com-o-co means the chief place of council, or King's House.

Pa-mun-key means where we took a sweat.[1]

War-ros-quy-oake means point of land. This was the original name of Isle of Wight County.

Nan-se-mond means fishing-point.

Ka-naw-ha means the river of the woods.

Kentucky means dark and bloody ground; or, according to other authorities, at the head of the river; long river; or long prairies.[2]

Ohio means the beautiful river; or, river of blood.

Roanoke was the same word they used to designate one kind of their shell money, and was probably given to the locality where these shells abounded.

Chesapeake means the mother of waters.

Appomattox means sinuous tidal estuary.[3]

Potomac means water flowing in cascades. The lower part of this river, to which such a name would be inappropriate, was, as we have seen, the **Co-hon-go-roo-ta**.

Patuxent means water flowing over mud.

Patapsco means water flowing over rocks.

---

[1] Campbell's *History of Virginia*, p. 193.
[2] Townsend's *United States*, pp. 57, 61, 63.
[3] Brown's *First Republic*, p. 194.

Pocomoke means broken by knobs or small hills.

Shenandoah means the daughter of the stars.[1]

Appalachian appears to signify those on the other side.

Tennessee, from one of the Cherokee villages, **Tenas See,** said to mean a curved spoon.

From Townsend, we learn that:

Accomac means land on the other side of the water.

Aquia Creek means muddy creek.

Alleghany River means the river of the **Allige-wi,** a tribe which preceded the Delawares.

Chickahominy means turkey-lick.

Miami River means stony river.

Muskingum means elk's face.

Rappahannock means the river of quick rising water.[2]

Some of the Indian names for places and streams in this part of the world, which they called **I-sen-a-com-ma-cah,** were:

Pa-qua-chowng was their name for the region known to us as the Falls of the James.

Accawmack was the name of the whole peninsula of the Eastern Shore. It was often spoken of as the Kingdom of Accomack.

The **Powhatan** River is now the James River.

The **Appamattuck** still retains its name, slightly altered in spelling.

---

[1] Irving's *Life of Washington,* vol. i., p. 39.
[2] Townsend's *United States,* p. 82.

The Qui-yough-co-han-ock was Chipoak Creek.

War-ras-quoy-ack Bay, pronounced War-ris-queak, was the name for Burwell's Bay.

The Nansemond retains its name as a stream.

The Chesapeake River, or "brooke" as Strachey calls it, is now the Elizabeth River.

The Chesapeake Bay retains its name.

The Chick-a-ham-a-ni-a retains its name slightly altered into Chickahominy.

Ke-cough-tan, pronounced Kik-o-tan, is now Hampton.

The Pamunck, or Pamunkey, is now the York.

Chin-quo-teck is now West Point.

The Yough-ta-mund is now the Pamunkey.

The Mat-ta-pa-ment is now the Mattapony.

The Pa-yan-ka-tank retains its name.

The O-pis-cat-u-meck was later called by the Indians the Top-pa-han-ock, then by the English the Queen's River, and now is called the Rappahannock.

The Pa-taw-o-meck was called by the English the Elizabeth, and is now called the Potomac. Its ancient Indian name appears to have been the Co-hon-go-roo-ta.

The Qui-yough River is now Bull Run.

The Paw-tux-ent in Maryland retains its name, slightly altered in spelling.

The Tock-wogh is now the Chester River.

The Wi-com-i-co River in Northumberland County still retains its name.

Mob-jack Bay retains its name.

On the Eastern Shore some of the Indian names which have been preserved, on the ocean side, are:
Chin-co-teague Bay, Inlet and Island.
As-sa-teague Island.
Me-tom-kin Inlet.
Wach-a-preague Inlet.
Great and Little **Mach-i-pon-go** Inlets.
Mock-orn Island.
And on the Bay side, there are:
Mat-ta-wo-man Creek.
Nas-wad-dox Creek.
Oc-co-han-nock Creek, the dividing line between Northampton and Accomac.
Crad-dock Creek.
Nan-qua Creek.
Pun-go-teague Creek and Town.
O-nan-cock Creek and Town.
Ches-con-es-sex Creek.
Mes-son-go Creek.
Po-co-moke Sound and River.
Big **An-ne-mes-sex** River.
Man-o-kin River.
Wi-com-o-co River.
Nan-ti-coke River and Point.
Chop-tank River, formerly the **Kus-car-a-wo-ak.**

Scattered through the eastern part of the State, mainly, the following Indian names have been retained:
Pungo, the name of a locality in Princess Anne.

Chuck-a-tuck in Nansemond.
Wash-i-kee in Greensville.
Po-quo-son and Mes-sick in York.
To-a-no in James City.
Nax-e-ra, Cap-pa-ho-sic, Wi-com-i-co, and Za-no-ni in Gloucester.
Mis-kim-on and Co-an in Northumberland.
Mach-o-doc in Westmoreland.
Tap-pa-han-nock and Nan-lak-la in Essex.
Man-ta-pike and Pow-can in King and Queen.
Ro-man-coke, Man-quin, Man-go-hick, and Co-ho-ke in King William.
Ma-to-a-ca and Win-ter-pock in Chesterfield.
Na-moz-ine Creek and Ro-wan-ta in Dinwiddie.
The Me-her-rin River and To-ta-no in Brunswick.
Chap-ti-co, O-lo, No-go, Pu-pa, and the Nottoway River in Lunenburg.
The Roanoke River in Mecklenburg.
Pas-sa-pa-tan-zy, A-qui-a, To-lu-ca, and Potomac Creek in Stafford.
Quan-ti-co, Ne-abs-co, Ca-thar-pin, and Oc-co-quan Creek in Prince William.
Ac-co-tink in Fairfax.
Kit-toc-ton Creek in Loudoun.
A-to-ka and So-we-go in Fauquier.
La-ko-ta in Culpeper.
Mas-sa-po-nax and Pan-i-en in Spottsylvania.
Nan-lak-i-a and Pas-sing in Caroline.
Tabs-cott, Lan-tan-a, Sha-ko, and Man-a-kin in Goochland.

Mat-to-ax in Amelia.
To-ro in Charlotte.
Or-rix in Bedford.
In the Valley of Virginia, the **Shen-an-do-ah** River:
The Big **Moc-ca-sin** Creek in Scott.
Ca-taw-ba Creek in Roanoke and Botetourt.
The **O-pe-quan** River, pronounced the Opéckon, which forms the boundary between Frederick and Clarke.
Row-an-ty and **Sappony** Creeks in Dinwiddie and Sussex.
Seneca Creek in Campbell.
Shaddock's Creek in Southampton.
Shock-oe Creek in Pittsylvania, and **Wa-qua** Creek in Brunswick.
Mountains which still bear their Indian names are the **Cacapon** which form the western boundary of Frederick, the **Alleghanies,** and the whole **Appalachian** Range. Qui-ra-uk, the name given by the Indians to the first settlers as that of the Blue Ridge, has disappeared.

We have only one sample of Indian poetry, and this is how we obtained it.
A slight advantage which the Indians once gained in an encounter was the occasion of much rejoicing on their part. They regarded it as a great victory, and made it the subject of a scornful war-song of triumph. This remarkable production is preserved for us by Strachey. He tells us:

Some Indian Words

"They have contrived a kind of angry song against us, in their homely rhymes, which concludeth with a kind of petition unto their Okeus, and to all the host of their idols, to plague the Tas-san-tas-ses[1] (for so they call us) and their posterities; as likewise another scornful song they made of us last year at the falls, in manner of triumph, at what time they killed Captain William West, our Lord General's nephew, and two or three more, and took one Symon Skove, a sailor, and one Cob, a boy, prisoners. That song goeth thus:

" Mat-a-ne-rew   sha-sha-she-waw   e-ra-wan-go
   pe-che-co-ma
Whe   Tas-san-tas-sa   in-o-shas-haw-ye-hoc-kan
   po-co-sack:
Whe whe, yah ha-ha ne-he wit-to-wa, wit-to-wa.

" Mat-a-ne-rew   sha-sha-she-waw   e-ra-wan-go
   pe-che-co-ma
Captain Newport in-o-shas-haw neir in-hoc na-
   ti-an ma-tas-san:
Whe whe, yah ha-ha ne-he wit-to-wa, wit-to-wa.

" Mat-a-ne-rew   sha-sha-she-waw   e-ra-wan-go
   pe-che-co-ma
Thomas Newport in-o-shas-haw neir in-hoc na-
   ti-an mon-cock:
Whe whe, yah ha-ha, ne-he wit-to-wa, wit-to-wa.

[1] The word ut-tas-san-tas-so-wa-ih meant stranger. This name which the Indians gave the English probably meant the strange people, the foreigners.

" Mat-a-ne-rew sha-sha-she-waw e-ra-wan-go
　 pe-che-co-ma
Po-chin Simon mo-sha-shaw nin-gon na-ti-an
　 mon-a-hack:
Whe whe, yah ha-ha ne-he wit-to-wa, wit-to-wa.

"Which may signify how they killed us for all our poc-ca-sacks, that is our guns, and for all that Captain Newport brought them copper, and could hurt Thomas Newport (a boy whose name indeed was Thomas Savage, who Captain Newport leaving with Powhatan to learn the language, at what time he presented the said Powhatan with a copper crown, and other gifts from his Majesty, said he was his son) for all his mon-a-chock, that is his bright sword, and how they could take Symon (for they seldom said our surnames) prisoner for all his tam-a-hanke, that is his hatchet, adding, as for a burden unto their song, what lamentation our people made when they killed him, namely, saying how they would cry whe, whe, etc., which they mocked us for, and cried again to us yah, ha, ha, Te-wit-ta-wa, Te-wit-ta-wa; for it is true they never bemoan themselves nor cry out, giving up so much as a groan for any death, how cruel soever and full of torment."[1]

Among the Indian words which were adopted by the English and which are still in use are:
　Pone, a word taken from their **Op-pone**, which

[1] *Historie of Travaile*, etc., p. 79.

meant bread. It is used now generally in connection with corn bread—a pone of corn bread.

Pocosin, land on which water stands in wet weather. The word signifies dreary.

Persimmon, the well-known wild fruit.

Hickory, the tough wooded tree with which we are familiar.

Chinkapin, the dwarf chestnut.

Opossum, or possum.

Raccoon, or coon.

Scuppernong, a sweet grape.

Hominy, the familiar article of food.

Barbecue, a word taken from their mode of roasting fish and animals whole.

Succotash, a dish of corn and beans mixed.

Paw-waw-ing, a word which meant the conjurations of the priest, has been preserved with an altered meaning.

Moccasin, the name of a deadly snake.

CHAPTER XX

THE TRIBES AND NATIONS

IT would probably be impossible to name all the Indian tribes living in Virginia in 1607. The division seems to have been, in some instances, into very small units. The inhabitants of one small village, being often spoken of as a tribe. The great divisions were, in the east, the Powhatan Confederacy, composed of many tribes; in the center of the State, the Man-a-kins or Mon-a-cans, and the Man-nah-o-acs; still farther to the west, in the mountainous part of the State, were the Shaw-a-nese, the Cher-o-kees, the Tus-ca-ro-ras, and others.

The center and heart of the Powhatan Confederacy was composed of the following six tribes, whose sovereignty Powhatan had inherited. These were his oldest and most faithful subjects. They were the Powhatans, the Pa-mun-keys, the Ar-ro-ha-tecks, the Ap-pa-mat-tucks, the Yough-ta-munds, and the Mat-ta-pam-i-ents, which we will now consider in order.

The Powhatans. This was Powhatan's own personal tribe, and numbered forty warriors. They lived on the north side of the James, in

Henrico County, near Richmond, which county is full of their arrow- and spear-heads, their tomahawks, pottery, mortars, and pestles. In all of his ancient, inherited, tribal headquarters, he had houses built after their manner like arbors, some thirty, some forty yards long, and at every house provision was made for him according to the time of his staying there. The King of this tribe was Taux Pow-ha-tan, which means "Little Powhatan," one of the great Powhatan's sons.[1]

Their chief town was named Powhatan, and was situated at Mayo's.[2]

This tribe is mentioned in the acts in connection with the following transaction:

"Me-tap-pin a Powhatan Indian being sold for lifetime to one Elizabeth Short by the King of Wainoake Indians who had no power to sell him being of another nation, it is ordered that the said Indian be free, he speaking perfectly the English tongue and desiring baptism."[3]

Such references as this in the Acts of Assembly which are given herein in connection with many of the tribes, insignificant apparently in and by themselves, yet serve not only to show the individual existence of the tribes thus mentioned, but they throw a strong light on the relations between these tribes and the Virginians, and the methods adopted by the Colonial Government of dealing with them and their tribal lands. In the case of some of the more obscure tribes these

---
[1] Smith, vol. i., pp. 116, 142.
[2] Burk, vol. iii., p. 89.   [3] 2 Hening, 155.

references are practically the only authentic, or easily accessible, authority we have to rely upon for the recognition by the Colony of these tribes as separate or distinct powers, at a time when the Indians constituted a political and military force which had to be reckoned with.

The Pa-mun-keys. Smith says, "Where the river [the York] is divided, the country is called Pamaunkee, and nourisheth near three hundred able men." This description included much of the area bounded by the Pamunkey and the Mattapony rivers. Their wer-ó-ance was O-pe-chan-ca-nough, the most bitter and aggressive of the enemies of the English. Their name was originally borne by the noble York, and the stream now called by their name was then styled the Yough-i-a-nund.[1] Their chief town was Ro-mun-cock.[2]

O-pe-chan-ca-nough's two brothers assisted in the government of this large tribe, and the three are spoken of by Strachey as the triumviri of that country.[3]

To write a history of the Pamunkeys would involve much of the colonial history of Virginia. They appear again and again upon its pages, and in the acts of the General Assembly. For many years they formed the heart and head of the opposing power. Originating with its cunning and relentless old king, and carried into execution in large part by their formidable warriors,

---
[1] Smith, vol. i., pp. 117, 142.   [2] Burk, vol. iii., p. 89.
[3] *Historie of Travaile into Virginia*, p. 62.

were the massacres of 1622 and 1644. But they finally became our allies, and fought side by side with us in our wars with other Indians.

This tribe, which is much older than the Commonwealth or Colony of Virginia, is still in existence, and forms an interesting link which connects the present with the long forgotten past.

On September 5th, 1908, the writer visited the reservation of the Pamunkey tribe, in King William County, about twenty-four miles east of Richmond. He was met at White House Station, on the Southern Railroad, by a member of the tribe, Mr. S. J. Sweatt, who acted as guide, and conducted him at once across the Pamunkey, taking the railroad bridge and causeway, as the nearest route. The causeway, which is a long one, built across the original channel of the river, was taken from the soil of the reservation. The guide represented this as being an invasion of their rights. He even said that they had had trouble in preventing two burial grounds being cut away for this work. They were saved, however, and stand out like little hills, on the green sward which now covers the part dug away.

The railroad runs through the reservation, nearly at its northern limit. The area of the whole tract is now only some seven hundred or eight hundred acres, having been subjected to successive reductions.

Our first visit was to the chief of the tribe, George Major Cooke. The chief was not at home, he was engaged in one of the proper ways an Indian chief would be engaged—he was fishing. Promises were held out to us that he would return in a short time, and meanwhile we were introduced to his squaw, his papooses, and his wigwam.

His squaw, in whom we viewed the successor to the queens of Pamunkey, is a typical Indian, in middle life, thin, and then engaged, for it was still early, in the affairs of housekeeping. Her name is Theodora Octavia Cooke, which compound of Greek, Latin, and English could hardly be considered as appropriate to her as would have been one of her own language. Around her was a goodly set of little Indians, but the two oldest sons were absent, being off with their father fishing, these two were Major Thomas Cooke, twenty years old, and Ottigney Pontiac Cooke, aged eighteen. With their mother were George Theo Cooke, a fine-looking young Pamunkey of seventeen, Captola Eulalia Cooke, a pretty girl of fifteen, Tecumseh Deerfoot Cooke, a handsome little fellow of eight, Dora Laughingwater Cooke, an attractive little girl of five, and Pocahontas Tarquinas Cooke, a sweet and pretty baby of two.

The house of the chief was a good-sized frame building, with outhouses and garden, and one of the first one meets with on entering the reservation. In this could be seen some pottery and bead-work, made by the members of the family. The pottery was all pipes, various devices being presented, such as the terrible warrior's head, the tomahawk, canoe, and other shapes. The bead-work was very pretty, taking the shape of women's belts, necklaces, and fobs.

While these things were being examined, our guide had gone to his house, which was not far distant, and now returned with a buggy, rather the worse for wear, drawn by a small, claybank horse. With this locomotive equipment we set off at a brisk trot, to view the reservation.

Our road was always down some green lawn, about thirty feet wide, bordered by cornfields, and enclosed by fences. These roadways were kept as a common of pasture by the tribe. The ruts cut by the carriages did not much disfigure them, and the general appearance of the whole place was made picturesque by these long stretches of green grass.

The place is called "Indian Town," and of course one would naturally expect to find at least one cluster of houses, to which the name would more particularly apply. But there is none such. The "Town" is a collection of small farms, ranging from ten to twelve acres, or thereabouts, in area. A large part of the reservation is still forest. The settlement gives one the impression of a well-populated rural neighborhood, the several houses being so near to each other, that from any one, you would be able to see probably three or four others. All are of frame, and most below the general average of size and appointment found among the smaller of the white farmers, although all are framed according to our general plans for such structures. Two were of two stories, and pretty good houses, but most are very small.

The cultivation of the land is the real support of these people. They still do a little hunting and fishing, but their territory has been so much reduced, and their right to roam, fish, and hunt in the neighborhood has been so curtailed, that this source of income can only be considered as an occasional addition to their more sure support, which is derived from tilling the soil, over which their warlike ancestors roamed at will.

The tribe is now reduced to about one hundred and ten, and there are some twenty-five of their houses on the reservation. Of these, about five are now unoccupied. The land belongs to the State of Virginia, held in trust by it for the tribe as a whole. No one thus owns any part of the soil in severalty. The various tracts are assigned to the head of a family for his life. The house is built at his expense, and is his property. If he die leaving a family, it will be allowed to remain in the possession of his widow or son, the youngest being preferred, if of sufficient age, and if he have the desire to continue to occupy it. The theory is, that every one must have a sufficient piece of land, and if there should be a demand made by a member, who was unprovided with land, if necessary, a part would be taken from him who held the largest piece.

We stopped on the roadside a Mr. Bradby, the former chief. He was very affable, his large round face smiling beneath a torn, straw hat. He looked the picture of health, but not particularly Indian. He was impressed with the need of education for his tribe, and thought that with better facilities, his brethren might distinguish themselves at the bar, in medicine, or other such liberal calling.

We visited several families. They received us very politely, were thoroughly friendly, and seemed to be pleased at the interest which they felt the outside world took in them. One of the most agreeable and interesting was a tall, and very powerful man, Mr. Samson, who, at ten in the morning, was sitting on his front porch shaving before a small round mirror, of a very irregular surface, hung up on the front of the house. He wore a small black moustache, but for all that, was an Indian all over. He was clad in a thick gray undershirt, corduroy pants, and rubber boots, though the day was dry and warm.

His house he had built with his own hands. It had two rooms which were just about large enough for him to move around in. He was a merry bachelor, possibly sixty years old, but who looked fifteen years younger. He did not know how old he was. When asked how he, so good looking a man, had escaped the fascinations of the fair sex, he laughed very heartily. His general defense for his conduct was that the women now were not what they used to be; they seemed to be of so much more flippant a nature than formerly, and not half so fond of hard work.

Mr. Samson did not seem to think, that in losing one of these modern helpmeets he had lost much, but yet, the possibilities of matrimony he still considered within his reach.

One old woman we called upon, the oldest member of the settlement, and who lived in one of the two best houses, was feeling so unwell that we did not stay long. She was about eighty years old. We found her sitting by a little wood fire, with a sunbonnet on. She had felt very cold in the early morning, and was still suffering, so we thought it kindness to leave her.

At every house was to be seen one or more guns. One family was cutting up apples to dry. Another was getting ready to move to New York where the father worked, the family coming down to Pamunkey during the school vacation season. This family had a very new house, which presented quite a contrast to most of the others. The mother of this family was a Chickahominy Indian. One of their daughters, who was present, was a buxom young squaw, very fair, and still attending school. When looking at her, we could not help thinking of the lonely, but very happy, Mr. Samson, who lived just a little bit down the road.

The guide thought the chief had probably caught enough fish by this time, so we drove down the verdant thoroughfares towards his home. These thoroughfares were soft enough for the horses feet, and pleasant enough to drive over, but they were not kept in the best condition.

Little labor seems to ever have been bestowed upon them. Where a lagoon passes across the road, it simply stays there; no effort is made to bridge it, nor fill up the road. At one place, a broad and deep pond occupied the road for some distance. Our driver calmly drove down into it, and kept going until he pulled up out of it, on the other side. All this had the charm of being just so perfectly natural.

When we reached the chief's house, we found that he had returned, and, having received the letters of introduction which we had left for him, he was very affable. He was tall, rather thin, a typical looking Indian, in appearance not an unworthy successor of O-pe-chan-ca-nough and Tot-to-pot-to-moy. Being asked if he minded having his photograph taken, he complained a little of the way he had to sit for pictures of which he never got a copy. But we promised to give him a copy of this picture, if he would honor us with a sitting. The question of costume then came up. The chief had been exhibited at the Jamestown Exposition, and, in order to present a proper appearance, had let his hair grow long, and has not cut it since. He promptly decided that his separate, individual picture he would have taken in costume, so, arranged in all the regalia of deerskin and beads, armed with spear, bow, arrows, and tomahawk, he stood in solitary grandeur while a kodak was snapped in front of him. And then, a group-picture, in his ordinary costume had to be taken, so the chief and his squaw, sitting side by side, surrounded by six of their offspring, were similarly tortured.

The guide, who was the second Pamunkey husband of a white woman, now took us to his house, one of the best on the reservation, where the writer was presented to this fair admirer of the Pamunkeys. She was a very nice looking young woman, with as dark complexion as many of the Indians. The house was surrounded by flowers, and presented a very tidy appearance.

There are only two houses of a public character on the reservation, the schoolhouse, a little, whitewashed affair, so small that you would never think it a public building, and the church. This latter is prettily situated in a tall grove of trees, and is of a respectable size. The Pamunkeys are all Baptists; Okee's reign is ended.

The authority of the chief, who is elected by the tribe, is more persuasive than otherwise. He is the titular head of the tribe, decides disputes on the reservation, keeps order, and represents the tribe in all its public affairs. Associated with him is a council of four.

The tribe pays no taxes to the State of Virginia, except the tribute imposed upon it in the early days of the settlement, when it became tributary to the English, acknowledging the superiority of the Crown of Great Britain. This tribute consists in game, which the chief delivers each year to the Governor of Virginia, at the State capitol, on New Year's day. According to the varying circumstances of the chase, it may

The Home of a Pamunkey Indian

be a deer, a wild turkey, ducks, or fish. The local tax imposed upon each man of the tribe is the sum of one dollar. The chief receives no salary, and this fund goes for other general purposes.

Little of the aboriginal Indian appears to-day in the settlement, for the houses, furniture, and costume correspond to those of the neighborhood, but the Indian physiognomy is presented perfectly in many cases, and these Pamunkeys, if dressed in the costume of their ancestors, could not be distinguished from those met with in 1607.

Their customs of marriage, and all such important matters, are now in conformity with Virginia law. The authority of the chief extends to the adjustment of small difficulties arising in the settlement, but punishment for homicide would be meted out by the regular courts of the Commonwealth. The chief has no sufficient force at his disposal to cope with such serious difficulties.

The Pamunkeys consider themselves a poor people. Their cultivation of the soil is fairly good, corn and peas being their chief products but they are not large proprietors, and they have to plant the same field over and over again allowing the land no time to rest. Many have gone outside for employment. The population of the tribe is about at a standstill. No marriages are now contracted with any but other Indians, or white people, the Pamunkeys holding themselves, as they do, superior to the colored people. The Indian type, presented by all the children the writer saw, was very distinct.

This little settlement represents the largest organized body of the formerly large number of Virginia Indians. As such, a deep historic interest attaches to them, not only for what they immediately represent, but also as constituting an exception to the general scheme of the construction of society, as at present organized; for here, on the banks of the river Pamunkey, there still exists tribal government.

The Mat-ta-po-nýs. These lived on the river now named after them, but which was originally called the Mat-ta-pa-ment, in what is now King William or King and Queen County. Their King was Wer-o-waugh.[1] They numbered one hundred and forty, and could muster thirty warriors.[2] They are said to have been a branch of the Pamunkeys.

This tribe was also called the Mat-ta-pam-i-ents or Mat-ta-pa-ments.

The following measure passed in 1662 shows that the Virginians were always ready to do justice to these people:

"It is ordered by the assembly that Lieutenant Colonel Goodridge be summoned to appear before the honorable governor and council at next quarter court to answer the complaint of the king of the Mat-ta-po-ny Indians concerning

[1] *History of Travaile into Virginia*, p. 62.
[2] Smith, vol. i., p. 117.

the burning of his English house,[1] and that the said Indian king have notice given him to be present."[2]

This tribe is also yet in existence and occupies a reservation in King William County. They number in all about fifty.

In 1894, trustees were appointed for the Matta-po-ni tribe in King William County: "Said trustees shall be governed by the laws now in force in regard to Indians and their reservations in this State; and, further, shall have the right upon the vote of the majority of the trustees, and also a majority of the members of the tribe above twenty-one years of age, to expel from their reservation any person who has no right upon said reservation, or any member of the tribe who shall be guilty of any unlawful offense: provided that any person expelled from said reservation shall have the right of appeal to the county court of King William from the decision of the trustees and the members of the tribe."[3]

The Ar-ro-ha-tecks. These lived in Henrico, a little below the Powhatans. Their military force was thirty warriors. The chief was Ash-u-a-quid.[4]

Their chief town was Ar-ro-ha-teck.[5]

The Ap-po-ma-tucks. This tribe lived on the river of that name, in Chesterfield County, and counted sixty warriors. Their wer-ó-ance was

---

[1] House built after the English method.   [2] 2 Hening, 155.
[3] Acts 1893-4, p. 973; 1895-6, p. 923.
[4] Smith, vol. i., pp. 116, 117, 142.   [5] Burk, vol. iii., p. 89.

Co-quo-na-sum. It was the Queen of this tribe who was appointed to bring Captain Smith water to wash his hands with, when he was carried captive before Powhatan. Their chief town was at Bermuda Hundred, near Petersburg.[1] It was assaulted by Sir Thomas Dale in December, 1611, in revenge for some injuries done by them, and taken without the loss of a man.[2] They were bitter enemies of the English, and were among those against whom Bacon conducted his campaign in 1676.

Over one of the small villages of this tribe ruled a sister of Co-quo-na-sum. In 1610 she lured fourteen of the English into her town, insisting upon their leaving their guns in the boat. The women were afraid of them, she said. The English were slaughtered to a man. In revenge, the town was burned, and many of the Indians slain.[3]

The Yough-ta-munds, also written **Yough-i-a-nunds.** They lived on the headwaters of the Pamunkey, which in that part bore this name, probably in Hanover County, or on the south side of the York, possibly in both places. The word "yough" in Indian meant four. We may surmise from this fact, that this tribe was a composite one.[4]

This tribe once numbered seventy, and its wer-ó-ance was Po-mis-ca-tuck.[5]

---

[1] Smith, vol. i., pp. 116, 117, 142, 162; Burk, vol. iii., p. 89.
[2] Stith, p. 124.   [3] *Historie of Travaile into Virginia,* p. 56.
[4] Smith, vol. i., pp. 117, 142.
[5] *Historie of Travaile into Virginia,* p. 62.

These six were the inherited tribes, the following were added to them, by the conquests or diplomacy of Powhatan.

We will first take the tribes on the James, or its tributaries and connections. They were:

The We-an-ocks. These lived in Charles City, Prince George and Surry counties, and claimed one hundred warriors. Their King was Ka-quoth-o-cun,[1] and their chief town, Wey-o-noke.[2]

This tribe is mentioned in the acts. It was their king who illegally sold the Powhatan Indian, already mentioned.

They are again mentioned in the acts, in 1693, when the Surry County Court was ordered "to assign a particular mark to each of the towns of the Weyonock Indians" by which all their hogs were to be marked, and providing penalties for purchasing any not properly marked.[3]

The Pas-pa-heghs. This tribe lived in James City and Charles City counties, and in their territory Jamestown was located. They numbered forty warriors, and their wer-ó-ance was Wo-chin-cho-punck. Their chief town was at Sandy Point, on the James. Wo-chin-cho-punck violently resented the intrusion of the English into his territories. He was taken prisoner by Captain Smith, and carried to Jamestown.[4] He escaped, and was finally killed by the English, on February 9, 1610.

[1] Smith, vol. i., p. 116.
[2] Burk, vol. iii., p. 89.
[3] 3 Hening, 109.
[4] Smith, vol. i., p. 223.

Captain Smith tells us that he kept "the king of Pas-pa-hegh in shackles, and put his men to double tasks in chains, till nine and thirty of their kings paid us contribution, and the offending savages sent to Jamestown, to punish at our own discretion: in the two years I stayed there, I had not a man slain." [1]

The king of this tribe had certainly good ground for his opposition to the Jamestown settlement. We are told of those who held Smith in captivity: "Much they threatened to assault our fort, as they were solicited by the king of Pas-pa-hegh, who showed at our fort great signs of sorrow for this mischance." [2]

The story of the death of this chief is thus told us by Strachey:

"Wo-chin-cho-punck, wer-ó-ance of Pas-pa-hegh, on whom on the 9th of February, 1610, whilst he, with a company of his people, was attempting some practice upon our old blockhouse at Jamestown, and had been for the same sulking about there some two or three days and nights, Captain George Percy, governor of the town, sent forth Ensign Powell and Ensign Waller to make surprise of him, if they could possibly, and bring him alive into the town; but they not finding him at any such advantage, yet loath to loose him, or let him escape altogether, set upon him (he being one of the mightiest and strongest savages that Powhatan had under him, and was therefore one of his champions, and one who had killed

[1] Smith, vol. ii., p. 100.   [2] Smith's *True Relation*, p. 28.

treacherously many of our men, as he could beguile them, or as he, at any time found them by chance single in the woods, strayed beyond the command of the blockhouse), and Powell running upon him, thrust him twice through the body with an arming sword[1]; howbeit, his people came in so fast, and shot their arrows so thick, as our men being unarmed[2] (in their doublets[3] and hose[4] only) and without pieces,[5] were fain to retire whilst the Indians recovered the wer-ó-ance's body, and carried it away, with a mighty quickness and speed of foot, and with a horrible yell and howling; howbeit, the lieutenant of the blockhouse, one Puttock, followed hard and over-reached one of the cro-nock-o-es, or chief men, and, closing with him, overthrew him, and, with his dagger, sent him to accompany his master in the other world."[6]

The Or-zi-nies. This tribe dwelt upon the north bank of the Chickahominy. The name of their village appears on the map as O-ze-nick, in James City County. Their wer-ó-ance was Kis-san-a-co-men. They were of an independent nature, and resented, and resisted, the payment of the tribute of corn, when demanded by Sir George Yeardley, after the departure of Sir Thomas Dale.[7]

The Chick-a-hom-i-nys. This tribe lived on

[1] A sword made especially for use in battle.
[2] Without their armor.
[3] An outer body-garment worn by men.
[4] A man's garment covering the legs and waist.   [5] Firearms.
[6] *Historie of Travaile into Virginia*, p. 59.   [7] Stith, p. 140.

the river named after them in New Kent County. They occupied a peculiar position of independence. At one time they were under Powhatan's authority, but freed themselves from it, and made treaties with the English on their own account, containing stipulations for their protection against him. They are described as a "dogged nation," who were too well acquainted with our wants, refusing to trade, with as much scorn and insolency as they could express. They had over three hundred warriors.[1]

Their chief town was Or-a-pax.[2]

Stith gives us this account of this tribe; writing of the year 1614, after the marriage of Rolfe and Pocahontas:

"The Chick-a-hom-i-nies were a stout, daring and free people. They had no wer-ó-ance, or single ruler, but were governed, in a republican form, by their elders. These were their priests, and some of the wisest of their old men, as assistants to them. In consequence of these principles of government, they took all opportunities of shaking off Powhatan's yoke, whom they looked upon and hated, as a tyrant. And, therefore, they had taken advantage of these late times of hostility and danger as well to the Indians as to the English, to assert their liberty. But now, seeing Powhatan so closely linked with the English, both in affinity and friendship, they were in great concern and dread, lest he should

---

[1] Smith, vol. i., pp. 116, 193; vol. ii., pp. 16–17.
[2] Burk, vol. iii., p. 89.

bring them again to his subjection. To prevent which, they sent ambassadors to Sir Thomas Dale; excusing all former injuries, and promising ever after to be King James's faithful subjects: That they would relinquish the name of Chick-a-hom-i-nies, and be called Tas-san-tes-sus, or Englishmen, and that Sir Thomas Dale should be their governor, as the King's deputy. Only they desired to be governed by their own laws, under their eight elders, as his substitutes.

"Sir Thomas Dale, hoping for some advantage from this, willingly accepted their offer. At the day appointed, with Captain Argall and fifty men, he went to Chick-a-hom-i-ny; where he found the people assembled, expecting his coming. They treated him kindly; and the next morning, having held a council, the peace was concluded on these conditions:

"That they should forever be called Englishmen, and be true subjects to King James and his deputies;

"That they should neither kill, nor detain, any of the English, or of their cattle, but should bring them home;

"That they should be always ready, to furnish the English with three hundred men, against the Spaniards, or any other enemy;

"That they should not enter any of the English towns, before sending in word, that they were new Englishmen;

"That every fighting man, at gathering their corn, should bring two bushels to the store, as a tribute; for which he should receive as many hatchets:

"That the eight chief men should see all this performed, or receive the punishment themselves; and for their diligence, they should have a red coat, a copper chain, and King James's picture and be accounted his nobleman." [1]

We have the following references and provisions in regard to them in the Acts of 1660:

"Upon the petition of Harquip the Mangoi of the Chickahomini Indians to have all the lands from Mr. Mallory's bounds to the head of Mattaponi River and into the woods to the Pamunkeys, it is accordingly ordered that the said land be confirmed to the said Indians by patent, and that no Englishman shall upon any pretense disturb them in their said bounds, nor purchase it of them unless the major part of the great men shall freely and voluntarily declare their consent in the quarter court or assembly.

"Whereas a certain grant hath been made to the Chickahomini Indians of certain lands in which tract Major-General Manwaring Hamond claimeth a divident [2] of two thousand acres granted him by patent, it is ordered, that the said Major-General Hamond be desired to purchase the same of the Indians or to procure their consent, for the preservation of the country's honor and reputation." [3]

[1] Stith, pp. 130, 131, 140, 149. [2] Dividend, a share or portion.
[3] A case of conflicting patents in which the English claimant is virtually ordered to make terms with the Indians in a manner satisfactory to them.

The Tribes and Nations 345

"Harquip, mangoi of the Chickahomini Indians, in behalf of himself and the other Indians the fourth day of April, 1661, did acknowledge before the grand assembly the sale of a parcel of land from the cliffs to the little creek to Mr. Philip Mallory, being formerly surveyed by Lt.-Col. Abrahall, and James Cole, containing seven hundred forty-three acres according to a survey of the same made for the said Mr. Mallory by George Morris the twentieth of June last." [1]

We have the following reference to them in 1662: "Whereas information hath been made that one Edward Dennis hath, without title or claim, seated himself in the Indian town of Chickahomini; it is therefore ordered that the said honorable the governor be pleased to send his warrant for the said Dennis, and as he finds occasion to give order for his continuance or removal." [2]

Members of this tribe still survive. As mentioned in the account of the Pamunkeys, one of the women met there, who had married into that tribe, was herself spoken of, and recognized as being originally Chickahomini.

The **Qui-yong-he-o-han-ocks**, also called the **Tap-pa-han-nas**. They lived in Surry and Prince George counties, and claimed sixty warriors. They are spoken of as "a small nation of Indians seated on the south side of the James, about ten miles above Jamestown." Their chief

[1] 2 Hening, 34, 35, 39.   [2] Ibid., 161.

was Pe-pis-cu-mah, also called Pe-pis-co. "This good king did ever affect the English above all others; and although he was very zealous to his false gods, yet he confessed, that the English God as much exceeded his, as their guns did his bow and arrows; and in time of drought he would often send presents to Captain Smith, to pray to his god for rain."[1]

The chief town was about Upper Chipoak Creek.[2]

There is a romance about Pe-pis-co. He fell in love with, and stole away from the terrible O-pe-chan-ca-nough, one of his "chief women." For this offense, Powhatan deposed him from being wer-ó-ance of this tribe, and put in his place, one of his sons, Tat-a-co-pe, then an infant, with his mother O-ho-lasc, as regent.

Pe-pis-co was suffered to remain in the country, and retained a little village upon the James, with some few people about him. He lost his kingdom, but he kept the woman he loved. Strachey tells us about this love affair. He says he made her "his best beloved," and that "she travels with him upon any remove, in hunting time, or in his visitation of us, by which means, twice or thrice in a summer, she hath come unto our town; nor is so handsome a savage woman as I have seen amongst them, yet, with a kind of pride, can take upon her a show of greatness; for we have seen her forbear to come out of her

[1] Smith, vol. i., p. 116; Stith, p. 99.
[2] Burk, vol. iii., p. 89.

The Tribes and Nations 347

quintan or boat through the water, as the others, both maids and married women, usually do, unless she were carried forth between two of her servants. I was once early at her house (it being summer time), when she was laid without doors, under the shadow of a broad-leaved tree, upon a pallet of osiers,[1] spread over with four or five gray mats, herself covered with a fair white dressed deer skin or two; and when she rose, she had a maid who fetched her a frontal[2] of white coral and pendants of great but imperfect colored and worst drilled pearls, which she put into her ears, and a chain, with long links of copper which they call Tap-o-an-tam-i-na-is, and which came twice or thrice about her neck, and they account a jolly[3] ornament; and sure thus attired with some variety of feathers and flowers stuck in their hair they seem as debonaire, quaint, and well pleased as (I wist) a daughter of the house of Austria behune[4] with all her jewels; likewise her maid fetched her a mantel, which they call put-ta-wus, which is like a side cloak, made of blue feathers, so artificially[5] and thick sewed together, that it seemed like a deep purple satin, and is very smooth and sleek; and after she brought her water for her hands, and then a branch or two of fresh green asshen[6] leaves, as for a towel to dry them."[7]

---

[1] Dried willow branches. [2] An ornament for the forehead.
[3] Beautiful. [4] Bedecked.
[5] Made with so much art or skill. [6] Ash.
[7] Strachey, *History of Travaile into Virginia*, pp. 57-8.

The War-as-coy-acks. These lived in Isle of Wight County, and could muster sixty fighting men. Their chief was Tac-kon-e-kin-ta-co. They appear frequently in the early history. Living on the same river, and between Jamestown and the sea, the settlers were forever passing by their territory. The king of this tribe gave Captain Smith kindly warning against Powhatan, when Smith was on his way to pay him a visit, telling him that Powhatan meant to kill him.

The name is pronounced War-ris-queek.

The following account of an incident in connection with this tribe and its wer-ó-ance is preserved by Strachey:

"Tac-kon-e-kin-ta-co, an old wer-ó-ance of Warraskoyack, whom Captain Newport brought prisoner with his son Tangoit about 1610, to our lord general,[1] lying then at Point Comfort, and whom again his lordship released upon promises and a solemn contract, made by the old man, to exchange with his lordship, after he should have gathered in his harvest, in August following, five hundred bushels of wheat, beans, and peas, for copper, beads, and hatchets; and for the better color (carrying away his son) and left a nephew (as he said) of his with his lordship, as a pawn or hostage, until the performance; howbeit, the imposture nephew, privy beforehand to the falsehood of the old man, watching his opportunity, leapt overboard one night (being kept

[1] Lord De la War.

The Tribes and Nations 349

in the *Delawar*[1]); and to be more sure of him at that time, fettered both legs together, and put a sea gown[2] upon him, yet he adventured to get clear by swimming, and either to recover the south shore, or to sink in the attempt. Which of either was his fortune we know not, only (if he miscarried) we never found his body nor gown, and the Indians of Warraskoyack would oftentimes afterward mock us, and call to us for him, and at length make a great laughter, and tell us he was come home; how true or false is no great matter; but indeed the old king, after that time, refused to perform the former bargain, for which his lordship, to give them to understand how he would not be so dealt withal, sent forth two companies, those of his lordship's own company, under the command of Captain Brewster, and some seamen, under Captain Argall, who fell upon two towns of his, and burnt them to the ground, with all their goodly furniture of mats and dishes, wooden pots and platters, for of this sort is all their goodly epitrapezia[3] or vessels belonging to their use for the table, or what else."[4]

In 1623, the tribe was attacked for the participation it had taken in the massacre of 1622.[5] And later, a fort, or "castle," was built by the English within its borders.[6]

[1] The ship named after Lord De la War.
[2] A skirted garment or wrapper meant to be worn at sea.
[3] Things put upon the table.
[4] Strachey, *History of Travaile into Virginia*, pp. 58-9.
[5] Smith, vol. i., pp. 116, 180.   [6] Stith, pp. 303, 322.

The tribe gave its name to one of the original eight counties into which the colony was divided.

The principal village of this tribe was War-as-coy-ack.[1] This was in the neighborhood of Smithfield.

The Nan-se-monds. This was a large tribe, living in the county named for them. They had two hundred warriors, and four wer-ó-ances, Wey-ho-ho-mo, Am-e-pet-ough, Wey-on-gop-o, and Tirch-tough.[2]

The following incident is told of them. In order to keep things quiet at Jamestown, Captain Smith sent one Martin off to make a settlement at Nan-se-mond. "That nation, having been reduced to subjection and contribution used him kindly; yet such was his unreasonable jealousy[3] and fear, that he surprised[4] the poor naked king, and his monuments[5] and houses, with the island, wherein he lived, and there fortified himself. But the Indians soon perceiving his fear and distraction, ventured to assault him; and they killed several of his men, released their king, and gathered and carried off a thousand bushels of corn; whilst he, in the meantime, never once offered to intercept them but sent to the President,[6] then at the Falls,[7] for

---

[1] Burk, vol. iii., p. 89.
[2] Smith, vol. i., p. 116; *Historie of Travaile into Virginia*, p. 59.
[3] Distrust of the Indians.   [4] Attacked without warning.
[5] The houses in which were deposited the embalmed remains of the Indian kings.
[6] Captain Smith.   [7] The falls of the James.

The Tribes and Nations 351

thirty soldiers. These were presently sent him from Jamestown."[1]

Their chief town was Nan-se-mond, situated on the river of that name, about the mouth of West Branch.[2]

In 1816, new trustees were appointed for the Nansemonds. These were empowered to make reasonable rules and regulations for the government of the tribe and the expenditure of the money held in trust for them. This was to continue so long as the tribe had any members still living. Any funds remaining were to be paid into the public treasury.[3]

The Ches-a-peaks. This tribe live in Norfolk and Princess Anne Counties, and according to Smith, in his day, numbered one hundred warriors.[4]

The tribe took its name, which means The Mother of Waters, from the bay and river which bordered its territories. The bay has kept its original name, but the Chesapeake River is now called the Elizabeth.[5]

Lane, who visited this tribe in 1585, said that "the territory and soil of the Ches-e-pe-ans (being distant fifteen miles from the shore), for pleasantness of seat, for temperature of climate, for fertility of soil, and for the commodity of the sea, besides multitudes of bears (being an excellent good victual), and great woods of sassa-

[1] Stith, p. 104.
[2] Burk, vol. iii., p. 89.
[3] Acts 1816-17, p. 174.
[4] Smith, vol. i., p. 116.
[5] Stith, pp. 13, 73.

fras and walnut trees, are not to be excelled by any other whatsoever."

The names of three of the towns of this tribe are known to us: Ap-a-sus, situated on the western side of the mouth of the Lynnhaven River; Ches-a-pi-ooc, on the western bank of that stream something more than half way to its source, and Ski-co-ak, situated on the eastern side of the Elizabeth River, on the site of the City of Norfolk. All were palisadoed as they appear on White and de Brÿ's map made in connection with the Roanoke Island settlement.

Ski-co-ak is mentioned in the earliest of all the accounts. Captain Barlow, in his report to Raleigh of the voyage made in 1584, says, measuring from Pom-e-i-ock: "Six days' journey from the same is situated their [the Indians'] greatest city, called Ski-co-ak, which this people [those of Roanoke Island] affirm to be very great; but the savages were never at it, only they speak of it by the report of their fathers and other men, whom they have heard affirm it to be above one hour's journey about it."

Lane also in speaking of this region said that the place of greatest strength of the king who ruled here was "an island, situate in a bay, the water round about the island very deep." From the geography of this region it would appear that this must refer to the same place.

A great Indian town therefore once existed here, but the later writers, Smith stating the military strength of this tribe at only one hundred, and Burk,[1] saying that the principal town of this tribe was about Lynnhaven, which would make it either Ap-a-sus or Ches-a-pi-ooc instead of Ski-co-ak, are explained by a statement in Strachey.[2] He tells us of the prophecy, already mentioned, made by the Indian priests to Powhatan, that from the east, through the Chesapeake Bay, a people would arise which would destroy his empire. He therefore, among others, waged war upon and destroyed the Chesapeaks, fearful of everything and everybody in that region.

Ski-co-ak, no doubt, at this time fell and its greatness vanished. In Strachey's time, he says, that the Indians who then occupied this territory were "new inhabitants," Powhatan having peopled the conquered territory with those on whom he could rely.

The Ke-cough-tans. These Indians lived in Elizabeth City County, their chief town being Ros-cows at, or near, Hampton. They had once been a large and powerful tribe, but had been reduced by war to twenty.[3]

Strachey gives us this account of the land of the Ke-cough-tans, which, including as it does Hampton and Old Point Comfort, is of more than ordinary importance:

"Po-chins, one of Powhatan's sons at Ke-cough-tan, was the young wer-ó-ance there at the

[1] Burk, vol. iii., p. 89.
[2] *Historie of Travaile into Virginia*, p. 105.
[3] Smith, vol. i., p. 116; Burk, vol. iii., p. 89.

same time when Sir Thomas Gates, lieutenant-general, took possession of it. It is an ample and fair country indeed, an admirable portion of land, comparatively high, wholesome, and fruitful; the seat sometimes of a thousand Indians and three hundred Indian houses, and those Indians, as it may well appear, better husbands[1] than in any part else that we have observed, which is the reason that so much ground is there cleared and opened, enough, with little labor already prepared, to receive corn, or make vineyards of two or three thousand acres: and where, beside, we find many fruit-trees, a kind of gooseberry, cherries, and other plums, the maricock,[2] apple, and many pretty copsies or boskes (as it were) of mulberry trees, and is (indeed) a delicate and necessary seat for a city or chief fortification, being so near (within three miles by water) the mouth of our bay, and is well appointed a fit seat for one of our chief commanders.

"Upon the death of an old wer-ó-ance of this place, some fifteen or sixteen years since (being too powerful neighbors to side[3] the great Powhatan), it is said Powhatan, taking the advantage, subtly stepped in and conquered the people, killing the chief and most of them, and the reserved he transported over the river, craftily changing their seat and quartering them

---

[1] Husbandmen.
[2] The maracock is the passion-flower. The fruit is of the size and color of a pomegranate.   [3] To be by the side of.

amongst his own people, until now at length the remainder of those living have with much suit obtained of him Pa-yan-ka-tanck, which he not long since (as you have heard likewise) dispeopled. They might have made of able men for the wars, thirty."[1]

On the York, the former "River of Pamunkey," were the following:

The Wer-o-wo-co-mo-cos. Thus were called those living at this place, which is the best known Indian settlement in Virginia, being "the chief place of council," and Powhatan's favorite residence. It was in Gloucester County, on the north side of the York, and is thus spoken of by Smith: "About twenty-five miles lower on the north side of this river is Wer-o-wo-co-mo-co, where their great king inhabited when I was delivered him prisoner; yet there are not past forty able men."[2] Smith is here not narrating his captivity, but the tribes in Virginia.

The principal town of this tribe was Wer-o-wo-co-mo-co, near Rosewell.[3]

The Kis-ki-acks. This tribe lived on the south side of the York, nearly opposite Wer-o-wo-co-mo-co. They numbered forty or fifty men. Their wer-ó-ance was Ot-ta-ho-tin. This place was one of Powhatan's strongholds.[4] The name of this tribe was afterwards corrupted by the

---

[1] *Historie of Travaile into Virginia*, p. 60.
[2] Smith, vol. i., p. 117.
[3] Burk, vol. iii., p. 89. [4] Smith, vol. i., pp. 117, 206.

English into Cheesecake, and so appears in the acts of the Grand Assembly.[1]

Their principal town was Kis-ki-ack, in York County.[2]

We have the following references to them in the early acts:

"Considering the great use and benefit the country may enjoy from the Chess-koi-ack Indians being kindly used by us, and being sensible that with the few guns they have amongst them they cannot prejudice us being a small, inconsiderable nation, it is ordered by the present Grand Assembly to show other Indians how kind we are to such who are obedient to our laws that the said Chis-koi-ack Indians quietly hold and enjoy the land they are now seated upon, and have the free use of the guns they now have, any act or order of assembly to the contrary notwithstanding."

"Whereas, by the report of Lieutenant-Colonel John Walker, who was appointed by the honorable Governor to enquire thereinto, it appears that Mrs. Mary Ludlow, relict and executrix of Lieutenant-Colonel Thomas Ludlow, deceased, entrencheth upon the Ches-qui-ack Indians' land at Py-an-ka-tanck. It is ordered by the Assembly that the said Indians enjoy their whole tract of land according to the said survey and that the said Ludlows' heirs enjoy the remainder of their patent, and further order that no other person enjoying or being seated on any part of

[1] Stith, p. 53. [2] Burk, vol. iii., p. 89.

The Tribes and Nations

the said Indians' lands possess the same but to be with all convenient speed removed, and the commissioners appointed by the right honorable Governor to enquire into and settle all differences and disputes concerning the said Indians' lands."[1]

The following eleven tribes are mentioned by Strachey as also being upon the Pamunkey, by which he meant the York and its branches:

The Can-taun-kacks, one hundred warriors, the chief, O-hon-na-mo.

The Mum-map-a-cu-nes, one hundred, their wer-ó-ance being Ot-ton-de-a-com-moc.

The Pa-ta-uncks, one hundred; wer-ó-ance, Es-sen-a-taugh.

The Och-a-han-nankes, forty, with the chief U-rop-a-ack.

The Cas-sa-pe-cocks, one hundred, with the chief Keig-hang-ton.

The Ka-pos-e-cocks, four hundred, with the wer-ó-ance Wey-a-mat.

The Pam-a-rekes, four hundred; wer-ó-ance, At-tas-quin-tan.

The Sham-a-pas, one hundred, with the wer-ó-ance Nan-su-a-punck.

The Or-a-paks, fifty; Powhatan himself being the wer-ó-ance.

The Chep-e-cho, three hundred with their wer-ó-ance O-pop-oh-cum-unck.

The Par-a-co-nos, ten; having only a Taux-wer-ó-ance,[2] At-tos-so-munck.

---

[1] 2 Hening, 39, 153.
[2] That is a little, subordinate, or vice-wer-ó-ance.

As being in command of these tribes and three others which are likewise included in our list, Strachey names O-pe-chan-ca-nough, Ke-quo-taugh, and Taugh-ha-i-ten, all three Powhatan's brethren, who he says are the triumviri, as it were, or three kings of a country called O-pe-chan-e-ke-no, upon the head of Pamunkey River, and these may make three hundred men.[1]

It is interesting to learn from this, that O-pe-chan-ca-nough's name was, like his brother Powhatan's, derived from that of a place. It was a territorial name, similar to that often borne by the nobles of other countries.

On the **Pa-yan-ka-tank** River lived a tribe of that name, which numbered about fifty or sixty serviceable men. They lived on the north side of the stream, near its mouth in Middlesex County.[2] Their principal town was at Turk's ferry.[3]

The **Pa-yan-ka-tanks,** who numbered forty to fifty when Strachey, that observant first secretary of the colony, wrote his account of his travels, are said by him to be the remains of the conquered Ke-cough-tans, transported there by Powhatan. The original Pa-yan-ka-tanks were destroyed, or reduced to slavery by Powhatan in 1608. They were then his neighbors and subjects. We have a brief account of this tragedy: "The occasion was to us unknown; but the

---

[1] *Historie of Travaile into Virginia*, p. 62.
[2] Smith, vol. i., pp. 117, 160.   [3] Burk, vol. iii., p. 89.

manner was thus performed. First, he sent divers of his men to lodge amongst them one night, pretending a general hunt, who were to give the allarum[1] unto an ambuscado[2] of a greater company within the woods, who, upon the sign given at the hour appointed, environed all the houses, and fell to the execution. Twenty-four men they killed outright (the rest escaping by fortune and their swift footmanship); and the long hair of the one side of their heads, with the skin cased off with shells or reeds, they brought away to Powhatan. They surprised also the women and children and the wer-ó-ance, all whom they presented to Powhatan. The locks of hair, with their skins, they hanged on a line between two trees; and of these Powhatan made ostentation, as of a great triumph, at Wer-o-wo-co-mo-co, not long after, showing them to such of the English as came unto him at his appointment, to trade with him for corn, thinking to have terrified them with this spectacle."[3]

On the Rappahannock more Indians lived than on any of the other rivers. The north side of this fine stream was covered with their villages. Among these tribes were:

The Cut-tat-a-wo-men. These lived on the north side of the river, in Lancaster County near the Chesapeake Bay. Here they had one

---
[1] Signal.   [2] Ambuscade.
[3] Strachey, *Historie of Travaile into Virginia*, p. 36.

branch of their tribe, with thirty fighting men, and another, much farther up the river, in King George County, of twenty. Their king was kindly disposed towards the English.[1]

Their principal town in King George was about Lamb Creek, and that in Lancaster, at Corotoman.[2]

The Rap-a-han-ocks. These were frequently called **Top-pa-han-ocks.** They also lived on the north side of the river named from them, and could count one hundred men.[3]

They are mentioned in the acts in the year 1662, and were thus protected in regard to holding their tribal lands:

"It is ordered by this present assembly upon the report of the committee for the Indian affairs, that Colonel Moore Ffantleroy enjoy at present no more of the land he is now seated upon than what is cleared with the houses built upon and marsh lying before it, and that he pay to the King of Rappahannock Indians fifteen matchcoats before he depart the town in part of thirty due per a former agreement, and the other fifteen when the differences between him and the said Indians shall be ended by the commissioners to be appointed by the right honorable Governor, provided they allow him five hundred acres of high land ground belonging to his said divident,[4] Provided if the said commissioners shall not

---

[1] Smith, vol. i., pp. 117, 185.   [2] Burk, vol. iii., 89.
[3] Smith, vol. i., pp. 117, 184-5.
[4] Dividend, that is, share of land due him.

The Tribes and Nations

determine the same then to be referred to the next assembly, and all other claims of the said Ffantleroy's to any other land of the said Indians are hereby declared void."[1]

Their principal town was on Rappahannock Creek, in Richmond County.[2]

The Nan-taugh-ta-cunds. These were also called Nand-tangh-ta-cunds. They lived on the south side of the river, in Caroline and Essex counties, and boasted one hundred and fifty men. Their king was friendly to the English.[3] Their chief town was at Port Tobacco Creek.[4]

The Mo-raugh-ta-cunds. These were also called the Mo-raugh-ta-ow-nas. They lived upon the north side of the Rappahannock, in Lancaster and Richmond counties, and had a fighting force of eighty men.[5] Their principal town was on Moratico River.[6]

The Pis-sa-secks. This tribe dwelt on the north side of the Rappahannock, in King George and Richmond counties. It is mentioned as having a king kindly disposed towards the English.[7] Their chief town was above Leeds town.[8]

The Do-egs. This tribe dwelt in Stafford County, not far from the site of Fredericksburg, on the north side of the Rappahannock. They are mentioned in connection with stealing the

---

[1] 5 Hening, 152.
[2] Burk, vol. iii., p. 89.
[3] Smith, vol. i., pp. 117, 160, 185.
[4] Burk, vol. iii., p. 89.
[5] Smith, vol. i., pp. 117, 184.
[6] Burk, vol. iii., p. 89.
[7] Smith, vol. i., p. 185.
[8] Burk, vol. iii., p. 89.

hogs of the early settlers at Jamestown, and later, in the acts of Assembly, as committing many murders of the English.[1]

On the Potomac lived several tribes, of whom we can name:

The Wigh-co-com-o-cos, who lived on the south side of the river, near its entrance into Chesapeake Bay. They numbered one hundred and thirty men.[2]

Their principal town was on Wi-co-com-i-co River, in Northumberland County.[3]

They were celebrated for being very small in size.[4]

The Cek-a-ca-wons. This tribe lived on the same side, as the above, a little farther up the river.[5]

Their principal town was on the Coan River.[6]

The Nom-i-nies. This tribe lived on the south side of the river, in Westmoreland County. A creek and cliffs fronting on the Potomac are named for them.[7]

The O-naw-man-i-ents. This was a tribe of one hundred living on this river.[8]

Their principal town was on Nomini River, in Westmoreland County.[9]

The Pa-taw-o-mekes. These gave their name finally to the whole river, which was at first

---

[1] 2 Hening, 193.   [2] Smith, vol. i., p. 118; 1 Hening, 515.
[3] Burk, vol. iii., p. 89.   [4] Smith, vol. i., p. 129.
[5] Smith, vol. i., p. 118.   [6] Burk, vol. iii., p. 89.
[7] Stith, p. 53.   [8] Smith, vol. i., pp. 118, 160.
[9] Burk, vol. iii., p. 89.

known as the Co-hon-go-roo-ta, at least from its junction with the Shenandoah, eastward to the Chesapeake Bay. They lived some distance up the stream, on the west side, in Stafford County. They numbered two hundred. Their wer-ó-ance was Jap-a-zows, the one who helped to kidnap Pocahontas, when Argall captured her. He is described as being an old friend of Smith, and so a friend of the whole English nation, ever since the first discovery of the country.[1]

Their principal town was on Potomac Creek, in Stafford County.[2]

In 1662, the King of the Potomacs was Wa-han-gan-o-che. He was tried before the Grand Assembly on a charge of high treason and murder and acquitted.[3]

The sale of several parts of their tribal lands is thus recorded:

"Whereas Wa-han-gan-o-che, king of the Po-tow-meck Indians, acknowledged before the committee appointed for the Indian business, the sale of that whole tract of land possest by Mr. Henry Mees in Potowmeck according to the bounds and marked trees which he confest were marked in his presence and with his consent, it is ordered by the assembly that the said Mees enjoy the said land to him and his heirs for ever.

"Whereas Wa-han-gan-o-che, king of the

[1] Smith, vol. i., pp. 118, 177; Stith, p. 127.
[2] Burk, vol. iii., p. 89. [3] 2 Hening, 149.

Potowmeck Indians, acknowledged before the committee for the Indians' business that he sold a parcell of land to Mr. Peter Austin, and hath received for the same ten matchcoats, and also promised to lay out the said Austin's land with marked trees, it is ordered by the assembly that the same being accordingly bounded, Mr. Austin enjoy the same to him and his heirs for ever.

"Upon the report of the committee appointed for settling the Indian business, it is ordered by the assembly that all differences of land between colonell Gerrard Fowke and Wa-han-gan-o-che, king of the Potowmeck Indians, be referred to such persons as the governour shall commissionate therein who are fully to end and determine the same.

"It is ordered by the assembly upon the report of the committee for the Indian businesses that all the differences of land between captain Giles Brent and Wa-han-gan-o-che, king of the Potowmeck Indians, be referred to the determination of such commissioners whom the honourable governour shall appoint therein."[1]

It would appear that this king had further trouble with the English, for we find, in 1665. that a part of the money with which a fort was to be built, was to be paid for by a levy of eighty thousand pounds of tobacco, "besides the sale of the king of Potomacks land." It would seem from this that his land was confiscated for the

[1] 2 Hening, 154, 205.

The Tribes and Nations 365

use of the public. As the trained bands of James City and Surry counties were to contribute six days' work towards the perfecting the fort, it is probable that it was to be built not far from the capital.[1]

The Taux-en-ents. This tribe lived on the western side of the Potomac, in Fairfax County. They numbered forty men. Their chief was Na-men-a-cus.[2]

Their principal town was at, or near Mount Vernon, General Washington's home.[3]

The Moy-a-ons. This tribe lived on the eastern side of the Potomac, in Prince George's County, Maryland. They are represented as friendly to the English.[4]

The Sec-o-wo-com-o-cos. This tribe lived on the north side of the Potomac, and had forty warriors.[5]

We also hear of the **Po-tap-a-cos,** with twenty men; the **Pam-a-ca-e-acks,** with sixty; and the **Moy-o-wance,** with one hundred.

The **No-cotch-tanks,** with eighty, are also mentioned as living on this river.[6]

On the Patuxent River lived the following:

The Paw-tux-ents. This tribe lived upon the east side of the river to which they gave the name, in Calvert County, Maryland. Their King was Na-men-a-cus.[7]

[1] 2 Hening, 220. [2] Smith, vol. i., p. 118; vol. ii., p. 61.
[3] Burk, vol. iii., p. 89. [4] Smith, vol. i., p. 177.
[5] Smith, vol. i., p. 118. [6] Smith, vol., i., p. 118.
[7] Smith, vol. i., pp. 118, 148, 183; vol. ii., p. 61.

The Ac-quin-ta-nack-su-aks. This tribe, with the one above, and the next, is merely mentioned as living on this river.

The Mat-ta-pan-i-ents. It is said of these three, that they could only muster two hundred and that "they inhabit together, and are not so dispersed as the rest. These of all others we found most civil to give entertainment."[1]

On the Eastern Shore, the tribes which were possibly under Powhatan's dominion were:

The O-zi-nies. This tribe lived in Queen Anne County, Maryland.[2]

The Kus-kar-a-wa-ocks. This tribe lived in Dorchester County, Maryland, on the river of that name, also called the Kus, and now, the Nan-ti-coke. They numbered two hundred.[3]

By some, this tribe is given greater importance than this statement would imply. One map, which the writer has seen, gives their name to all the region now known as the Eastern Shore of Maryland, and a large part of Delaware, as if they were an independent confederacy.

The Tants Wigh-co-com-i-cos. This tribe lived in Worcester County, Maryland, on the Po-co-moke, or Wigh-co River.

Smith says of these two tribes: "The people of those rivers are of little stature, of another language from the rest, and very rude."[4]

The Gin-gas-kins. We know nothing of this

---

[1] Smith, vol. i., p. 118.
[2] *Ibid.*, p. 120.
[3] *Ibid.*, p. 120.
[4] *Ibid.*, p. 120.

tribe except that in 1813, the tribal holding of lands by the Gin-gas-kin Indians, in the county of Northampton, was done away with, and an equitable division of the lands was made to the members of the tribe, to be held by them separately, in fee simple. These lands were to be free from taxes so long as they should be held by the members of the tribe or their descendants.

The Ac-co-han-ocks. This tribe lived just about on the boundary line of Accomac and Northampton counties, on the Bay side. They numbered forty men. Their king was Kep-to-peke.[1]

Their principal town was on the Ac-co-hon-noc River.[2]

The Ac-cow-macks. This tribe lived nearly at the south end of Northampton County. They numbered eighty warriors. Captain Smith said of the wer-ó-ance of this tribe: "This king was the comeliest, proper, civil savage we encountered." He is elsewhere spoken of as the "laughing king." He says, in general, of this tribe, that it "doth equalize any of the territories of Powhatan, and speak his language." The soil is also praised, and the good harbors for small vessels. On the whole, we are informed that this was one of the very best of the tribes.[3]

Their chief town was about Cherton's, in Northampton County.[4]

---

[1] Smith, vol. i., p. 120; vol. ii., p. 61.
[2] Burk, vol. iii., p. 89. This river is now called Occohannock Creek.
[3] Smith, vol. i., pp. 120, 173; vol. ii., p. 63.
[4] Burk, vol. iii., p. 89.

We have the following reference to them in the acts of 1660:

"Whereas the Indians of Accomack have complained that they are very much straitened for want of land, and that the English seat so near them, that they receive very much damage in their corn, It is ordered that the right honorable the governor give commission to two or three gentlemen with a surveyor living on this side the bay (that have no relation to Accomack), to go over thither, and lay out such a proportion of land for the said Indians as shall be sufficient for their maintenance with hunting and fishing excluded, And that the land so laid out to be so secured to the Indians that they may have no power to alienate it, or any part of it hereafter to the English."[1]

We have attempted, not without difficulty, to enumerate the many tribes which were under Powhatan's rule. We are by no means satisfied that there are not mistakes in the above list; we may both have inserted tribes which do not belong there, and omitted others which do. The sources of information on the subject are none too clear.

It will be observed that some of these tribes bore the names now given to the rivers in the State. A few of our Indian names of rivers are due, no doubt, to the fact that they were so called, not because such or such an Indian word would be a good name to apply to such or such a

[1] 2 Hening, 13.

The Tribes and Nations

stream, but the Meherrin River was the Meherrin River, because the Meherrin Indians lived upon that river, and so on. Conversely, the rivers, which were, of course, much older than the tribes, and which had been named by them, gave their names to many of the tribes living on them, among these clearly are the Potomacs, the Rappahanocks, the Chesapeaks, the Patuxents, the Chickahominys, the Appomattox, and so on. Captain Smith, himself, writing of this fact in his *General History* says: "The most of those rivers are inhabited by several nations, or rather families of the name of the rivers."

Other tribes evidently took their names from the places where they lived. Among these were the Pamunkeys, the War-as-coy-acks, the Nanse-monds, the Ac-co-macs. The Cherokees, however, derive their name from their descent —Sons of Fire they called themselves.

How much of interest lies locked up in these names, most of which will remain untranslatable forever!

The domain ruled by Powhatan was surrounded by enemies who were forever at war with it. Among these may be most conspicuously mentioned the **Man-a-kins,** or **Mon-a-cans,** and the **Man-na-ho-acks.** Both of these powers lay to the west, the first on the headwaters of the James, and the latter on the headwaters of the Rappahannock. It was from this region that the colony had endless trouble, and many of its defensive measures, after its first struggles with those nearer Jamestown, were directed towards stopping the incursions of these enemies, who were not only enemies of the English, but of the native Indian population, which lived in the portion of Virginia first occupied by the English.

Strachey tells us in speaking of the different nations of Indians in Virginia: "The people differ not much in nature, habit, or condition, only they are more daring upon us; and before we erected our forts amongst them, there was ever enmity, and open wars, between the high and low country, going by the names of Mon-o-cans and Powhatans."[1]

The **Man-na-ho-acs,** included eight tribes, these were:

The **Man-na-ho-acs,** who lived in Stafford and Spottsylvania counties; the **Shack-a-ko-nies,** in Spottsylvania; the **Whon-ken-ties,** and the **Taux-i-tan-i-ans** in Fauquier County; the **Teg-ni-na-ties,** and the **Has-si-nun-ga-es,** in Culpeper; the **Ont-ponies,** and the **Ste-gar-a-kies** in Orange County.[2] The last seven paid tribute to the Man-na-ho-acs.[3]

The **Mon-a-cans** included five tribes:

The **Mon-a-cans,** who lived on the James, above the falls, and numbered thirty warriors, their chief town, Ras-sawck, being in the fork of James River[4]; the **Mon-a-sic-cap-a-noes,** who

---

[1] *Historie of Travaile into Virginia*, p. 27.   [2] Burk, vol. iii., p. 89.
[3] *Historie of Travaile into Virginia*, pp. 102, 104.
[4] The southeastern extremity of Goochland County.

lived in Louisa and Fluvanna counties; the Mon-a-has-san-oes, who lived in Bedford and Buckingham counties; the Mas-sin-a-cacs, who lived in Cumberland; and the Mo-hem-en-choes, who lived in Powhatan County.[1] The four last paid tribute to the Mon-a-cans.[2]

The Mas-sa-wo-mecks. Strachey thus describes this tribe:

"Beyond the mountains, from whence is the head of the river Patomac, do inhabit the Massa-wo-mecks (Powhatan's yet mortal enemies) upon a great salt water, which by all likelihood may either be some part of Canada, some great lake, or some inlet of some sea, that may fall into the west ocean or Mar del sur.[3] These Massa-wo-mecks are a great nation, and very populous, for the inhabitants of the heads of all those rivers, especially the Pa-taw-o-mecks, the Pawtux-unts, the Sas-ques-a-han-oughes, the Tockwoghs, are continually harbored[4] and frightened by them, of whose cruelty the said people generally complained, and were very importunate with Captain Smith, and his company, in the time of their discovery, to free them from those tormentors, to which purpose they offered food, conduct, assistants, and continual subjection, which were motives sufficient for Captain Smith to promise to return with sufficient forces to constrain the

[1] Burk, vol. iii., p. 89.
[2] *Historie of Travaile into Virginia*, pp. 102, 104.
[3] South Sea, the Pacific Ocean.
[4] Forced to keep their harbors.

said Mas-sa-wo-mecks; but there were in the colony at that time such factions and base envies, as malice in some, in some ignorance, and cowardice in others, made that opportunity to be lost.

"Seven boats full of these Mas-sa-wo-mecks, the discoverers before mentioned, encountered at the head of the bay, whose targets, baskets, swords, tobacco-pipes, platters, bows and arrows, and everything, showed they much exceeded them of our parts; and their dexterity in their several boats, made of the barks of trees sewed together, and well luted[1] with gum and resin of the pine tree, argueth that they are seated upon some great water. Of these, likewise, it may please the Lord General again to inform himself, as circumstances and occasion shall serve to turn against Powhatan."[2]

Toward the north, other tribes were the **Tockwoghes**, who lived in a strongly fortified town, on a river of that name, now called the Chester,[3] and the **At-quan-a-chuks**, who lived in Delaware.

In this direction we also hear of the **Sen-e-dos**, who occupied the north fork of the Shenandoah until 1732, when they were exterminated by hostile tribes from the south. And the **Tus-ca-roras**, whose villages were near Martinsburg, in the present county of Berkeley.[4]

---

[1] Having the cracks or openings closed.
[2] Strachey's *Historie of Travaile into Virginia*, pp. 104–5.
[3] Smith, vol. i., p. 182.
[4] Peyton's *History of Augusta County*, p. 6.

This was presumably a branch of the great nation of that name which was well known.

The **Cin-e-las**, on the Upper Potomac, are mentioned, but not much is known of them.

And the **Pas-cat-a-way** tribe, on the headwaters of the Chesapeake, is also mentioned. They were alive and gave trouble to the Virginia and Maryland authorities as late as 1699.[1]

Strachey gives us this account of the **Sus-que-han-nocks**; who lived still farther to the north:

"Upon the river inhabit a people called the Sus-que-sa-han-oughs; they are seated two days higher than was passage for the discoverers' barge; howbeit, sixty of the Sus-que-sa-han-oughs came to the discoverers with skins, bows, arrows, targets, swords, beads, and tobacco-pipes for presents.

"Such great and well-proportioned men are seldom seen, for they seemed like giants to the English,—yea, and to the neighbors—yet seemed of an honest and simple disposition, with much ado restrained from adoring the discoverers as gods. These are the most strange people of all those countries, both in language and attire; for their language it may well beseem their proportions, sounding from them as it were a great voice in a vault or cave, as an echo: their attire is the skins of bears and wolves; some have cassocks made of bears' hides and skins, that a man's neck goeth through the skin's neck, and the ears of the bear are fastened to his shoulders

[1] Sainsbury *Abstracts*, vol. ii., pp. 110–15.

behind, the nose and teeth hanging down his breast, and at the end of the nose hangs a bear's paw; the half sleeves coming to the elbow were the necks of bears, and the arms through the mouth, with paws hanging in a chain for a jewel; his tobacco-pipe three-quarters of a yard long, prettily carved with a bird, a deer, or with some such device, at the great end, sufficient to beat out the brains of a horse. Likewise their bows, and arrows, and clubs, are suitable to their greatness; these are scarce known to Powhatan.

"They can make well near six hundred able and mighty men, and are palisadoed in their towns to defend them from the Mas-sa-wo-mecks, their mortal enemies. Five of these chief wer-ó-ances came aboard the discoverers, and crossed the bay with them in their barge; the picture of the greatest of them is portrayed, the calf of whose leg was three-quarters of a yard about, and all the rest of his limbs so answerable to that proportion, that he seemed the goodliest man they ever saw; his hair the one side was long, the other shorn close, with a ridge over his crown like a coxcomb; his arrows were five quarters[1] long, headed with flints or splinters of stones, in form like a heart, an inch broad, and an inch and a half or more long; these he wore in a wolf's skin on his back for his quiver, his bow in the one hand and his club in the other."[2]

They included, or were otherwise known as

[1] Of a yard.
[2] Strachey's *Historie of Travaile into Virginia*, p. 39.

the Con-es-to-gas, and occupied a large area to the north of the Chesapeake Bay, and appear to have been a separate confederacy.[1]

It is said that the Sus-que-han-oughs originally occupied the headwaters of the Chesapeake Bay, but were driven out by the Cin-e-la tribe and took up their residence on the upper waters of the Potomac, which was supposed to be one of their favorite places of residence, as the remains of their villages are more numerous in this region than elsewhere in the Valley.[2]

In 1662, the colony took this action in regard to them:

"Upon the report of the committee appointed for the Indian affairs it appearing that the Susque-han-nock and other Northern Indians, in considerable numbers, frequently come to the heads of our rivers, whereby plain paths will soon be made which may prove dangerous consequence, and also affront the English and destroy their stocks and get the whole trade from our neighboring and tributary Indians; it is ordered by this assembly that for prevention and of other injuries to the English from the Marylanders for the future, that the honorable governor cause by proclamation a prohibition of all Marylanders, English and Indians (which they have already done to us), and of all other Indians to the northward of Maryland, from trucking, trading, bartering, or dealing with any English or Indians to

---

[1] The *American Anthropologist*, vol. xi., p. 260.
[2] Peyton's *History of Augusta County*, p. 6.

the southward of that place, and that, by commission from the governor, Colonel Wood be impowered to manage the said business."[1]

The Not-to-ways settled on the river which still bears their name, at a late period, some time after 1665. Their principal town was in Nansemond or Southampton County, very near the North Carolina line. They are first mentioned in the acts in 1693, when the County Court of Surry County, which then stretched to the North Carolina line, was ordered to designate certain marks with which all swine owned by the Indians of the various towns of this tribe should be marked.[2] In 1728, Colonel Byrd speaks of them as "the only Indians of any consequence now remaining within the limits of Virginia." Nottoway Town, as their last stronghold was called, then numbered about two hundred inhabitants.

The condition of this tribe, as it existed in 1734, is presented to us in an act of Assembly passed to enable them to sell a part of their lands, thus: "Whereas the Nottoway Indians are possessed of a large tract of land, laid off in a circle of six miles diameter, lying and being on the north side of Nottoway River, in the county of Isle of Wight; and of one other large tract of land, of six miles square, lying and being on the south side of the said river, in the county aforesaid: And, whereas, that nation is of late reduced, by wars, sickness, and other casualties, to a small number, and

[1] 2 Hening, 153.   [2] 3 Hening, 109.

among those that remain, many are old and unable to labor or hunt, so that one of the said tracts will be sufficient for them, and more than they are able, in their present circumstances, to cultivate, or make any use of."

Permission was therefore granted to the chief men of the Nottoway nation to sell the circular tract of six miles in diameter, with the consent of their trustees, John Simmons, of Isle of Wight, and Thomas Cocke and Benjamin Edwards, of Surry, who were appointed to see the act duly executed. No one person was allowed to buy more than four hundred acres, and all the formalities of the transfer, which was to vest a fee simple title in the purchaser, were minutely prescribed, including the making of livery of seisin upon the land. One tract of four hundred acres was to be purchased at what was to be adjudged a reasonable price, for a glebe for the use of the parson of the parish wherein the land lay. The trustees themselves were not to purchase any of the land without the consent of the Governor and Council.[1]

About 1800, the Nottoways, residing in the County of Southampton, were authorized to sell three hundred acres of their land; and in 1803, they were allowed, under the direction and with the approbation of their trustees, to sell all of their lands lying on the north side of Nottoway River. The money arising from the sale of the lands was to be applied by the trustees in the

[1] 4 Hening, 459.

manner they thought best for the benefit of the tribe, so long as any of them were living. Should the tribe become extinct, the money or any part of it which was left, was to be paid into the public treasury.[1]

In 1816, new trustees were appointed for the Nottoways. These trustees were empowered to make reasonable rules and regulations for the government of the tribe and for the expenditure of the money held in trust for them, which was to continue so long as any number of the tribe were living. Any funds remaining on hand were then to be paid in to the public treasury.[2]

In 1819, this tribe was reduced to only twenty-six persons. They owned a tract of land containing 3912 acres. This being more than they needed for agricultural purposes, 3000 acres of it were authorized to be divided and sold for their benefit. The trustees of the tribe and the Indians were to unite in making the deeds of conveyance. The purchase money was to be invested for the benefit of the tribe.[3]

The Indians objected to this, as being too much land to be sold, and it was soon afterwards reduced to 1124 acres which was to be thus disposed of.[4]

In 1838, a plan was adopted whereby the members of the tribe could have their parts of the land belonging to them set aside so as to be

---

[1] 1 Shepherd's *Statutes at Large*, 274; 3 ditto, 36.
[2] Acts, 1816–17, p. 174.
[3] Acts, 1818–19, p. 198.   [4] Acts, 1820, p. 92.

held separately in fee, but this was only to apply to those who were not likely to become chargeable to any part of the Commonwealth.[1]

The Me-her-rins, whose name still lives in the designation of one of our rivers, are said to have been a branch of the fierce Sus-que-han-nas, who were enemies of the Powhatans.

This tribe settled in Virginia after the arrival of the white man, some time after 1665. They lived on the Me-her-rin River. In 1753, a parish bearing their name was formed in the southern part of Brunswick and Greensville counties. This was a fierce and warlike tribe.

The Oc-ca-nee-chees were a small but very important nation which dwelt in this same region, in what was later Mecklenburg County. Their chief town was near Clarksville, close to the Carolina border, and situated upon an island in the Staunton, or Roanoke, River. It was defended by three strong forts, and was a celebrated center of trade for the other Indians for hundreds of miles. It was no doubt this fact that made their language the universal medium of communication as stated by Beverley.[2]

In 1676, when this tribe came into special prominence on account of events connected with Bacon's Rebellion, its king was Per-si-cles. He is described as a very brave man and ever true to the English, but during the tragic events of that year he was finally brought into hostility to them, and was killed in the battle which then

---

[1] Acts, 1838, p. 213.   [2] Beverley, book 3, p. 24.

occurred, Nathaniel Bacon being in command of the Virginians.

The Tu-te-loes also lived upon the Me-her-rin River. This tribe was connected with the Carolina Indians, probably the Cho-wan-ocs.[1]

West of the Mon-a-cans and Man-na-ho-acks lay the mountains. These were in the possession of many powerful and terrible tribes. The most prominent of these tribes were the following:

"**The Shaw-a-nese**, the most considerable of the Algonquin tribes, had their principal villages east of the Alleghanies, near the present town of Winchester, but their possessions extended west to the Mississippi River. Foote asserts[2] that the Shaw-a-nese owned the whole Valley of Virginia, but had abandoned it. He gives no authority for the statement, and we have found none in our researches. Of all the Indian tribes with whom our ancestors came in contact, the Shaw-a-nese were the most bloody and terrible, holding all other men, as well Indians as whites, in contempt as warriors, in comparison with themselves. This estimate of themselves made them more restless and fierce than any other savages, and they boasted that they had killed ten times as many white people as any other Indians did. They were a well-formed, active, and ingenious people, capable of enduring great

[1] Jefferson's *Notes on Virginia*, p. 97.
[2] Second Series, p. 159.

privations and hardships, were assuming and imperious in the presence of others not of their own nation, and sometimes very cruel."[1]

"That portion of the valley now embraced within the county of Augusta, is not known to have been the home or fixed residence of any tribe of Indians at the period of its settlement, nor is it known that it was not the home of some tribe or branch of a tribe. Such red men as Lewis met on entering Augusta, in 1732, were friendly, and so continued for over twenty years.

"That the country had been, previous to 1732, permanently occupied, is indicated by the remains of barrows,[2] cairns[3] and ramparts, composed of mingled earth and stones, found at different points in the county, notably near Waynesboro, on Lewis Creek, a few miles below Staunton; on Middle River near Dudley's mill, and at Jarman's Gap, north of Rockfish. The cairn at Jarman's Gap is probably sepulchral, and may have been intended and used as a place of worship.

"The Valley of Virginia was, in 1716, when visited by Spotswood, without extensive forests, but the margins of streams were fringed with trees; there were pretty woodlands in the low grounds, and the mountain sides were densely

---

[1] Peyton's *History of Augusta County*, p. 5.
All quotations from Peyton's *History of Augusta County* are reproduced by the permission of L. W. H. Peyton, the personal representative of Col. John Lewis Peyton.   [2] Burial mounds.
[3] Heaps of stones, often for sepulchral purposes.

covered with timber trees. The wood destroyed by autumnal fires was replaced by a luxuriant growth of blue grass, white clover, and other natural grasses and herbage. The spontaneous productions of the earth were everywhere numerous and abundant, and there were many varieties of game and wild animals. The luxuriance of the vegetation evinced the fertility of a soil which required only the hand of art to render it in the highest degree subservient to the wants of man. But the nomads of the valley were averse to improvement; their indolence refused to cultivate the earth, and their restless spirit disdained the confinement of sedentary life. To prevent the growth of timber and preserve the district as pasture, that it might support as much game as possible, and that the grass might come forward in the early spring, the savages, before retiring into winter quarters, set on fire the dry grass and burnt over the country. The absence of trees in an extensive quarter of the county northwest of Staunton, led our ancestors to style it 'The Barrens,' a name that it still bears, though it is interspersed at this time by handsome woodlands, the growth of the last eighty years.

"The two principal non-resident tribes who frequented this fine country in 1716–1745 were the **Delawares** from the north and the **Ca-tawbas** from the south. At the time Augusta was settled, 1732, a bloody war was progressing between these tribes, and the valley was the theater of action. In this war other tribes now and again participated as the allies of one or the other party, and it was at a battle on the north fork of the Shenandoah, in the county now bearing that name, that the Sen-e-dos tribe was exterminated. There is a burial place there eighteen to twenty feet high and sixty feet in circumference, filled with human bones, which testify to the truth of this tradition."[1]

We have no map giving us the names and location of the Indian villages in this portion of the State, as we had from Smith's map, of the eastern and central portion, nor have we at hand material for the composition of such a map.

An account of some of their settlements and antiquities is thus given us by Kercheval:

"On the banks of the Co-hon-go-ru-ton [Potomac], there has doubtless been a pretty considerable settlement. The late Col. Joseph Swearengen's dwelling house stands within a circular wall or moat. When first known by the white inhabitants, the wall was about eighteen inches high, and the ditch about two feet deep. This circular wall was made of earth—is now considerably reduced, but yet plainly to be seen. It is not more than half a mile from Shepherdstown.

"For what particular purpose this wall was thrown up, whether for ornament or defense, the author cannot pretend to form an opinion. If it was intended for defense, it appears to have

[1] Peyton's *History of Augusta County*, pp. 5, 9.

been too low to answer any valuable purpose in that way.

"On the Wap-pa-tom-a-ka, a few miles below the forks, tradition relates that there was a very considerable Indian settlement. On the farm of Isaac Vanmeter, Esq., on this watercourse, in the county of Hardy, when the country was first discovered, there were considerable openings of the land, or natural prairies, which are called 'the Indian old fields,' to this day. Numerous Indian graves are to be seen in the neighborhood. A little above the forks of this river a very large Indian grave is now [1850] to be seen. In the bank of the river, a little below the forks, numerous human skeletons have been discovered, and several articles of curious workmanship. A highly finished pipe, representing a snake coiled round the bowl, with its head projected above the bowl, was among them. There was the under jaw bone of a human being of great size found at the same place, which contained eight jaw teeth in each side of enormous size; and what is more remarkable, the teeth stood transversely in the jaw bone. It would pass over any common man's face with entire ease.[1]

"There are many other signs of Indian settlements all along this river, both above and below the one just described. Mr. Garret Blue, of the county of Hampshire, informed the author, that

[1] Peyton thinks this was the bone of some animal. *History of Augusta County*, p. 7.

The Tribes and Nations

about two miles below the Hanging Rocks, in the bank of the river, a stratum of ashes, about one rod in length, was some years ago discovered. At this place are signs of an Indian village, and their old fields. The Rev. John J. Jacobs, of Hampshire, informed the author that on Mr. Daniel Cresap's land, on the north branch of the Potomac, a few miles above Cumberland, a human skeleton was discovered, which had been covered with a coat of wood ashes, about two feet below the surface of the ground. An entire decomposition of the skeleton had taken place, with the exception of the teeth: they were in a perfect state of preservation.

"On the two great branches of the Shenandoah there are now to be seen numerous sites of their ancient villages, several of which are so remarkable that they deserve a passing notice. It has been noticed, in my preceding chapter, that on Mr. Steenbergen's land, on the north fork of the Shenandoah, the remains of a large Indian mound are plainly to be seen. It is also suggested that this was once the residence of the Senedo tribe, and that that tribe had been exterminated by the southern Indians. Exclusive of this large mound, there are several other Indian graves. About this place many of their implements and domestic utensils have been found. A short distance below the mouth of Stony Creek (a branch of the Shenandoah), within four or five miles of Woodstock, are the signs of an Indian village. At this place a gun barrel and several iron tomahawks were found long after the Indians left the country.

"On Mr. Anthony Kline's farm, within about three miles of Stephensburg, in the county of Frederick, in a glen near his mill, a rifle was found which had laid in the ground forty or fifty years. Every part of this gun (even the stock, which was made of black walnut) was sound. Mr. Kline's father took the barrel from the stock, placed the breech on the fire, and it soon discharged with a loud explosion.

"In the county of Page, on the south fork of Shenandoah River, there are several Indian burying grounds, and signs of their villages. These signs are also to be seen on the Hawksbill Creek. A few miles above Luray, on the west side of the river, there are three large Indian graves, ranged nearly side by side, thirty or forty feet in length, twelve or fourteen feet wide, and five or six feet high. Around them, in circular form, are a number of single graves. The whole covers an area of little less than a quarter of an acre. They present to the eye a very ancient appearance, and are covered over with pine and other forest growth. The excavation of the ground around them is plainly to be seen. The three first mentioned graves are in oblong form, probably contain many hundreds of human bodies, and were doubtless the work of ages.

"On the land of Mr. Noah Keyser, near the mouth of the Hawksbill Creek, stand the remains of a large mound. This, like that at Mr.

Steenbergen's, is considerably reduced by plowing, but is yet some twelve or fourteen feet high, and is upwards of sixty yards round at the base. It is found to be literally filled with human skeletons, and at every fresh plowing a fresh layer of bones is brought to the surface. The bones are found to be in a calcareous [1] state, with the exception of the teeth, which are generally sound. Several unusually large skeletons have been discovered in this grave. On the lands now the residence of my venerable friend, John Gatewood Esq., the signs of an Indian village are yet plainly to be seen. There are numerous fragments of their pots, cups, arrow points, and other implements for domestic use, found from time to time. Convenient to this village there are several pretty large graves.

"There is also evidence of an Indian town in Powell's Fort, on the lands now [2] owned by Mr. Daniel Munch. From appearances, this too was a pretty considerable village. A little above the forks of the Shenandoah, on the east side of the South Fork, are the appearances of another settlement, exhibiting the remains of two considerable mounds now entirely reduced by plowing. About this place many pipes, tomahawks, axes, hominy pestles, etc., have been found. Some four or five miles below the forks of the river, on the southeast side, on the lands now owned by Capt. Daniel Oliver, is the site of another Indian village. At this place a con-

[1] Reduced to a soft chalky condition. [2] 1850.

siderable variety of articles have been plowed up. Among the number were several whole pots, cups, pipes, axes, tomahawks, hominy pestles, etc. A beautiful pipe of high finish, made of white flint stone, and several other articles of curious workmanship, all of very hard stone, have been found. Their cups and pots were made of a mixture of clay and shells, of rude workmanship, but of firm texture.

"There are many other places, on all our watercourses, to wit, Stony Creek, Cedar Creek, and O-pe-quon, as well as the larger watercourses which exhibit evidences of ancient Indian settlements. The Shaw-nee tribe, it is well known, were settled about the neighborhood of Winchester. What are called the 'Shawnee cabins,' and 'Shawnee springs,' immediately adjoining the town, are well known. It is also equally certain, that this tribe had a considerable village on the Babb's march, some three or four miles northwest of Winchester.

"**The Tus-ca-ro-ra** Indians resided in the neighborhood of Martinsburg, in the county of Berkeley, on the Tus-ca-ro-ra Creek. On the fine farm, now owned by, and the residence of, Matthew Ranson, Esq. (the former residence of Mr. Benjamin Beeson), are the remains of several Indian graves. These, like several others, are now plowed down; but numerous fragments of human bones are to be found mixed with the clay on the surface. Mr. Ranson informed the author, that at this place the under jaw bone of a human being was plowed up, of enormous size; the teeth were found in a perfect state of preservation.

"Near the Shannondale springs, on the lands of Mr. Fairfax, an Indian grave some years since was opened, in which a skeleton of unusual size was discovered.

"Mr. E. Paget informed the author that on Flint Run, a small rivulet of the South River, in the county of Shenandoah, a skeleton was found by his father, the thigh bone of which measured three feet in length, and the under jaw bone of which would pass over any common man's face with ease.

"Near the Indian village described on a preceding page, on Capt. Oliver's land, a few years ago, some hands in removing the stone covering an Indian grave discovered a skeleton, whose great size attracted their attention. The stones were carefully taken off without disturbing the frame, when it was discovered that the body had been laid at full length on the ground, and broad flat stones set round the corpse in the shape of a coffin. Capt. Oliver measured the skeleton as it lay, which was nearly seven feet long."[1]

"Among the most formidable of the Indian nations with which the Virginians came into contact and collision was the nation of 'the **Cher-o-kees,** who occupied the upper valley of the Tennessee River and the high lands of Carolina, Georgia, and Alabama. The Cher-o-kees

[1] Kercheval's *History of the Valley*, pp. 34 *et seq.*

were the tallest and most robust of the southern tribes, their complexions brighter than usual with the red men, and some of their young women were nearly as fair and blooming as European women. They owed allegiance to the **Mus-co-gul-ges,** who stood at the head of a confederacy composed of **Cher-o-kees, Sem-i-noles, Chick-a-saws, Choc-taws, and Creeks,** and it is probable that bands from all of these tribes, or at least warriors, accompanied the Cher-o-kees, in their annual visits to the Valley. Without exception, these southern Indians were proud, haughty, and arrogant, brave and valiant in war, ambitious of conquest, restless and perpetually exercising their arms, yet magnanimous and merciful to a vanquished enemy when he submitted and sought their friendship and protection.'

"The Cherokees are known to have been visited by De Soto as early as 1540; but their interior position kept them long from any intercourse with the white settlers on the seacoast of Carolina. The first white man who is known to have resided among them was one Cornelius Dougherty, an enterprising, but lax-principled Irishman, who established himself as a trader in one of the Cherokee towns in 1690."[1]

"The word 'Cheera,' in the language of this tribe, means fire, and the warriors were called Cher-ra-kee, meaning sons of fire, that is, of the divine element, and their priests were called Chee-ra-tag-he, men of divine fire. This word

[1] Peyton's *History of Augusta County,* p. 6.

The Tribes and Nations 391

Cher-ra-kee, which applied only properly to the braves, came gradually to distinguish the whole tribe, although their nation was called by themselves Tsa-rag-hee.

"According to their own traditions, they came originally from the far west, but when first known to the Europeans, they occupied a country forming now the upper portion of Georgia, Alabama, and Mississippi, and the part of Tennessee south of the Little Tennessee River.

"The government of the tribe was that of an elective monarchy, more absolute in time of war than in peace, and subject to deposition at any time. It was held at the time of the Revolution, when this tribe was an ally of Great Britain, by O-con-o-stot-a, one of the greatest war chiefs of this nation, who held sway over it for half a century. Under him was the half- or vice-king, who was second in command, and acted in his stead in case of the sudden death of the monarch. These two rulers with the chieftains, or princes of the scattered villages, composed the supreme council of the nation, which sat at E-cho-ta, their capital, and decided all important questions in peace and war. But over the archimagus or king, and even the supreme council, was the great and good spirit who was the guardian of the Cher-o-kee, and who uttered his will through the beloved man or woman of the tribe.

"During and after the Revolution, this office was held by a woman, who often thwarted the deliberate and deeply concerted plans of the great council of the nation, with the great O-con-o-stot-a at its head.

"The Cher-o-kees had no large cities, nor even villages, but dwelt in scattered townships in the vicinity of some stream where fish and game could be found in abundance. A number of their towns, bearing the musical names of Tal-las-se, Tam-ot-tee, Chil-how-ee, Cit-i-co, Ten-nas-see, and E-cho-ta, were, at the opening of the Revolutionary War, located upon the rich lowlands lying between the Tel-li-co and Little Tennessee Rivers.[1] About one-third of the tribe occupied these settlements, and they were known as the **Ot-ta-ri**, or, among the mountains, Cher-o-kees. About the same number were located near the headwaters of the Savannah, in the great highland belt, between the Blue Ridge and the Smoky Mountains,[2] and they were styled **E-rat-i**, or, in the valley, Cher-o-kees. Another body, among whom were many Creeks, and which was somewhat more numerous and much more lawless than either of the others, occupied towns along the Tennessee, in the vicinity of Lookout Mountain. These, from their residence near the creek of that name, were known as **Chick-a-mau-gas**."

"These three bodies were one people, governed by one archimagus, and at this time they

---

[1] Monroe County, Tennessee, covers all of this area.
[2] The Great Smoky Mountains divide North Carolina and Tennessee. The Blue Ridge runs to the east of them.

numbered in all about thirty thousand people, between three and four thousand of whom were 'gun men,' or warriors."

"E-cho-ta, which was located on the northern bank of the Tel-li-co, about five miles from the site of Fort London, and thirty southwest from the present city of Knoxville,[1] contained their great council-house, and was the home of the archimagus, and the beloved woman, or prophetess of the tribe. It was their sacred town, or 'city of refuge.' . . . Once within the limits of E-cho-ta, an open foe, or even a red-handed criminal, could dwell in peace and security. The only danger was in going and returning. It is related that an Englishman, who in self-defense had slain a Cherokee, once fled to this sacred city to escape the vengeance of the kindred of his victim. He was treated here with so much kindness that after a time he deemed it prudent to leave his asylum. The Indians warned him against the danger; but he ventured forth, and on the following morning his body was found on the outskirts of the town, pierced through and through with a score of arrows."

"E-cho-ta contained a hundred or more cabins and wigwams, scattered along the bank of the stream, on both sides of a broad avenue, shaded with oaks and poplars, and trodden hard with the feet of men and horses. A little apart from the other wigwams, and more pretentious than

---

[1] A point in Loudon County, Tennessee, would correspond with this description.

the rest, was that of the prophetess. Beside it was its 'totem'—an otter in the coils of a water-snake. . . . Near by was the house of O-con-o-stot-a, and not far off, the grand council-house of the tribe, occupying a spacious opening, circular, of a tower-shaped construction, twenty feet high, and ninety in circumference. It was rudely built of stout poles, plastered with clay, and had a roof of the same material, which sloped down to broad eaves that gave effectual protection to the walls from the rain. Its wide entrance was covered with a couple of buffalo skins hung so as to meet together in the middle; but it was without windows, an aperture in the roof, protected by a flap, serving to let the smoke out, and the light in, just enough to make more sensible the gloom that shrouded the interior. Low benches, neatly made of cane, were ranged around the circumference of the room; and on these sat the warriors of the tribe when they gathered to the great councils; but they were cleared away when the braves met here to perform their green-corn dance."

"In the rear of each lodge was a small patch of cleared land, where the women and negro slaves—stolen from the white settlers over the mountains—cultivated beans, corn, and potatoes, and occasionally some such fruits as pears, plums, and apples."[1]

---

[1] Kirke's *Rear-Guard of the Revolution*, pp. 13-25. All quotations from this work are reproduced by permission of D. Appleton & Company, Publishers.

The important part which the Cher-o-kees were destined to play in the history of the Colonies, as allies of England during the Revolution, amply justifies this extended notice of the tribe.

West of the Cherokee settlements, on the other side of the mountains, was a vast region stretching to the Mississippi, which was entirely uninhabited. Until the year 1769, there could not be found any permanent habitation of man in this region. It was the hunting ground and battle-field of the Indians, claimed by hostile tribes, but occupied by none.[1]

It is interesting to know that a few descendants of the Cher-o-kees are still living in Virginia, in Amherst County, where they and their ancestors have been settled for the last one hundred and twenty-five years. They are the descendants of several old Cherokee warriors, who dropped off from a band of pilgrims on their return from a visit to the "Great White Father." There is a mixture of white blood in the clan, which now numbers from two hundred and fifty to three hundred persons. They are known locally as "Issues."

The name "Issue" was derived from an illogical association of words and ideas which arose before the civil war, when free negroes were called "free issue." These people were dark, but not slaves nor negroes, but were classed by the whites somewhat with them, and

[1] Kirke's *Rear-Guard of the Revolution*, p. 13.

given part of the designation of free negroes—Issues.

The name "Issues" is disliked by them, and they proudly call themselves Indian men and Indian women, and keep much aloof from both the whites and the negroes. The family names recognized by them are Johns, Branham, Adcox, and Willis, names taken from the whites, and one Indian name, Redcross. They live the obscure life of agricultural tenants, or small farmers.[1]

In the course of the history of the country at large, the relation of the State of Virginia to some of the Indian tribes presented many curious phases. In 1861, when the War between the States broke out, the Secretary of the Interior of the United States Government held in trust for the Choctaw tribe of Indians registered bonds of the State of Virginia amounting to $450,000. This tribe of Indians, living in the southwest, had been taken under the protectorate of the Confederate Government, as that tribe had "united themselves with the Confederate Government." This made them allies of Virginia. Interest was due, and the Indians wanted their money, but Virginia would not pay it to the Federal authorities for them. The State therefore declared cancelled the bonds as then held by the Secretary of the Interior of the United States, and issued others in their place, to the Secretary of the Treasury of the Confederate

[1] *The Southern Churchman*, vol. lxxii., No. 53.

States. And, in 1864, a similar arrangement was made with regard to $90,000 of bonds, so held for the Cherokee Indians.[1]

The Cherokee nation continued as a political body until midnight of June 30, 1914. It was then dissolved. The tribal funds amounting to $600,000 was divided among its forty-one thousand members. Commissioner Sells of the Indian Office called on that day for the resignation of all Cherokee officials.

At the time of its dissolution the Cherokees were the largest of the five civilized tribes. Under the laws of Congress it was intended that all of these civilized tribes should dissolve as nations in 1906. Congress, however, extended the time in the discretion of the Indian Office.

At the time of its dissolution one of its members was a Senator of the United States from Oklahoma, and received about $15 as his portion of the tribal funds.

The other four nations which made up the "Five Civilized Tribes" were the Choctaws, Chickasaws, Creeks, and Seminoles.

Another powerful nation was the **Ca-taw-bas,** whose headquarters were on the Ca-taw-ba River, in South Carolina.

The Catawba River rises in the Blue Ridge Mountains, North Carolina, near Morgantown. It runs east and then south into South Carolina, where it is known for some distance as the

[1] Acts 1861-2, p. 34; Acts 1863-4, p. 9.

Wateree, but after the confluence of the Broad River, it takes the name of Santee and under this name empties into the Atlantic Ocean. It crosses the boundary line of North and South Carolina about at its center.

The Catawba territory stretched toward the east from this river to the Yadkin, and on the west, by reason of a treaty made with the Cherokees, to the Broad River. It lay on both sides of the boundary between North and South Carolina.

The largest village of this tribe was in York County, South Carolina, on the Catawba River. This was probably the place called Catawba Town by the Virginians.

The Catawbas were probably the bravest and most enterprising of all the southern tribes. They are known to have gone as far north as Pennsylvania, to wage war with the Five Nations, and they repeatedly engaged in battle with the Northern Indians in the Valley of Virginia. The battle of Hanging Rocks was fought between this nation and either the Mohawks or the Delawares.[1]

In 1682, this tribe could put 1500 warriors in the field. By the year 1756, from the combined effects of small-pox, and other deadly diseases, and from constant and bitter warfare with the Iroquois, Cherokees, Shawanese, Delawares, and other nations, they were reduced to about four hundred fighting men, the remnants of over twenty different tribes.

[1] Peyton's *History of Augusta County*, p. 6.

The Tribes and Nations 399

Before this date, however, peace had been made between them and the Cherokees. The Broad River, which still bounds Cherokee County, South Carolina, on the east, was made the boundary between them. And in 1751, their wars with the Iroquois were terminated by a conference at Albany. But they were still at war with western Indians.

The Catawbas became firm allies of Virginia. They fought on the side of the colonies in the war against the Tus-ca-ro-ras, during the years 1711, 1712, and 1713; and again with them against the French and Indians. They failed to keep their promise to send a force to assist Braddock, but fought on the side of Virginia and the Carolinas against England in the Revolutionary War.

In 1756, the king of the Catawbas was Heigler. After having been a firm friend of Virginia, he was killed near his own village by a small party of his ancient enemies, the Shaw-a-nese, in 1762.[1]

Other tribes to the south were the **Man-go-ags**, the **Chaw-ons**, and the **We-op-e-medgs**, the last two on the Virginia–Carolina State line. The We-op-e-medgs lived nearest the seacoast, the Chaw-ons to the west of them.

The colony also came into contact with the

---

[1] *The Virginia Magazine of History and Biography*, vol. xiii., notes pp. 227, 238, 260.

Delawares, who frequented the Susquehanna River in Pennsylvania.[1]

They were a powerful body of Indians, in possession of the eastern part of Pennsylvania, and the whole of New Jersey. They do not seem to have occupied the State of Delaware, which took its name not from them, but from Lord De la War.

Other tribes with which Virginia came into contact and sometimes in conflict were the **Wyandots,** and the **Mingoes,** the latter a branch of the Iroquois which had settled on the Ohio and its branches. The Delawares and Shawanese were also Iroquois tribes which migrated to this section about 1728, coming from the French settlements in Canada. The **Miamis** formed another tribe which settled in what is now Ohio. They were also called **Twigh-twees.** They were the most powerful confederacy of the west, combined four tribes, and extended their influence even beyond the Mississippi. Their principal town was Pi-qua. The **Chick-a-maw-gas,** in Tennessee, and the **Six Nations** of New York, also come before us, and play their part in Virginia's history.

Among the Indian settlements which came into historical prominence as the colony extended farther and farther west may be mentioned Shanno-pins town, a Delaware village, on the southeast side of the Alleghany River, two or three

[1] Peyton's *History of Augusta County,* p. 6.

miles above Pittsburg, and Logstown, on the north bank of the Ohio. This was later named Fort Mackintosh, and now the town of Beaver, in the county of that name, in the State of Pennsylvania, about twenty-five miles down the river from Pittsburg. This was the stronghold of Tan-a-cha-ris-son, the Seneca chief of the mixed tribes which had migrated to the Ohio. He was surnamed the "half-king," as not wholly an independent sovereign, being still subordinate to the Iroquois Confederacy. We meet with him at the period of Washington's journey to Fort Duquesne.

Charters Old Town and Sewickley Old Town from ten to fifteen miles up the Alleghany on its western shore, Queen Al-li-guip-pe's town, on the site of the present McKeesport, were also well-known Indian towns in Pennsylvania, in that portion of it once claimed by Virginia.

In the old Virginia territory west of the Ohio Indian towns abounded. Its tributary streams, the Muskingum, the Hockhocking and the Scioto all had their waters guarded by Indian towns and villages.

Virginia's power and influence having been felt, and government established by her as far west as the Mississippi, and northwest to the Great Lakes, she came in contact with all these tribes and nations and many others.

In common with the Indians in the rest of North America, these tribes and nations, as already stated, were engaged in endless warfare among themselves, in the prosecution of which, when they captured their enemies, they practiced all the cruelties which a savage imagination could suggest. Among other enormities, they sometimes practiced cannibalism. We are told in particular of the **Po-cough-tro-nacks,** a tribe which lived beyond the Falls, who ate men.[1]

"These vagrant tribes camped or resided at great distances from each other, were widely dispersed over a vast country, and any connection between them and particular localities was of so frail a texture that it was broken by the slightest accident.

"The different tribes or nations were small in number as compared with civilized societies in which industry, arts, agriculture, and commerce have united a vast number of individuals whom a complicated luxury renders valuable to each other.

"No accurate information exists as to the numbers composing these tribes, but it is most probable they did not exceed a few hundred warriors each. At the landing of the Pilgrims in 1620, the number of Indians in New England did not exceed 123,000, and a few years later the number was greatly reduced by a plague. It is probable that the Indian population of Virginia was larger at this time, as the climate of our Valley and State is generally better adapted to the wants of man than that of New England.

[1] Smith's *True Relation*, p. 36.

The Tribes and Nations 403

Bancroft, however, ventures the opinion that the whole Indian population east of the Mississippi and south of New England did not, in 1620, exceed 180,000.

"Detached parties of armed barbarians from the Northern and Western tribes occasionally came to the Valley, and the Mas-sa-wom-ees penetrated to Eastern Virginia and were a terror to the low-land tribes. Armed parties also visited the Valley from the five nations situated on the rivers and lakes of New York—the Mohawks, O-nei-das, O-non-da-gas, Cay-u-gas, and Sen-e-cas."[1]

In the course of its laborious, and often tragic, westward progress, Virginia came into contact or conflict with these many, and often powerful, tribes. War and campaigns followed, diplomacy and treaties, conflicting interests adjusted, and compromises agreed upon, boundary lines established between the white man and the red man, grants of land, and conquests of territory.

It also involved treaties of alliance and cooperation with some of these Indian tribes, and with the other English settlements, sometimes hampered by local jealousies and self-interest. Some of these hostile Indians, too, were not unsupported by powerful European influence. France was their ally, and Virginia had to contend with her trained soldiers as well as with the savage foe.

[1] Peyton's *History of Augusta County*, pp. 6-7.

The varying circumstances of this ever onward and ever widening movement found Virginia now waging war in the western forests, to stop the slaughter of her people on the frontier; building forts without number and palisades of enormous length; now sending troops to the aid of Carolina, threatened with destruction by the Indians of the south; or debating with Maryland, Pennsylvania, and New York the terms of a treaty between the Indians and the English Colonies at Lancaster or Albany.

Picturesque figures move across the stage, and incidents as strange, and often as horrible, as war only can produce, marked the struggle.

From movements of armed forces covering the distance from Cape Henry to the heart of the Northwest Territory, and from Carolina to Fort Duquesne, down to hand-to-hand encounters in the log cabins of the pioneers, as the Indians in small bodies roamed through the settlements, the soil was too often drenched with the blood of the contending races. It was a life-and-death struggle between them for the possession of the very soil on which they lived.

The Indians were no mean antagonists. Born to war, and bearing pain and torture with stoical indifference and Spartan-like fortitude, the Indians of Virginia defended their possession of the land they had inherited as any other warlike nation would have done.

Awed at first by the new foe they had to deal with, whom they regarded with superstitious

The Tribes and Nations

dread, protected as he was, also, by coats of mail and master of those terrific fire-arms and thundering cannon, the Indians, during the period of the colony's greatest weakness, were at a disadvantage. This became less as time went on, for he became familiar with the white man, and no longer feared him as he had. They gradually became supplied, too, with similar arms, and the old inequality between them disappeared.

Thus the Indian power long continued formidable, and threatened the settlements with total destruction.

CHAPTER XXI

CONCLUSION

SUCH was the people which sparsely occupied a nearly unbroken wilderness among whom was now to be attempted the planting of European civilization and the Protestant form of the Christian religion.

It was no small task which was undertaken. These brave pioneers faced death in many forms. They faced the dangers of the sea, the dangers of an unknown land; they faced sickness, privation, and enemies civilized and uncivilized. They left behind them the familiar scenes of childhood, their homes and their kindred, and all that men hold dear on earth. When they turned their ships toward the setting sun, and began to plow the deep waters of the broad Atlantic, how little could they tell what was in store for them in the great unknown whither they were sailing, and whether they would accomplish their purpose and again behold the beloved scenes of Old England, or leave their bones to bleach upon the sands of a distant continent!

It may be that they fully realized the grandeur of their work, and were inspired by the thought that they, as well as the great leaders who directed them, were actors in a drama of worldwide significance, and that their names and their deeds would deserve to be remembered by the generations of their race which were to follow them—and we do so honor and record them.

INDEX

A

Accomac, special mode of fishing, 95–96; towns in, 152, 155; Empress of, 155; kingdom of, 155, 316; town of, on site of Cape Charles, 157; word, 316; tribe, 367–368
Accounts, how kept, 84
Acquia Creek, word, 316
Adultery, women careful not to be suspected of, 34; how women punished for, 81, 173; unpardonable offence, 81; how men punished for, 172, 173
Adventurers, meaning of the word, 22–23
Agriculture, conducted by the women and children, 80, 102, 104; basis of classification as between barbarous and savage, 101–102; importance of, 102; system of corn-planting and gathering, 103–104, 136; cultivation of tobacco, 106–108; how land cleared of trees, 109, 110, 134; of the Cherokees, 394
Ahone, name of the benign deity, 250
Alexandria, site of Indian town, 157
Algonquin Indians, 26; pottery of, 119–127
Alleghany, the word, 316
Allies, Indian, of Virginia, 326–327, 396, 397, 399; of the Indians against Virginia, 403
Altar-stones, see Pawcorances
Amherst County, some Cherokees still in, 395
Animals in the forest, 28
Appalachian, the word, 316

Appamattox, the town, 155; on site of Petersburg, 157; huskanawing at, 197; name, 315, 316; the tribe, 324, 337–338
Aprons, women clothed with, 58
Arbors, houses like, 96
Archery, skill in, 96–97
Aristocratic, Indian government, 133–134, 165, 169
Arrows, how made, 42–43, 112; uses, 42–43; fishing with, 42, 95, 98; heads, 112; stone, discussed, 113–114; where made, 114–119
Assaomeck, town on site of Alexandria, 157
Assemblies, see Public meetings
Augusta County, tribes in, 380–383
Authorities, this book based on, vii.–xv.
Axes, uses of, 110; how made, 112; stone, discussed, 113–114; where made, 114–119

B

Bacon, Nathaniel, in command against the Occaneechees, 379–380
Bald-eagle described, 94–95
Barbecue, style of cooking meat, 47, 67–68
Barbers, women as, 33–34, 62
Bark, shields made of, 112, 173, 176
Barlow quoted, 110, 352
Barrens, The, in Augusta County, 381–382
Barrow, see Mound
Barter, trading by, 44

Index

Baskets, 76; how made, 110; use in pottery-making, 121–122, 125
Bassets, seat of Eltham at Machot, 151
Bathing to harden, 60
Battle, between the Patomecks and Massomecks, 176–177; of Point Pleasant, won by the Virginians, 182; Okee carried into, 243; of Hanging Rocks, 398
Beads, for coronets, 36, 42, 63; use of, in marriage ceremony, 77
Beans, general article of food, 68, 73; widely cultivated, 73; planted with the corn for a support, 103. *See* Food
Beards, Indians generally wore none, 33; pulled out by roots, 36; some priests wore, 233
Beaufort County, North Carolina, Indian town in, 159
Beaver, uses of, 43; eaten, 69; Pennsylvania, site of Indian town, 401
Bedford County, tribes in 371
Beds, of earth, 130; of sticks, etc., 132, 137–138, 140; covered with mats, 132; how slept on, 138, 140
Belts made of peak, etc., 46
Berkeley County, West Virginia, tribes in, 372–373, 388–389
Bertie County, North Carolina, Indian tribe in, 158
Beverley, Robert, writings, xiv.–xv.; quoted, 35, 41, 44, 46, 47, 56, 57, 59, 60, 62, 63, 64, 67, 72, 73, 74, 81, 84, 85, 86, 91, 99, 109, 112, 128, 130, 185, 194, 231, 233, 234, 243, 253, 258, 265, 286, 287
Big Knives, the Indians' name for the Virginians, 182
Black boys, a servant class, 169
Board, children put on, 61
Bodyguard, Powhatan's, 275; Grangenimeo's, 283; his wife's attendants, 283
Bonds of Virginia held by Choctaws and Cherokees, 396–397
Bones, chains of, 61, 63
Bows, made of locust wood, 112; of witch-hazel, 112

Bracelets, 55; worn by men and women of condition, 37; made of pearls or beads of copper, 40, 55; or of peak or runtees, 46
Branches of trees as clôthes, 64–65, 87
Bronze Age, bodies burnt, 217
Brown, Alexander, quoted, ix.
Brunswick County, tribes in, 379
Buckingham County, tribes in, 371
Bull Run, Indian name for, 317
Burial, customs: body put on scaffold, 201–202; body buried, 202; body burnt, 202; riches buried with body, 202–203; mourning for a king, 203; mounds, chapter on, 204–222; *see* Mounds
Burk quoted, 80–81, 171–172
Burnt, bodies, 217; offerings to the Evil Spirit, 262
Byrd, Colonel Wm., Indians lived in his pasture, 155

C

Cabins, picture of, 57; for man to protect corn, 68; unclean, 189
Cabot, discovery of, foundation of claims of England, 2
Calumet, or pipe of peace, 49–52
Calvert County, Maryland, town in, 152; tribes in, 365
Camden County, North Carolina, town in, 158
Cannibalism, 402
Canoes, of birch, 48–49; fishing in, 93–96; of trunks of trees, 95, 109, 176; making of, 109–111
Cape Charles, site of Indian town, 157
Capital punishment, how inflicted, 172–173
Caroline County, tribes in, 361
Carteret County, North Carolina, Indian town in, 159
Catawba, tribe, 26, 382–383, 397–399; Roanoke Island settlers came in contact with, 27; became allies of Virginia, 399; town, 398
Cattle, Indians had none, 45, 71

Index 411

Ceremony of marriage, breaking string of beads over joined hands, 77; none when presents accepted, 79-80
Chains, of pearl, worn by the princes, 40; and by women, 59
Charles City County, towns in, 146, 147, 155; tribes in, 339
Cherokees, a branch of the Iroquois, 26; where located in Virginia, 324; the tribe, 389-397; meaning of the name, 390-391
Chesapeake, houses of a, town, 150; name, 315; river, 317; bay, 317; tribe, 351-353
Chester River, Indian name for, 317
Chesterfield County, tribes in, 337
Chickahominy, Smith captured on, 97; town of, 156, 345; word, 316; river, 317; tribe, 341-345; form of government, 342-343; treaty with Dale, 342-344; troubles over lands sold by King of, 344-345
Chiefs, see Weroances
Childbirth, women easily delivered, 60; how child treated, 60, 61
Children, Indian, born white, 32, 36, 131; how carried, 59-60, 62; how hardened, 60; how treated when born, 60; named by father, 61; on boards, 61; greased, 61; wait on parent, 62; how dressed, 62; use of bow and arrow, 62; work of, 75-76; part played by, in agriculture, 80, 102; disposition of in divorce, 82; large number desired, 82; care of sachem, 171; yearly sacrifice of, 191, 223-224, 252; altar-stones used to instruct, 230; sacrifice of, due to the priests, 237
Chinkapin, the word, 323
Chipoak Creek, Indian name for, 317
Chowan, County, North Carolina, towns in, 158; tribe, 380
Church government vigorous in Virginia, 23-24
City of Refuge, 393

Civilized tribes, 397
Cleopatre, daughter of Powhatan, 274
Clock, meaning of the word, note, 231
Cloth, Indians made, 125
Clothes, mantle, 37; skins, 40, 41-42; fashions, 53-59; matchcoats, 57; deerskins, 62; of women, 64; thread for, 95
Cockarouse, title of honor for bravery, 92; must have been huskanawed, 195
Cockle shell, used as money, 47; as a spoon, 75
Cohongoroota, river, 315, 363, 383
Cohonks, winters called, 84; years reckoned by, 84; moon of, 84
Colcraft, Henry R., quoted, 214
Color, of Indians, 32, 36; partly due to smoke, 131
Columbus, discovery by, foundation of claims of Spain, 2
Common people, given to stealing, 35; headgear, 37; clothes, 37; bareheaded, 56; their souls not believed to be immortal, 241-242
Conch shell, 46, 64
Confederate Government, Choctaws and Cherokees allies of, 396-397
Conjuration, particular case of, 227-229; performed in the Occaneeche language, 260
Conjurer, see Priests and Conjurers
Cooking, boiling, 66; fish, 66; meat, 66-67; done with little care, 67-68; seasoning 68. See Food
Cooks, 62
Copper, chains and bracelets of, 40, 53, 54, 55, 61, 63
Corn, Indian, 47, 73, 74, 76, 80, 84; fields, 58, 102; bread, 68; gathering, 84; moon, 84; importance of, 103; how planted and gathered, 103-104; the King's, how planted and gathered, 104-105, 136; how protected, 136; annual feast at corn gathering, 263-264
Coronet, 36, 46, 56

Council, great, of nation, power of, 171
Counting, system of, 84; pastime involving, 86
Courtship, 78, 80
Cowee range, 266
Crawford, Colonel Wm., his death, 300–301
Creation, Indians' belief as to, 239–240, 254–258
Crown, sent by James I. to Powhatan, use of, at time of corn planting, 104; descent of, through female line, 170; kept in the god's house at Orapax, 251
Cruelty of the Indians, 44–45, 181–182
Crystal altar-stone for sacrifice, 253
Culpeper County, tribes in, 370
Cumberland County, tribes in, 371
Cushaws, preserved, 69; described, 73; cultivated, 73
Customs, welcome to chief, 43; walking, 44; dances, 45; traveling, 47; receiving strangers, 49–52; entertaining strangers of condition, 52

D

Dances, war, 45; one arranged by Pocahontas, 64–65; feature of yearly festival, 85; two kinds described, 86–87; every night, 87; one like the Hornpipe, 88; at the matchacomoco, 175; one form of devotion, 230
Dare County, North Carolina, Indian town in, 159
Day, how divided, 84; none more holy than another, 229, 251–252; "A, in an Indian Village," 288–309
Dead, bodies of the kings, see Mummies; fate of the, decided by Mahomny, 261–262
De Bry, pictures engraved by, 37–39
Deer, plentiful, 40; skins used as dress, 62; how flayed, 62; feeding-grounds, 73; how hunted, 97, 99–100; stalking, 97–98; use of, when killed, 99, 100; the Great Deer, 256–257
Descent of the Crown, 170
Despotism, Powhatan's rule a, 165–166, 167–168, 174–175; Burk's statement as to authority, 171
Devil worship, 249, 250, 251, 252, 259–260; names for, 306. *See* Religion
District of Columbia, tribe in, xii.; quarries and workshops in, 114–119
Divination and enchantment, frequency of, 262
Divisions, political, of land, 165, 167
Divorce, husband could at will, 78, 79, 80, 81; right of wife to, 80, 81; children how disposed of in case of, 82
Domestic animals, lack of, 71
Dorchester County, Maryland, tribes in, 366
Drink, water, principal, 70; appetite for strong, 70–71
Drums, how made, 85–86, 87; none used in war, 177
Duffield match-coat, 57
Dutch, love of the Indians for the, 180–181

E

Ear-rings, 40, 41, 54, 55, 59
Eastern Shore, towns on, 155; kingdom of Accomack, 155, 316; Still Pond, 265–266; tribes on, 366–368
Echota, capital city of the Cherokees, 391–394
Edenton, site of Indian town, 158
Edict of Nantes, 11, 15
Eltham, seat of the Bassetts, 151
Embalming, 47, 198, 199–200. *See* Mummies
Empress of Accomac, 155
Enchantment, frequency of, 262
England, claim of, to Virginia, 2; King of, at the head of movement to found Virginia, 19–21; policy of, in regard to the Indians, 30, 236
English, Indian name for the, 321, 343; Indian words adopted into the, 322–323

Index 413

Ensenore, mourning for, 203; views in regard to immortality of the white men, 242–243
Essex County, towns in, 156; tribes in, 361
Estates, private, on sites of Indian villages, 157
Europe, condition of, in sixteenth and seventeenth centuries, 1–15; powers of, which laid claim to Virginia, 2–3

F

Faces carved on posts, 85, 244, 249, 264
Fairfax County, tribes in, 365
Falls Church, Indian workshop near, 117–118
Falls of the James, 161–164; Indian name for, 316
Father, children named by, 61; daughters bought of, in marriage, 77–78; oaths on manes of dead, 248–249
Fauna of the Virginia forest, 28–29
Fauquier County, tribes in, 370
Feasts, how attended, 40; one described, 85; held at night, 137
Feathers as ornaments, 37, 39, 41
Female, title to the Crown by descent through, 170
Feudal system, the Indians' virtually a, 129
Field, picture of Indian, 42
Fire, always kept burning in cabins, 66, 131; how lighted, 66, 109, 111; water, 70–71; every night for amusement, 87; fishing, 93–94; hunting, 97, 99–100; always kept with the mummies of the kings, 199
First fruits, 262
Fiscal system of Powhatan, 165–166, 167
Fish, see Food
Fishing, women enjoy seeing, 63; spring diet, 71; chapter on, 91–96; weirs, 91–92, 94, 95–96, 98; catching sturgeon, 92–93; by fire, 93–94; in canoes, 93–96; hawk, picture of, 94; nets, 95; hooks, 95; lines, 95; bait tied on, 95; shooting fish with arrows, 95, 98; in Accomac, 95–96; care taken in, 96
Flora of the Virginia forest, 28
Fluvanna County, tribes in, 371
Flying-squirrels, 73
Food, constituted the Indians' principal riches, 44, 71; amount consumed, 66, 74, 76; grace before, 74; but little stored up, 101; waste of, 67, 70, 100; for various seasons, 71–72; no cattle nor domestic fowls, 70–71, 73; herbs not used as, 69; had no salt, 68; used ash of hickory, etc., for seasoning, 68; cooks, 62; how cooked and served, 47, 66, 67, 68, 70, 74–75, 76; all sorts of flesh used as, 68, 76; feasts, 40, 85, 139; some mentioned:
  acorns, 71
  apricots, 73
  beans, 68, 73, 103
  bear's oil, sauce for dried meat, 47
  beaver, 68
  bread, made of corn, wild oats, sunflower seed, 68; or tuckahoe, 70; how baked, 68, 72; eaten alone, 68
  cherries, 73
  chinkapins, 69
  corn, see Corn
  crabs, 71–72
  cushaws, 69, 73
  dried fish, flesh, and oysters, 72
  earthnuts, 69
  fish, quantity of, 40, 73; how dressed, 66, 68; how cooked, 66, 67, 74; season for, 71–72
  goats, 73
  gourds, 73
  grapes, 73
  grubs, 68
  hominy, 67, 74
  macocks, 73
  maracocks, 73
  matcocks, 69
  melons, 69, 72–73, 102

Food—*Continued*
  mulberries, 71–72
  muskmelons, 73
  nectarines, 72–73
  nuts, 69, 71
  oil of acorns, sauce for dried meats, 47, 69, 71
  onions, wild, 69
  oysters, 71–72
  peaches, 69, 73
  peas, 68, 73
  plums, 73–74
  potatoes, 73
  pulse, 68
  pumpkins, 69, 73, 102
  roasting ears, 68–69
  rockahomonie, for traveling, 47–48
  roots, 69–70
  simlins, 73
  snakes, 68
  squirrels, 71, 73
  strawberries, 69, 71–72
  terrapin, 68, 71–72
  tocknough berries, 72
  tortoise, land, 72
  truffles, 69
  tuckahoe, 69–70
  turkeys, 71
  turtles, 68
  venison, 76
  walnuts, 69, 71, 73
  wasps, 68
  water, pond, preferred, 70
  watermelons, 73
  wheat, a kind of, 73
Football, 88
Forest, covered with grapevines, 27; principal trees, 28; flora and fauna of, 28–29; often uninhabited, 96; clear of underbrush around the towns, 138
Fort, West's, 144; Algernoone, 148; at Warascoyack, 349; Mackintosh, 401
Forum, one in each town, 87, 134, 135, 136–137
Fowls, abundance of, 73; no chickens nor peacocks, 73; how hunted, 99; how dressed, 68. *See* Food
France, claim of, to Virginia, 2; policy of, in regard to the Indians, 30; an ally of the Indians, 403

Frederick County, tribes in, 380–381; towns in, 386
Fredericksburg, site of Indian town, 157
Freedom of religion, involved in wars of sixteenth and seventeenth centuries, and in the colonization of Virginia, 4–15; existed nowhere at that time, 18
Fruits, *see* Food
Funeral, rites, chapter on, 198–203
Furs, wreath of, 37; for use, 45

G

Game, seasons for, 71–72; kinds of, 73, 97; where found, 96; part of most valued, 99, 100; fowls abundant, 99; large, how hunted, 99–100. *See* Hunting
Gates County, North Carolina, Indian town in, 158
Gloucester County, towns in, 142, 145–146; tribes in, 355
Glover, Thomas, writings, xiv.; quoted, 45, 93, 106, 129, 189, 202, 235
Glue, of deer sinews and horns, 43, 112; of turpentine, 112
God, *see* Religion
Gourds, 62, 73, 75; for rattles, 86, 87; use in pottery-making, 121–122
Government, feudal in its nature, 129; of the Indians, aristocratic, 133–134; essentially a hierarchy, 165, 173; Powhatan's, despotic, 166; taxes of, under Powhatan, oppressive, 167; descent of the Crown, 170; of the Chickahominies, 342–343; of the Cherokees, 391–392; political connection between the tribes weak, 402
Grangenimeo, brother of Pemisapan, 283
Grapevines, profusion of, 27–28
Graves, pottery found in, 120; Indian in northwestern part of State, 381–389
Greasing, of the hair, 36; children, 61
Great, Hare, leg nd of the, 255–258; Deer, legend of, 256–257

Index 415

Greensville County, tribes in, 379
Gustavus Adolphus, 13

H

Hair, of Indians, black, 33; men's, half shaven, 33-34, 54-55; worn long, 39; cut fancifully and painted, 36; tied in knot under ears, 39; cut like a cock's comb, 39-40, 41, 57; few beards, 54, 57; front part of women's cut short, 58; women's put up in knot, 61; of maids cut short in front and sides, 63; of married women all long, 63
Hammer, weapon like a, 176
Hamor, Ralph, writings, xiii.; quoted, 151
Hampshire County, West Virginia, Indian relics in, 384-385
Hampton, Indian fields at, 102; site of Indian town, 157
Hanover County, towns in, 149, 153; tribes in, 338
Happy hunting grounds, 261-262
Hare, native animal, 73; the Great, legend of, 255-258
Hariot, Thomas, writings, vii.; sent over by Raleigh, vii.; pictures, 37-39; quoted, 39, 40, 55, 57, 61, 62, 65, 66, 76, 85, 105, 134, 135, 201, 230, 239
Heaven, the Indians' belief in regard to, 240, 241-242, 257-258, 261-262; Indian word for, 306. *See* Religion
Hell, the Indians' belief in regard to, 240, 241, 261-262; words for, 240, 306. *See* Religion
Henrico County, towns in, 145, 325; tribes in, 324-325, 337
Henry III. on throne of France when this history begins, 3
Henry IV. assassinated, 12
Heraldry, marks on the body in the nature of coats of arms, 42
Hertford County, North Carolina, Indian town in, 158
Hickory, ash of, for seasoning food, 68; nuts, 69; liquor made from, 69; Indian name for milk, 69; the word, adopted into the English, 323
Holmes, W. H., quoted, 119
Holy days, none specially observed, 229, 251-252
Hours, no distinction of, 84
Houses, and towns, chapter on, 128-140; string used in construction of, 95; for hunting, 96, 101, 139-140; corn stored in dwelling, 104; axes and hatchets used in building, 110; Indians lived in, 128; not tents, 138; set about the towns irregularly, 130, 134, 139; how built, 130-132, 133, 139; fire in, 131, 137, 140; only one room, 131, 135; flowers near, 133; built by the rivers, 137; all of one pattern, 139; built under trees, 139; king's larger, 139; scæna by, 140; not kept clean, 189; grand council, of the Cherokees, 394
Howe quoted, 212-216
Hunger, Indians patient of, 70; effect of, reduced by tightening their girdles, 70
Hunting, chapter on, 96-101; of deer, favorite sport, 40, 97-98, 99-100; care taken in, 96; how conducted, 96, 97, 99, 100-101; houses built for, 96, 101, 139-140; use of fire in, 97, 99-100; deer-stalking, 97-98; of fowls, 99
Husband, duties of, 80; effect of plurality of wives on, 82-83
Huskanawing, chapter on, 191-197; where done, 144, 191, 196, 197; how often practiced, 191, 195; only the choicest youths selected for, 195; essence of the rite, 195-196; cockarouses and priests must have been through, 195; wysoccan, a mad potion given in, 196; those treated must forget the past, 196-197; Okee's part in, 193-194, 197
Hyde County, North Carolina, towns in, 157, 159

Index

I

Idols, *see* Religion

Ill-breeding punished by the weroances, 168

Immortality of the soul, *see* Religion

Indian, file, 44; fashion and domestic construction of, society, 53–76; summer, 89–90; old fields, 102, 134; chiefs, *see* Weroances; towns, *see* Towns; names of places in Virginia, 318–320; words adopted into the English, 322–323; relics in northwestern part of the State, 383–388; allies of Virginia: Pamunkeys, 326–327; Choctaws, 396; Cherokees, 397; Catawbas, 399. *See* Indians

Indians, character of, chapter on, 25–52; in Virginia belonged to the neolithic Stone Age, 25; classed as barbarous, 25; of the Algonquin stock, 26; distribution of, in eastern part of the United States, 26–27; at war among themselves, 27, 129, 173, 382–383, 401–402; character and attainments, 29–30, 34, 174, 175–176, 181–182; policies of Spain, France, and England in relation to the, 30; color and features, 31–32, 36, 59, 63, 131; hair, 33, 36, 39, 41; paints used by, 32–33; clothes, 37, 41–42; shoes, 37; marked on the back, 40–41; all lived in towns, 128–129; able-bodied, 33, 35–36; long-lived, 44, 76; most frequent diseases of, 185–190; patient of hunger, 70; moderate in eating, 66, 76; excessive in eating, 74; bodies alter with their diet, 72; wasteful, 67, 70, 100; prone to drunkenness, 70–71; cruel, 44–45, 181–182, 300–301; care-free original condition, 98–99, 100; economic effect produced by the coming of the English, 101; marriage among, 77–83; occupations of men and women, 75–76, 102, 104, 110; quarries and workshops, 114–119; manufactures, 125; as traders, 34–35; standard of honesty, 35; differences in language, *see* Language; in council, 170, 177–178, 179–181; the Virginians adopted forms of speech of, 178–179; called the English by their first names, 322; all except the priests protected by the orders of King James, 236; love of the, for the Dutch, 180–181; reservations for, 327, 336; trustees appointed for, 351; troubles caused by northern, 375–376; characteristics of the southern, 390

Injury, never forgotten, 34; revenge for, 35

Interpreter, Spelman, an, xii.

Interruption, punished, 168; none in public meetings, 177–178

Iron, Indians lacked, 112

Isle of Wight County, town in, 149; tribes in, 348

"Issues," some Cherokees called, 395–396

J

James I., the head of the movement to found Virginia, 19–21; sent crown, etc., to Powhatan, 104, 251; Powhatan protected by orders of, 236

James City County, towns in, 144–145, 146, 149; tribes in, 339, 341

James River, falls of, 161–164; Indian name for, 316; tribes on, 339–355, 369–371

Jamestown, in the territory of the Paspaheghs, 339

Jefferson quoted, 204–210

Johah, shout of approbation, 180

Jones quoted, 35, 44, 55, 74, 79, 81, 134, 261

Jopassus, Spelman lived with, xi.; sold Spelman to Argall, xii.; account of creation, 254–258; brother of Powhatan, 272; King of the Potomacs, 363

Index

K

Kanawha, name, 315
Kecoughtan, Indian fields at, 102, 354; described and destroyed, 148; site of Hampton, 157, 317; sacrifice of children at, 191; tribe, 353–355; town, 354–355; conquest of, 354–355; tribe transported to Payankatank, 358–359
Keightley quoted, 288
Kent County, Maryland, town in, 151
Kentucky, name, 315
Kercheval quoted, 89, 383
Kewas, an idol, see Religion
Kewasowok, plural of Kewas, 240
King, title of, 168; the embalmed kings, and funeral rites, chapter on, 198–203; the Laughing, 274, 367; the Half King, 391, 401; Indian Kings, see Weroances
King George County, tribes in, 360, 361
King William County, Pamunkeys live in, 327; Mattaponys live in, 336–337
King and Queen County, Beverley lived in, xv.; town in, 151
King William County, towns in, 156
Kingdom, of Accomack, 155, 316; term may apply to small number, 156
Kiskiack, town, 146, 356; tribe, 355; allowed to have guns, 356; their land secured to them, 356; owned land at Payankatank, 356
Kiwasa, or Kewasa, an idol, see Religion

L

Lancaster County, town in, 147; tribes in, 359–360, 361
Land, separate use of, 133, 139, 168; size of tracts of, 138; separate tracts for tribes, 139, 165, 167; conveyed by the weroances, 169; tribal, 325; sales of, by King of the Chickahominy tribe, 344–345; secured to the Kiskiacks, 356; disputes in relation to, adjusted, 356, 360–361, 363–364; secured to the Rappahannocks, 360–361; controversy with the King of the Potomacs, 363–365; of the Gingaskins, 366–367; secured to the Accomacks, 368; of the Nottoways, 376–379; unoccupied, between the mountains and the Mississippi, 395
Lane, map of expedition of, 160; quoted, 239, 242, 351, 352
Language, differences in, very great, 33; each town had separate, 134, 285–286, 287; no written, 285; that of the Occaneeches a general, 286; long words, 286–288; paucity of the Indian, 287; "A Day in an Indian Village," 288–309; "The Lovers' Quarrel," 309–311; "The Troublesome Traveler," 312–314; "The Quarrelsome Chiefs," 314; names of places, meaning of, 315–316; other Indian names of places, etc., 316–320; Indian verses, 320–322; words adopted into the English, 322–323
Laughing King, 274, 367
Laws, political, and art of war, chapter on, 165–182; no written, 167–168; will of the chief is law, 167–168; title to the crown, 170; enforcement of criminal, 172–173; Indians not without, 172; how summoned for war, 174–175
Leaves, not used as food, 69; as covering, 64–65, 87
Letters, Indians had none, 167
Liquor, made from hickory nuts, 69; no other drinks, 70; Indians' fondness for, 70–71
Loggs Town, seat of Queen Alliguippe, 179
London Company, established Virginia, 21; overthrown by the King, 21
Longevity, Indian over 160 years old, 44; general among the Indians, 76

Louisa County, tribes in, 370–371
"Lovers', The, Quarrel," 309–311

M

Machicomuck, the temple, 240
Matchacomoco, a grand council, 175
Machot, town, 151–152
Machumps says grace at Dale's, 74
Macocks, a kind of pumpkin, 73; for rattles, 87
Mahomny, the god who decides the fate of the dead, 261–262, 305
Mamanahunt, site of, 146; not at first under Powhatan's rule, 147
Manakins, where settled, 324, 369–370; tribes ruled by, 370–371
Mannahoacks, tribes ruled by the, 369–370
Mantles of turkey-feathers, 53
Map, Smith's, 141; of towns in Virginia, 142; of towns in North Carolina, 160; de Brys, 160
Maracock, fruit of the passion flower, 73
Marietta, mound at, 210–211
Marks, on the backs of Indians, 40–41, 42
Marriage, chapter on, 77–83; wives bought, 77, 78; ceremony of, 77, 79–80; of the kings, 78; courtship, 77–80; polygamy, 77, 78, 79, 80; duties of the consorts, 80; divorce, 78, 79, 80, 81
Married women, how distinguished from maids, 63; see Wives
Maryland founded, 14; freedom of religion compulsory in, under its charter, 18; trade with, prohibited, 375–376
Massachusetts, difference between, and Virginia, 15–18
Massomeck, battle between, and Potomac, 176–177
Matachanna, daughter of Powhatan, 274

Match-coats, large mantles, 37; formerly worn only by the old, 57; meaning of, 58; children carried in, 59–60; used as mats, 131
Matcocks, fruit of the passion flower, 69
Materia medica, knowledge of the priests, 186; roots and barks of trees, 187, 188–189; Indian medicine very strong, 189; given in large doses, 190; antidote for snake-bites, 186, 190; mad potion for huskanawing, 195–196; wighsacan a purgative, 184; puccoon used as a medicine, 188–189, 229
Mats, used to sit on, 62, 75, 131; picture of, 75; made by women, 76; made of bents, 76; used for doors and partitions in houses, 131; covering for beds, 132; carried about for hunting-houses, 139–140; interior of temples divided by, 245
McGee, W. J., quoted, 161–164
McKeesport, Pennsylvania, site of Indian town, 401
Mattapament, town, 152 river, 317; tribe, 324, 336; see Mattaponys
Mattapamients, the tribe, 324, 336, 366; see Mattapony
Mattapony, river, 317; the tribe, 336–337; still existent, 337
Meat, see Food
Mecklenburg County, tribes in, 379
Medicine, Indian practices in regard to, 183–190; knowledge of, monopolized by the priests, 183, 186–187, 194; use of rattles, 183, 185; treatment of wounds, 183–184, 190; treatment of ulcers, hurts, and swellings, 184, 185, 190; purgation, 184; dropsy, 184; sweating, 184, 185, 187; sweating - house, 187–188; swellings how treated, 185; use of sucking, 185; use of charms, 185; use of burning wood, 185–186; use of smoking and scratching, 186; snake-

Index

Medicine—*Continued*
bites, 186–187, 190; vomiting a bad omen, 190; bleeding or cupping not used, 190; fractures cured, 190; *see Materia Medica*
Meherrin, tribe, 379; river, tribes on, 379, 380
Metaphor, Indian fondness for, 178–181
Miami, tribe, 26; word, 316
Middlesex County, tribes in, 358–359
Milk called hickory, 69
Mobjack Bay, 317
Moccasins, shoes, how made, 37, 56–57
Monacans, *see* Manakins
Money, made of conch shell, 46; fixed in value, 47; wives bought with, 77
Montoac, name of many gods, 239. *See* Religion
Months counted by moons, 84
Moons, months counted by, 84; names of, 84
Morters made by women and children, 76
Mounds, one opened by Mr. Jefferson, 204–210; theories in regard to origin of, 204–205; well known to the Indians, 209; some located, 209–210; one at Marietta, 210–211; one at Moundsville, 211–222; stone found in 215–216; origin of those in Virginia, 222; in the Valley of Virginia, 381–389
Moundsville, mound at, 211–221
Mount Vernon, town near, 365
Mourning for the dead Kings, 203
Mummies, bodies preserved by barbecuing, 47; of the kings, how protected, 132, 198, 200, 201, 251; another mode of preservation, 198–200; where kept, 199, 249–250; guarded by the priests, who stayed with them, 199, 200; removed by the Indians, 203, 253
Murder, how punished, 172; rare, 173
Music, pastime, 86; singing, 86; every night, 87; instruments of, 85–86, 87
Musical instruments, pipes, 85; drums, 85–86, 87; rattles, 86, 87; no trumpets, 177
Muskingum, word, 316

N

Nails, length of Indian women's, 59; kept long to skin deer, 62
Names, given by parents, 60; soon given to child, 61; given by father, 61; meaning of, of places, 315–316; Indian, for places, etc., 316–320; origin of Powhatan, 269, 358; origin of Opechancanough, 358; origin of names of the tribes, 142, 368–369; Indians used only first names of the English, 322
Nansemond, town, 149; towns in, 149, 156; the name, 315; river, 317; tribe, 350–351; tribes in, 350, 376–379
Nation, term may apply to small number, 156. *See* Tribes
Necklaces, worn by ladies of distinction, 64
Nets, fish, and other kinds made, 125
New England settled, 13
New Kent County, tribes in, 341–342
Newport, Capt. Christopher, commander of second expedition to Virginia, 19
Norfolk, site of Indian town, 157
Norfolk County, Indian tribe in, 351–353
Northampton County, towns in, 152, 155; tribes in, 366–367
Northumberland, County, towns in, 156
Nuns, faces like, on posts, 85, 244, 249, 264

O

Oaths, the keeping of, 248–249; on manes of dead father, 248–249
Occaneeches, adoration and conjuration performed in language of, 260; theirs a general language, 286; tribe, 379

Ohio, name, 315; Indian towns on, 401
Oil, of acorns, sauce to dry meat, 47; bear's, same use, 47; women keep skin clean with, 64; no sweet oils, etc., used in embalming, 199; used to keep the skin of the mummies from shrinking, 200
Okee, see Religion
Old Fields, Indian, English name for their tracts, 102; always fertile, 102, 134
Opechancanough, whether a brother of Powhatan, 268, 271–272; Pepisco steals one of his women, 346–347; origin of his name, 358; see also xii., 145, 147, 151, 283, 326
Opitchapan succeeded his brother Powhatan, 271–272
Orange, the Prince of, life-work and death, 5–9
Orange County, tribes in, 370
Orapax, town, 152; Cakeres an idol at, 251; crown and other articles kept at, 251; tribe, 357; Powhatan weroance of, 357
Origin of the world and mankind, 239–240, 254–258
Oysters, pearl gotten from, 47; as food, 71–72; abundance and size, 72; dried, 72

P

Page County, Indian towns in, 386
Paint, Indians decorated with, 36, 40, 56, 64, 175
Palisade, picture of, 58; surrounded most towns, 130, 132, 134; what kept within, 132
Pamlico County, North Carolina, Indian town in, 159
Pamunkey, place, 44; corn destroyed at, in 1624, 103; river now the York, 142, 317, 326; present, river, formerly the Youghtamund, 170, 326; towns of, in 1705, 156; huskanawing at, 196, 197; still in possession of principal seat of the priests, 226–227; the name, 315; the tribe, 324, 326–336;

visit to the Reservation, 327–336
Paquippe lake, 61
Parkman referred to in connection with Indian burials, 222
Pastimes, watching fishing, etc., 59, 63; yearly feast, 85; singing, music, and games, 86; nightly music and dancing, 87; one form of dance, 88; football, 88; kicking small ball, 88
Patapsco, name, 315
Patuxent, town, 152; name, 315; river, 317; tribes on the, 365–366; tribe, 365
Pawcorances, sacrifices made on them, 230; the crystal altar-stone, 253–254; commemorated events by, 230, 254; used to instruct children, 254; the bird called, 254
Pawwawing days, 90; sorceries of the Indians so called, 233
Payankatank, river, 317; country peopled by the Kecoughtans, 354–355; the Kiskiacks owned land at, 356; tribes on, 358–359; tribe, 358–359; destroyed by Powhatan, 358–359
Peace, pipe of, 49–52; making of treaties of, 178; how marked, 178
Peak, for coronets, 36–37, 56; for necklaces and bracelets, 42, 64; valued for ornament, 45; various uses of, 46; passed as money, 46, 306; made from the conch shell, 64
Pearls, chains and bracelets of, worn by princes, 40, 55; supply of, 47; worn by virgins of good parentage, 62–63; buried with the dead, 202–203
Pepisco, romance of, 346–347
Percy, Capt. Geo., writings, viii.; at a huskanawing, 191; quoted, 248
Perquimans County, North Carolina, town in, 158
Petersburg, site of Indian town, 157
Philip II. on throne of Spain when this history begins, 3; the enemy of Virginia, 11

Index 421

Philip III., the enemy of Virginia, 11
Pictures, White's, 37–39, 124
Pilgrim Fathers, 15–18
Piney Branch, workshop on, 114–116
Pipes, of conch shell, 46; of peace, 49–52; for music, 85; of clay, 122
Places, Indian names for, 315–320
Pocahontas, dance arranged by, 64–65; daughter of Powhatan, 273, 274; name, 274, 315; Opachisco her uncle, 275
Pochone, see Puccoon
Pocomoke, name, 316
Pocones, see Puccoon
Poetry, specimen of Indian, 320–322
Point Pleasant, battle of, won by the Virginians, 182
Political laws, and the art of war, chapter on, 165–182; title to the crown, 170; weroance and sachem, 170–171; connection between the tribes was weak, 402
Polygamy, custom, 77, 80; on the part of the kings, 78; status of wives, 79; reason for, 82; effect on the husbands, 82–83
Pomeiock, pictures relating to, 36–39, 135; Indians of, how marked, 41; aged men of, how dressed, 57; chief women of, how dressed, 61; described, 134–135; mentioned, 157
Pompions, cultivated, 69, 73; shells for rattles, 86
Pond, water preferred, 70; artificial for water supply, 135
Popogusso, Hell, 240, 241, 261–262
Population, not so great here as in West Indies, 82; greater than supposed, 130; estimates of, 279–280, 402–403
Posts, faces carved on, 85, 244, 249, 264
Potomac, town, 151; battle with Massomeck, 176–177; Quioquascacke a god of the, country, 251; the name, 315; river, 317; tribe, 362; tribes on the,

xii., 362–366, 371–372, 373, 383
Pots, how set for cooking, 66; made of clay, 110, 119–127; general form of, 122; uses of, 123. See Pottery
Pottery, made by women, 65–66, 76; manufacture of, 119–127; decoration of, 123–127; relation to basketry, 125
Pouncing, general custom, 40, 53–54, 56, 58–59, 61; nationality shown by, 42; described by Strachey, 59; how done, 63; designs of, on body, same as that on pottery, 124
Powhatan, origin of the name, 144, 269, 358; other names given him, 269; origin of his family, 268; where born, 267–268; belonged to the Powhatan tribe, 324; eighty years old when the English came, 267; personal appearance, 267; temperament, 270–271; four brothers and two sisters, 170, 271–272; three brothers lived at Pamunkey, 170; his wives, 272, 273, 276; care of his wives 78; his children, 272–274, 346; one of his councilors, 274; inherited rule over six tribes, 268, 270; his bodyguard, 275; the night-watch, 275; his treasure-house, 275–276; his chief holy house, 224–225; regarded as a demigod, 166; his power, 276; territory conquered by him, 270; bounds of his empire, 269–270; population of his empire, 279–280; number of kings under him, 268–269, 276; tribes subject to him, 324–368; despotic rule of 166, 342; his priests responsible for destruction of the Roanoke Island settlement, 235–236; destroyed the Chesapeaks, 353; destroyed the Payankatanks, 358–359; Mamanahunt long independent of him, 146–147; fiscal system, 165–166, 167; oppressive taxes, 167; punishments ordered by, 277–278; had many enemies, 173; was

Powhatan—*Continued*
weroance of the Orapax tribe, 357; Werowocomoco favorite residence, 142; resided at Machot, 152; owned Orapax, 152; offered to sell Capahowasick, 145–146; disturbed by prophecies, 280–281, 282; protected by order of King James, 236; policy of, in dealing with the English 278–279; demoralization of his court due to the coming of the English, 281; died at Orapax, 153; the rule as to the succession to his crown, 170; succeeded by his brother Opitchapan, 271; fate of, as compared with Pemisapan, 283–284; tribe, 268, 270, 271, 273, 324–326; town, 144; town, on site of Richmond, 156–157

Powhatan County, tribes in, 371

Priests, and conjurers, chapter on, 223–237; their attire, 225–226, 230–231, 231–232; conjurer's dress, 232; black bird above ear as badge of office, 231; deemed semi-divine, 193–194; their souls deemed immortal, 241–242; lived well, 233–234; their power, 165, 252; constituted an hierarchy, 165, 173, 223, 342; ruled the Chickahominies, 342; decided questions of war, 173; were specially trained in medicine, 186, 183–190, 194; must have been huskanawed, 195; keepers of the mummies of the kings, 199; stayed with the mummies, 199, 201; opposition of, to the white man, 223–224, 235–237, 238; principal seat of, 224–227; sacred house near Uttamussack, 224–225; devotions of, 226, 229, 230; no special holy days, 229, 251–252; conjuration of, 227–229, 231; of Secota described, 230–231; some wore beards, 233; belief in their supernatural powers, 233; producing rain, 233, 234–235; office of, never held by women, 234; made the people believe, 260; control over worshipers in Okee's temple, 247, 260; redeem an Okee fallen in battle, 243; good, highly valued by the weroances, 249; prophecies of, in relation to Powhatan's empire, 280–282; destruction of the Roanoke Island settlement due to, 236; denounced by Whittaker, 233–234; Strachey thought they should be destroyed, 235–237

Prince George County, town in, 155; tribes in, 339, 345–346; Maryland, town in, 152; tribe in, 365

Princess Anne County, tribe in, 351–353

Prophecies, 280–281, 282, 353

Protestantism, extension of, involved in the colonization of Virginia, 4–15; contest between, and Roman Catholicism, 5–15

Proudfit, S. V., quoted, 114, 153

Public meetings, for war, etc., 170; decorum of, 177–178; how treaties conducted, 178–181

Puccoon, a root, 229; paint made from, 32–33, 54, 264; used as medicine, 188–189, 229

Punishment, for adultery, 81, 172; for murder, 172; for robbery, 172; capital, how inflicted, 172–173; "cruel and unusual," 181–182

Puritanism, contrast between reasons of, for colonization, and those which caused the settlement of Virginia, 15–18

Putin Bay, Werowocomoco on or near, 143

Q

"Quarrelsome, the, Chiefs," 314

Quarries, Indian, 114–119

Quebec founded, 11

Queen, title of, 168; Aliguippe, 179, 401

Queen Anne County, Maryland, tribes in, 366

Quioccos, *see* Religion

Quioccosan, *see* Religion

Quiver, of rushes, 40; bark, 42; skin, 42

R

Rain, power of priests to produce, 233, 234–235; offerings for, 251
Raleigh, Sir Walter, opposes the policies of Spain, 7–12
Rappahannock, town, 156; word, 316; river, names for, 317; tribes on the, 359–362, 369–370; tribe, 360
Rattle, picture of child with, 62; musical instrument, 86, 87; use in medicine, 183
Rattlesnake root, cure for snake-bite, 186–187
Reeds, knives made of, 43
Refuge, city of, 393
Regions, Pamunkey, 44; Secotan, 160; Weapemeoc, 160; Newsioc, 283; Pomuik, 283; Isenacommacah, 316
Reincarnation, 242, 258
Relics, Indian, in northwestern part of the State, 383–388
Religion, freedom of, involved in the wars of the sixteenth and seventeenth centuries, 4–15; nature of the Indians', 238; the Indians', described by Whittaker, 252–253; the Indian governmental system of, 249; Occaneeche the language of, 260; tutelar deities of towns, 247–248, 251; the priests made the people believe, 260; Indian priests resented attack on their, 223–224; Indians reticent about, 238, 244, 258; medicine a part of, and not to be disclosed, 186–187; Quioccosan or Machicomuck words for temple, 305; temples surrounded by posts with faces on them, 244, 264; the temple at Pomeiock, 135; idols placed in the temples to protect the mummies of the kings, 198, 240, 250, 305; Beverley's visit to the Indian temple, 243–248; part played by conjurers and priests in Okee's temple, 247; altar-stones, 230, 253–254; see Pawcorances; frequency of sacrifice, 263; religious relics carefully kept by Indians, 132; no special holy days, 229, 251–252; seasons observed in, 263–264; devotions, 226, 229–230, 254; frequency of divinations and enchantments, 262; various objects of worship, 249; the Devil chief object of worship, 249, 251, 259–260, 262; necessity for worshiping him, 259–260; Riokosick and Riapoke names for the Devil, 306; Okee the malignant deity, 250–251, 259–260, 305; his part in huskanawing, 193–194, 197; protected the mummies of the kings, 198, 240, 250, 305; carried into battle, 243; the name Okee a generic term, 247–248, 305; the idol Okee described, 246, 247, 250, 252; burnt offerings and first fruits given to, 262; Ahone the great and good god, 250, 259, 305; names of the gods Okee, Quioccos, Kiwasa, 239, 247–248, 305; Cakeres and Quioquascacke, 251; Montoac a general word for gods, 239, 305; one great god, 239; Rawottonemd their word for god, 305; Kewas, an image of god in the form of a man; plural Kewasowok, 305; Quiyoughcosoughs, the name for petty gods and their affinities, 305; Quioccos the idol which dwelt in the temple, 305; Mahomny the god who decides the fate of the dead, 261–262, 305; gods have human forms, 240; sun worship, 248; the good spirit of the Cherokees, 391; the evil spirit of the Cherokees, 266; his habitation, 266; sanctity of oaths, 248–249; rite of huskanawing, 191–197; grace before meals, 74; first fruits, 262; tobacco subject of sacrifice, 262–263; sacrifice to running streams, 265; pyra-

Religion—*Continued*
midical stones and running streams types of the immutability of the deity, 264, 265; the giant's footprint, 265; Still Pond, 265–266; Jopassus' account of creation and the, of the Indians, 254–258; the Great Hare, 255–258; belief in the immortality of the soul, 240–243, 257–258, 261, 262; applied to weroances and priests, 241–242; did not include the common people, 241–242; journey of the soul after death, 257–258; the Happy Hunting Grounds, 261; the Barren Hunting Grounds, 261–262; the doctrine of reincarnation, 242, 257–258; belief that the white men were dead men returned to life, 242–243; Popogusso their word for Hell, 306; Mounshaquatuuh, their word for Heaven, 306; Pepisco's appreciation of the God of the English, 346

Reservations, Pamunkey, 327–336; Mattapony, 336–337

Revenge, never forget injury, 34; case of, 35; form of private justice, 45–46, 393; tobacco, the Indians', on the White Man, 105

Riches, food principal, 44; Indians had little, 45. *See* Treasure

Richmond, site of Indian town, 144, 145, 157

Richmond County, towns in, 149, 156, 361; tribes in, 361

Rivers and streams, names of, 315–316

Roads, Indian running north from Werowocomoco, 143; along the north shore of the York, 143

Roanoke, ornament, 42, 45; money, 47, 307; town of, 157; name, 315

Roanoke Island, settlement came in contact with the Catawbas, 27; town, pictures relate to, 39; Indians, how marked, 41; costumes, etc.,
55; climate, 55; king of the country around, 203; settlement's destruction due to Powhatan's priests, 235–236

Roasting-ear, picture of boy with, 62; a favorite food, 68–69; in picture of man and wife at dinner, 75; time, a division of the year, 84

Robbery, how punished, 172

Rock Creek, workshops on, 116

Roman Catholicism, its efforts to suppress Protestantism, 4–15

Rose Hill, quarry, 117, 118

Rosewell, Werowocomoco, at or near, 143, 355; Indian roads near, 143

Running streams, worshiped, 265

Runtees, made of the conch shell, 46; use of, as ornaments, 46, 307; picture of boy with necklace of, 62

S

Sachem, office of, 170–171

Sacrifice, yearly, of children, 191, 223–224, 252; altar-stones for, 230, 253; the crystal altar-stone, 253; principal devotion consisted in, 253–254; tobacco, object of, 262–263; frequency of, 263; to running streams, 265

Scalp-lock, long lock preserved for distinction, 36; half of the hair allowed to grow, 54–55

Scarecrow, picture of cabin used by, 58; regular feature of agriculture, 136

Seasons, and festivals, chapter on, 84–90; how divided, 84; those observed religiously, 263–264

Secota, pictures relating to, 37–39, 135–136; described, 135–136; mentioned 159; priests of, 230–231

Secotam, Indians of, how marked, 41; region, 160, 283

Servants, black boys, 169

Shawanese, tribe, 26, 380–381; where located, 324

Shelly, Werowocomoco at or near, 143

Index 425

Shenandoah, name, 316; Indian towns on, 385-389
Shenapin town, incidents of treaty held at, 179-180
Shields, of bark, 112, 173-174, 176
Shoes, how made, 37, 56
Sickness, *see* Medicine
Sieges, Indians not capable of making, 182
Singing, calculated to affright rather than delight, 86; further described, 86
Six Nations, location of, among the Algonquin Indians, 26; incident of a treaty with, 180-181; came in contact with Virginia, 400
Skicoak, town on site of Norfolk, 157
Skins, 53; of birds, 54; how dressed, 57, 104; of persons, how hardened, 60; how kept, 64; part of game most valued, 99, 100
Slaves, how married women punished for adultery might become, 81; stolen from the white men by the Indians, 394
Smith, Capt. John, writings, viii.; taken captive by hunting-party, 97; map, 141; quoted, 34, 42, 53, 58, 60, 71, 75, 85, 96, 111, 137, 229, 243, 287, 369
Smithfield, site of Indian town, 157, 350
Smoke, houses full of, 131
Snake, as earring, 54; eaten as food, 68; bite of, how cured, 186-187, 190
Socobec, town, on site of Fredericksburg, 157
Soul, belief in immortality of, 240-243; journey of, after death, 257-258. *See* Religion
Southampton County, tribes in, 376-379
Spain, claim of, to Virginia, 2; policy of, in regard to the Indians, 30; the Chickahominies engage to fight against, 343
Spelman, Henry, writings, x.-xiii.; head cut off, 151; quoted, 54, 61, 73, 76, 77, 88, 99, 103, 139, 172-173, 175, 183, 201, 233, 251;
Spinning, how done, 95
Spoon, 75; picture of cockleshell used for, 75; those used by the Indians very large, 75
Spots, on body, from bleeding, 40
Spottsylvania County, tribes in, 370
Spring, the budding of, one of the Indians' divisions of the year, 84
Stafford County, tribes in, 361, 362-363, 370; town in, 363
Stags, moon of, 84
Stealing, common people given to, 35
Still Pond, 265-266
Stockings worn more generally by old people, 57-58
Stoicism, pain borne with, 44-45
Stone Age, Virginia Indians belonged to neolithic, 25; workshops of, 112-119; implements of, discussed, 113-114; bodies unburnt during, 217
Stones, heap of, raised to commemorate treaties of peace, 178; used to typify qualities of the deity, 264-265
Stools of earth, 130, 131
Strachey, Wm., writings, viii.-x.; quoted, 31, 59, 65, 71, 72, 74, 78, 82, 94, 102, 112, 133, 135, 140, 165, 166, 170, 191, 198, 202, 223, 224, 227, 235, 241, 249, 255, 287, 321, 370
Strangers, how received, 49-52; of condition, how entertained, 52, 62
Sturgeon, how caught, 92-93
Suffolk, site of Indian town, 157
Summer, highest sun, Indian division of the year, 84; Indian, meaning of, 89-90
Summons, to war, how served on warriors, 174-175
Sun, highest, one of the divisions of the year, 84; worshiped as a god, 248
Superstitions, continual fire in the home, 66; suggested in connection with pottery, 121; as to vomiting, 190; in regard

Superstitions—*Continued*
to huskanawing, 193-194; in regard to lightning and thunder, 194, 229, 259-260; passing sacred house at Uttamussack, 224-225; conjuration and sorcery, 227-229; in regard to the white men, 242-243, 404-405; various objects of worship, 249; the bird pawcorance, 254; baskets of stones, 265; running streams, 265; giant footprint, 265; Still Pond, 265-266; prophecies as to the destruction of the realm, 280-282. *See* Religion
Surry County, Indian towns in, 144, 155; tribes in, 339, 345-346
Susquehannocks, one of the Six Nations, 26; large in stature, 33, 373-374; described, 373-376; tribe, 373-376, 379
Sweating-house, medical treatment with, 187-188
Sword, of wood, 174

T

Tablet, breast ornament, 41, 46
Tahahcoope, son of Powhatan, 274
Tappahannas, Oholasc regent over, 272; tribe, 345, 360
Targets of bark, 112, 173-174, 176
Tattooing, *see* Pouncing
Taxes, paid in tithes, 165-166, 167; oppressive, 167
Temple, at Pomeioc described, 135; mummies of the kings kept in, 199; Beverley's visit to the, of Okee, 243-248; and priest in the territory of each weroance, 249; built at the cost of the weroances, 249; how constructed, 249; surrounded by posts with faces carved on them, 264; called quioccosan or machicomuck, 305. *See* Religion
Tennessee, word, 316
Textile art, 125-127
Thanksgiving, how expressed, 88
Thread, how made, 95; uses of, 95

Timberneck Bay, Werowocomoco, on or near, 142
Time, how divided, 84
Tithes exacted by Powhatan, 167
Titles of honor, sachem, 171, 302; cockarouse, 92, 168-169, 302; weroance, 168, 169, 302; borrowed from the English, 168-169; woman queen, 302; cronockoes, 302; mamanatowick, 269, 302; veroanee, 302; mangoi, 344, 345; beloved man, 391
Tobacco, pipes of peace, 49-52, 73; used most by men with many wives, 83; shown in pictures, 102; Indians' revenge, 105; described by Hariot, 105-106; how used, 105-106; cultivation of, 106-108; worm, 108; object of sacrifice, 262-263
Tockwogh, town, 151; river, 317; tribe, 372
Tomahawk, adorned with peak and runtees, 46; picture of, 75; buried as sign of peace, 178
Tombs of the kings of Secota, 137
Tomlinson, A. B., quoted, 211
Tools, files of beaver teeth, 43; knives of split reeds, 43; shells for razors, 33-34; bones for fish-hooks, 95; cockle shells for spoons, 75; thread made of grass, 95; axes made of stone, 112; weapon like a pickaxe, 174
Toppahanock, river, 317; tribe, 360
Torture, of prisoners, 44-45; general among the Indians, 181-182; particular case of, 300-301
Towns, and houses, chapter on, 128-140; located, chapter on, 141-160; picture of, 58; Indians lived in, 128-129; 134; each, ruled by a king, 128-129, 133-134; size of, 129-130, 138, 139, 352-353; palisadoed, 130; generally small, 133; distance apart, 134; forums in, 134, 136-137; when removed, 134; usually by

Index 427

Towns—*Continued*
rivers, 137, 138–139; woods clear around, 138; generally on a hill, 138–139; map of, in Virginia, 142; John Pory visits, 152; map of, in North Carolina, 160; often had same name as tribes, 142; all had tutelar deities, 247–248; at Turk's Ferry, 358; on the Wappatomaka, 384; in Hampshire County, W. Va., 384–385; on the Shenandoah, 385–386; in Frederick County, 386; in Page County, 386; in Pennsylvania, 400–401; west of the Ohio, 401; some mentioned in this volume:
Accohanock, 367
Accomack, 157, 367
Acquack, 149
Anoeg, 270
Apasus, 352
Appamattox, 155, 157, 338
Appocant, 145, 149, 277
Aquascogoc, 41, 159
Aquohanock, 152
Arrohateck, 145, 337
Assaomeck, 157
Capahowasick, 145–146
Catawba town, 398
Catokinge, 158
Cekacawon, 362
Charters Old Town, 401
Chawanook, 158
Chawopoweanock, 144
Chepanow, 158
Chesakawon, 147
Chesapeake, 150, 352
Chickahomonie, 156, 345
Chiconessex, 155
Chilhowee, 392
Citico, 392
Corotoman, 360
Cotan, 159
Croatoan, 159
Cuttatawomen, 360
Dasamonquepeuc, 159
Echota, 391, 392, 393–394
Gangascoe, 155
Gingoteque, 155
Gwarewoc, 159
Hatorask, 159
Kecoughtan, 102, 148, 157, 191, 354–355
Kiequotank, 155

Kiskiack, 146
Loggstown, 401
Machopongo, 255
Machot, 151, 152
Mamanahunt, 146
Mantoughquemeo, 157
Mascoming, 158
Matchopungo, 155, 255
Matomkin, 155
Mattapanient, 152
Mattpament, 152
Menheering, 156
Mequopen, 159
Metpowem, 158
Mohominge, 145
Monahassanugh, 270
Moratuc, 158
Moraughtacund, 361
Moysonec, 145
Muscamunge, 158
Nacotchtanke, 153–154
Nanduye, 155
Nansemond, 149, 156, 351
Nantaughtacund, 361
Newsioc, 159
Nominy, 150
Nottoway, 155
Occahanock, 155
Occaneeche, 379
Ohaunook, 158
Onancoke, 152, 155
Onawmanient, 362
Orapax, 152–153, 251, 271, 275, 342, 357
Ozenick, 146, 149, 341
Ozinies, 146
Pamunkey, 44, 156, 224
Panawaioc, 159
Paquiwoc, 159
Paspahegh, 144–145, 339
Pasptanzie, xii.
Pasquenoke, 158
Patawomek, 151, 251
Pawtuxunt, 152
Payankatank, 358
Piqua, 400
Pissacoack, 149
Pissaseck, 361
Pomeiock, 36–39, 41, 57, 61, 134–135, 157, 352
Port Tabago, 156
Potomac, 363, 383
Powhatan, 144, 157, 325
Pungoteque, 155
Quiyoughcohanock, 144, 191, 346

428 Index

Towns—*Continued*
  Ramushowog, 158
  Rappahannock, 156, 361
  Rassawck, 370
  Roanoke, 157
  Romuncock, 326
  Secota, 58, 62, 135–136, 159
  Sectuoc, 159
  Sewickley Old Town, 401
  Shenapin Town, 179–180, 400–401
  Skicoak, 157, 352–353
  Sockobeck, 157
  Tallassee, 392
  Tamottee, 392
  Tandaquomuc, 158
  Tauxenent, 365
  Tennassee, 392
  Tockwogh, 151, 372
  Tramasquecoock, 159
  Uttamussack, 224–227, 253
  Waratan, 158
  Warraskoyack, 149, 157, 350
  Werowocomoco, 142–143, 271, 315, 355
  Wicocomoco, 156, 362
  Wokokon, 160
  Wyanoke, 147, 155, 339
  Yawtanoone, xi., 251
  See Maps, 142, 160
Toyatan succeeded his brother Powhatan, 271–272
Trading, by barter, 44; with Maryland prohibited, 375
Traveling, food during, 47–48; skill shown in, 96
Treasure, hidden, 71; buried with the dead, 202–203; Powhatan's guarded by an idol, 251
Treaties, *see* Public meetings; with the Chickahominies, 342–344
Trees, principal, 28; how felled, 109, 110, 134; around towns, 138; houses under, 139; planted to commemorate treaties of peace, 178
Tribes, and nations, chapter on, 324–405; of Indians in eastern part of the United States, 26–27; origin of names of, often same as rivers, etc., 142, 368–369; the weroances alone sold the lands of, 169; how located in Virginia, 324;

under Powhatan, 324–368; the five civilized, 397; some of the, mentioned in this volume:
  Accohanocks, 270, 367
  Accowmacks, 270, 367
  Acquintanacksuaks, 366
  Anacostans, xii.
  Anoeg, 270
  Appomattucks, 268, 270, 337–338
  Arrohatecks, 268, 270, 324, 337
  Atquandachuks, 372
  Bocootawwonough, 270
  Cantaunkacks, 357
  Cassapecocks, 357
  Catawbas, 26, 382–383, 397–399
  Cayugas, 26, 403
  Cekacawons, 362
  Chawons, 269, 399
  Chawonoaks, 269
  Cheescake, *see* Kiskiack
  Chepechos, 357
  Cherokees, 26, 324, 389–399
  Chesapeaks, 280, 351
  Chickahominies, 341–345
  Chickamawgas, 392, 400
  Chickasaws, 27, 390, 397
  Chippewas, 26
  Choctaws, 27, 390, 396, 397
  Cinelas, 373, 375
  Conestogas, 375
  Creeks, 27, 390, 392, 397
  Cuttatawomen, 359
  Delawares, 26, 382, 398–401
  Doegs, 361
  Erati, 392
  Eries, 26
  Foxes, 26, 73
  Gingaskins, 366
  Hassinungoes, 370
  Hurons, 26
  Illinois, 26
  Iroquois, 26, 398–399, 400, 401
  Kaposecocks, 357
  Kecoughtans, 273, 353
  Kickapoos, 26
  Kiskiacks, 355–357
  Kuskarawaocks, 366
  Manakins, 324, 369–370
  Mangoags, 369, 399
  Mannahoacks, 324, 369–370

Index

Tribes—*Continued*
Maskoki, 26
Massawomecks, 270, 371–372, 374
Massawomees, 403
Massinacocs, 371
Mattapaments, 336–337
Mattapamients, 268–270, 336–337
Mattaponys, 336–337
Meherrins, 379
Miamis, 26, 400
Mingoes, 400
Mobilians, 26
Mohawks, 26, 403
Mohegans, 26
Mohemenchoes, 371
Monacans, 324, 367–370
Monahassanoes, 371
Monasiccapanoes, 370
Moraughtacunds, 361
Moraughtaownas, 361
Moyaons, 365
Mummapacunes, 357
Muscogulges, 390
Nandtaughtacunds, 361
Nansemonds, 350
Narragansetts, 26
Natchez, 27
Nocotchtanks, 365
Nominies, 362
Nottoways, 376–379
Occaneeches, 379
Ochahannankes, 357
Ojibwas, 26
Onawmanients, 362
Oneidas, 26, 181, 403
Onondagas, 26, 181, 403
Ontponies, 370
Orapaks, 357
Orzinies, 341, 366
Ottari, 392
Ottawas, 26
Pamacaeacks, 365
Pamarekes, 357
Pamunkeys, 44, 103, 156, 196, 197, 226–227, 268, 270, 315, 324, 326–336
Paraconas, 357
Pascataway, 373
Paspahegs, 339–341
Patauncks, 357
Patawomecks, 362–365
Patawuxents, 365
Payankatanks, 358
Pequots, 26
Pissasecks, 361
Pocoughtronacks, 402
Potapacos, 365
Pottawatomies, 26
Powhatans, 268, 270, 271, 273, 324–326
Quiyongheohanocks, or Tappahannas, 272, 345
Rappahannocks, 360
Secowocomacos, 365
Seminoles, 27, 390, 397
Senecas, 26, 401, 403
Senedos, 372, 383, 385
Shackakonies, 370
Shamapas, 357
Shawanese, 26, 324, 380, 388, 398, 399, 400
Six Nations, 26, 398, 400
Stegarakies, 370
Susquehannocks, 26, 33, 373–376, 379
Tants Wighcocomicos, 366
Tappahannas, or Quiyongheohanocks, 272, 345, 346
Tarratines, 26
Tauxenents, 365
Tauxitanians, 370
Tegninaties, 370
Tockwoghes, 269, 372
Toppahanocks, 360
Tsaraghee, 391
Tuscaroras, 26, 324, 372, 388, 399
Tuteloes, 380
Twightwees, 400
Wampanoags, 26
Warascoyacks, 149, 157, 348
Weanocks, *see* Wyanoke
Weopemedgs, 399
Werowocomocos, 142–143, 355
Whonkenties, 370
Wighcocomocos, 33, 156, 362
Winnebagos, 26
Wyandots, 400
Wyanoke, 147, 155, 339
Youghianunds, 338
Youghtamunds, 268, 270, 271, 324, 338
Tribute Indians reduced to, 146, 154
Triumviri of Opechanekeno, 326, 358

Trustees appointed for Indian tribes, 351, 378
Tuckahoe, an edible root, 69–70
Turkey-feather, mantles, 53; arrows fledged with, 112
Turpentine, glue of, 112
Tuscaroras, a branch of the Iroquois, 26, 372; where located, 324, 372; the Catawbas fought with Virginia against, 399
Tutelar deities, all towns had, 247–248, 251
Tyrrell County, North Carolina, Indian town in, 159

U

Unoccupied region between the mountains and the Mississippi, 395
Uppowoc, see Tobacco
Uttamussack, principal seat of the priests, 224–227; its location, 226; crystal cube at, 253

V

Valley of Virginia, tribes of the, 380–390; "The Barrens," 381–382; scene of Indian battles, 398, 403
Vegetables, see Food
Verazzano, voyage of, foundation for claims of France, 2
Virginia, a leading motive for the colonization of, was the extension of Protestantism, 4–15; difference between, and Massachusetts, 15–18; would not tolerate Roman Catholics, 18, 23–24; founding of, by the King of England, 19–22; scope of the undertaking, 21–22; religious principles of the founders long adhered to, 23–24; why so respected, 23–24; Indians of, how classed, 25–26; flora and fauna of the, forest, 27–29; kind of country first occupied, 29; policy of, in regard to the Indians, 30–31; bonds of, held by Choctaws and Cherokees, 396–397; westward progress of, 403-405; Company, the colony established by, 21; Indian name for, 316
Virginians, adopted figurative language of Indians, 178; adopted Indian method of fighting, 182; called by the Indians the Big Knives, 182

W

Wahanganoche, disputes with over sales of land, 363–365
Walking, Indian mode of, 44
Walnut, 69, 71, 73
Wampum peak, made of conch shell, 46; use of, in treaties, 179–180; used as money, 306–307
War, art of, and political laws, chapter on, 165–182; method of, 45, 175–177, 182; for women, 82, 173; with the Pamunkeys in, 1624, 103; continual among the Indians, 129, 173, 382–383, 401–402; begun after due consultations, 170, 173, 175; authority of the commander, 171–172; the priests generally decide question of, 173; how warriors summoned for, 174–175; Indians timorous in action, 175–176; and cruel, 176; dance, 45; whoop, 117; Virginians adopted Indian method of, 182; idol carried into battle, 243; Virginia's westward progress, 403–405
Warraskoyack, town, 149; on site of Smithfield, 157; tribe, 348–350; name, 315; bay, 317
Washington County, North Carolina, town in, 159
Water, Indians' principal drink, 70; pond, preferred, 70; artificial, supply by town, 135
Weanoack, town burned, 147; tribe, 339
Weapons, kinds used, 174, 176
Weighing, difficulty in Indians understanding, 34–35
Weirs, fishing, how made, 91–92, 94, 95–96, 98

Index 431

Weroances, meaning of the word, 269; how dressed, 39, 172; how wives selected, 78; had many wives, 77, 79; planting and gathering their corn, 104–105; their houses, 139; power of, 165–166, 168, 171; taxes due by, 166; number of, 166; ill-breeding punished by, 168; lands sold by them, not by the tribe, 169; office of, 170–171; how distinguished, 172; ruled by the priests, 165, 173; how their bodies preserved after death, 47, 198, 199, 200; how their mummies guarded, 199–200; protected by the orders of King James, 236; their souls believed immortal, 241–242; each had a temple and priest in his jurisdiction, 249; were builders of the temples, 249; some mentioned in this volume:
  Amepetough, 350
  Ashuaquid, 337
  Attasquintan, 357
  Attossomunck, 357
  Canasateego, 180–181
  Coquonasum, 337–338
  Ensenore, 203, 242–243
  Essenataugh, 357
  Grangenimeo, 283
  Harquip, 344
  Heigler, 399
  Jopassus, xi., xii., 254–258, 272, 363
  Kaquothacun, 339
  Kecatough, 272, 358
  Keighangton, 357
  Keptopeke, 367
  Kequotaugh, see Kecatough
  Kissanacomen, 146, 341
  Menatonon, 283
  Namenacus, 365
  Namontack, 273
  Nansuapunck, 357
  Nantaquaus, called the Laughing King, 274, 367
  Oconostota, 391–392, 394
  Ohonnamo, 357
  Opechancanough, xii., 145, 147, 151, 268, 271, 272, 283, 326, 346–347, 358
  Opitchapan, 271–272
  Opopohcumunck, 357
  Ottahotin, 355
  Ottondeacommoc, 357
  Pemisapan, 203, 242–243, 283, 284
  Pepisco, 346–347
  Pepiscumah, see Pepisco
  Persicles, 379–380
  Pinmacum, 283
  Pochins, 273, 353
  Pomiscatuck, 338
  Poonens, 158, 283
  Powhatan, see Powhatan
  Tackonekintaco, 348
  Tahahcoope, 346
  Tanacharison, 391, 401
  Tatacope, see Tahahcoope
  Taughhaiten, 358
  Taux-Powhatan, x., 273, 325
  Tirchtough, 350
  Tottopottomoy, 333
  Toyatan, see Opitchapan
  Uropaack, 357
  Wahanganoche, 363
  Werowaugh, 336
  Weyamat, 357
  Weyhohomo, 350
  Weyongopo, 350
  Wingina, see Pemisapan and Wingina.
Wochinchopunck, 339–341
Werowocomoco, location, 142–143; roads from, 143; rivaled by Machot, 152; tribe, 355
Westmoreland County, towns in, 149, 150; tribes in, 362
Westphalia, treaty of, 14–15
West's fort, 144
West Point, Indian name for, 317
White, John, pictures, 37–39, 124; sent over by Raleigh, 39; map, 160
White peak, uses of, 46
Whiteside Mountain, the home of the Spirit of Evil, 266
Whittaker quoted, 139, 166, 173, 233, 252
Wiccocomoco, see Wighcocomocoes
Wicomico River, 317
Wife, see Wives
Wighcocomocoes, tribe small in stature, 33; town, 156; tribe, 362

Wigwam, 130; see Houses
William the Silent, 5-9
Wingina, marks on his subjects, 41; on his brother-in-law's subjects, 41; southern limit of kingdom, 159; sick when English first appeared, 282; his allies and enemies, 283; took the name of Pemisapan, 283; planned extermination of the English, 283; death of, 284
Winters, years reckoned by, 84; called cohonks, 84
Wives, bought with money, 77; plurality of, 77, 78, 79, 80, 82; of the kings, 78; care of Powhatan's, 78; status of, 79; duties of, 80; right of divorce, 80, 81; gotten by skill in hunting, 96
Wolves, quantity of, 28; native animal, 73
Women, of Secotam, 58; pastimes of, 59; carrying children, 59-60; love of children, 60; waited on by children, 62; how employed, 62, 75-76; behavior of, 62-64; kept skin clean with oil, 64; dress of young, 62-63, 64, 65; how to tell married, 63; breasts, 63, 64; young, gay, 63-64; makers of pottery, etc., 65-66, 75-76; served meals, 76; wars for, 82; threads made by, 95; on hunting-parties, 96; agriculture conducted by, and children, 80, 102; under care of sachem, 171; sometimes sachems, 171; never priests nor conjurers, 234; constituted part of the delights of heaven, 261; dress of one described, 346-347
Worcester County, Maryland, tribes in, 366
Words, some Indian, 285-323; see Language
Workshops, Indian, 114-119
Worsaae quoted, 112, 217
Wounds, see Medicine
Wreath worn by women about the head, 58
Wreck of Christian ship about 1564, 111
Wysoccan, a mad potion given in huskanawing, 196

Y

Year, how divided, 84
Yeardley forces payment of tribute, 146
York, river, formerly Pamunkey, 142, 326; town on the, 145-146; tribes on the, 355-359
Youghtamund, river now the Pamunkey, 170, 317, 326; the tribe, 324, 338

www.ingramcontent.com/pod-product-compliance
Lightning Source LLC
Chambersburg PA
CBHW071618230426
43669CB00012B/1977